100 Woodblock Prints of Edo Culture

From the Ukiyo-e Collection of the Tobacco and Salt Museum

Yoshiko Yuasa
Edward F. Domino

NPP Books

NPP Books, P.O. Box 1491, Ann Arbor, MI 48106, USA

Printed in USA

International Standard Book Number: 978-0-916182-18-2 (Soft cover, 8.5" by 11")
Previously ISBN: 978-0-916182-16-8 (Soft cover, 210mm by 297mm)
Library of Congress Number: 2008926254

Acknowledgements

We owe our sincere gratitude to Mrs. Nobuko Gerth. Her understanding of the Japanese language and culture was most helpful in her careful editing. She provided us with many valuable suggestions and contributed to the clarity and enrichment of the book.

The English text of this book was set in Century Old Style and Helvetica Neue.

The paper used meets the minimum requirements of the American National Standard for Information Sciences. Permanence of Paper for Printing Library Materials, ANSI Z39.48-1984.

www.nppbooks.com

Preface

The purpose of this work is to make available to the general public a small set of Japanese woodblock prints called ukiyo-e. One hundred were selected from the extensive collection of ukiyo-e in a special museum located in Tokyo, Japan. The Tobacco and Salt Museum has a superb collection of woodblock prints devoted to the history of both tobacco and salt and their impact over the centuries on Japan.

In the present volume, descriptions in both English and Japanese accompany each print. Those in English are purposely detailed. We wished to take the reader "by the hand" and describe what each ukiyo-e reveals in a unique period in Japanese history. References to tobacco and its use are to be viewed as part of the Japanese concept of shikohin as described in the Introduction by the Museum Director, Dr. Yoshihiko Ohkawa.

Each original print is made available through the kindness of the Tobacco and Salt Museum. Most are unknown to Westerners. The viewer/reader of this selected collection from the Museum's archives is given a visual and written tour of Japanese Edo period culture. Like a series of snapshots, each of the prints provides a view of a unique cultural experience. Members of Edo society used small amounts of tobacco which was smoked in very small bowl pipes called kiseru. These pipes were of various lengths and sizes. Using tea and small amounts of tobacco were common recreational and pleasure-seeking activities of Edo society.

We thank the many persons who helped to bring this publication to fruition. We especially thank Dr. Ohkawa for permitting and supporting this joint endeavor.

Our task has not been easy. We apologize for any errors, omissions, or misinterpretations and wish they be brought to our attention for future correction.

Yoshiko Yuasa
Curator, Curatorial Department
Tobacco and Salt Museum
1-16-8 Jinnan, Shibuya-ku
Tokyo, Japan 150-0041

E.F. Domino, M.D.
Professor of Pharmacology
University of Michigan
Ann Arbor, MI 48109 USA

Contents

INTRODUCTION

Tobacco as Part of Culture and the Ukiyo-e Collection of the Tobacco & Salt Museum

The definition of "culture" differs widely among scholars and dictionaries. One common definition is the arts and other manifestation of human activity collectively, either specifically or generally. We may refer, for example, to the culture of the Edo Period in Japan as in this book, or the culture of the 20th Century. Human activities vary and are manifested in art, literature, music, theater, architecture, consumer goods, etc. Anthropologists also use the term to include technology, science, and moral systems. In accordance with the dictionary definition, "culture" is the physical and spiritual result which human beings have created by working with nature. On the other hand, Mr. Ryōtaro Shiba, a famous Japanese novelist, defines "culture" as something which seems to have no rationale behind it but gives one comfort and pleasure. I would like to recommend this definition of "culture." There are many things that come under this category. For instance, arts such as paintings, music, novels, movies, plays, or food, clothing, shelter, and shikohin may be mentioned. Shikohin is a Japanese term that denotes drinks and eatables consumed not for nourishment but for pleasure. Coffee, tea, alcohol, and tobacco are examples. A most important concept is that culture has diversity. There is no one culture common for all human beings. It is essential for humans to be exposed to the diversity of culture by members. We should do this publicly and broadly.

Tobacco is a typical aspect of many cultures. In the beginning, tobacco was used for religious purposes. The oldest example of tobacco use is a relief of the Maya smoking god discovered at the Palenque ruin in Mexico. By decoding Mayan characters, it has been verified that this relief was made in 692 A.D. A replica of the relief can be viewed at the Tobacco & Salt Museum in Tokyo, Japan.

Tobacco was introduced into Europe after Christopher Columbus arrived in the West Indies in 1492. It was originally used as a medicine. Various products such as pipes and chewing tobacco, cigars, snuff, and water pipe tobacco became popular, depending on country or region. When tobacco was introduced into Japan is unclear, but it is thought to be around the end of the 16th to the beginning of the 17th Century. In the Edo period, the culture of using a Japanese pipe called kiseru for smoking thin cut tobacco leaves (Hosokizami) became popular. Various smoking accessories such as cases for kiseru, tobacco pouches, and tobacco trays were widespread among common people. Some sophisticated people, including Kabuki players in the Edo period, are shown in drawings of ukiyo-e (wood block prints).

During the latter half of the 19th Century, cigarettes were mass produced and their use became fashionable throughout the world. This trend of excessive use of cigarettes is now considered a bad habit. Nowadays, it should be emphasized that smoking may be enjoyed only in modest amounts.

Museum's History

The Tobacco & Salt Museum was established in 1978 by the Japan Tobacco & Salt Public Corporation. The purpose of the Museum is not only to introduce the history and culture of tobacco and salt, but also to investigate related cultural materials. The collection of the materials was started in 1932 by the Monopoly Bureau of Ministry of Finance. We have continued efforts to collect various tobacco related materials. As of March 31, 2007, the total number is now more than 230,000, and the number of ukiyo-e is 1,748. As a result, the quality of the collection and the exhibition related to tobacco is considered excellent.

For this book, the curator of the museum, Ms. Yoshiko Yuasa, has selected 100 suitable ukiyo-e from the Museum's collection. She and Professor Edward Domino have provided explanations for each ukiyo-e, mainly in English and complementarily in Japanese.

I believe that most of the readers of this book will be able to enjoy the beauties of these ukiyo-e. I would like to express my sincere thanks to Professor Domino for his contributions to this book.

The importance of tobacco in the Edo period of Japan has been well described by Mr. Timon Screech in 2004 in the volume Smoke - A Global History of Smoking edited by S. L. Gilman and Z. Xun, Reaktion Books, London, ISBN 1 86189 2004.

Finally, I would like to request many parties to support our Museum. It is my desire to make this museum more enjoyable and relevant to the general public in understanding the Japanese cultural history.

Yoshihiko Ohkawa, Ph.D.
Director, Tobacco & Salt Museum

THE UNIQUENESS OF JAPANESE WOODBLOCK PRINTS[1]

Paper and Printing

Paper and printing from woodblocks has a very ancient history. The concept of printing came first. How and where did it start? Who invented printing? Its beginnings lie in the ancient Near East about 5,000 years ago. Sumerians were the earliest printers, as evidenced by their impressions on clay from stone seals. The use of seals spread from Mesopotamia to India and then to China. The Chinese applied ink to seals and impressed them on wood or silk. By the 2nd Century AD, they had invented paper. By the 9th Century, they were printing pictures from woodblocks. These ideas spread throughout the world, especially in nearby Japan. Each civilization developed its own unique pictorial designs printed from wooden blocks onto paper. Northern Europeans had developed designs with religious significance by the end of the 14th Century, such as the woodcut of St. Christopher ca. 1435. However, in Japan woodcut designs were unique, emphasizing scenes from daily life. The patience and skill of the Japanese craftsmen who cut depressions into wood to depict the extremely thin raised lines for rain, for example, are most impressive.

In Japan - The World of Ukiyo-e

Pictures depicting festivals, kabuki players, pleasure quarters, and other forms of entertainment became available, primarily for wealthy aristocrats, during the Azuchi-Momoyama period (1568-1600). In the Edo period (1603-1868), such prints became increasingly popular. They were mass reproduced. The prints were known as ukiyo-e (literally, pictures of the floating world). The term "floating world" needs further explanation. An object which displaces its own weight in air, gas, or fluid becomes weightless. It tends to rise, move gently, or drift. Ideas may float or drift by in one's mind. Hence, pleasant scenes provide a dream-like quality.

Ukiyo-e is a combination of three different words. The Japanese pronunciation of "uki" has two different meanings. One is to have fun, be merry and happy. A second meaning is to float. Both meanings are applicable to the depicted scenes. The Japanese word "yo" means world and "e" picture. Hence, ukiyo-e is a picture of a dream-like world of fun and happiness.

Early black on white print is known as sumizuri-e. However, with increased popular demand, different woodblock printing techniques were developed. The prints with the background colored by hand were known as tan-e. Two to three colored woodblock prints were called benizuri-e. By the mid-18th Century, Edo artists and printing craftsmen advanced their techniques to multicolored (polychrome) woodblock prints called nishiki-e, literally brocade pictures.

In contrast to early ukiyo-e which were painted singly, the nishiki-e prints were mass produced. Since individual prints were relatively inexpensive, they were easily affordable to the general public. Their availability made them useful souvenirs.

---

[1] A rewritten version of Japanese and English text describing the permanent exhibit (Fifth Floor) of Japanese woodblock prints in the Edo Museum, Tokyo, Japan (reproduced with permission).

Forms of Ukiyo-e

Single hand-painted pictures are called nikuhitsu-ga. Multiple pictures were bound in a book format. The early ukiyo-e were printed ink pictures, colored by hand. With the advent of color ink in the mid 18th Century (1765), there was a change from black and white to multicolored block printing using separate woodblocks for each color. Vegetable or plant dyes were widely used. The immense popularity of the polychrome woodblock of ukiyo-e rose hand in hand with general interest in common life during the mid 17th Century. Scenes from pleasure quarters, Kabuki plays, birds, flowers, and landscapes, etc. became their favorite subjects.

The Process

The artist made the original drawing. However, this was just the beginning of a complex process involving collaboration of artists, engravers, and printers. Artists like Harunobu, Kiyonaga, Utamaro, Sharaku, Toyokuni, Hokusai, and Hiroshige are some of the better known. The steps used included chiseling and preparation of each woodblock color. When the engraving process was complete, the printing process began. This involved as many as 21 or more separate steps to produce a single printed ukiyo-e. Since this process was easily repeated, a large number of reproductions could be made of the original single print drawn by the master artist who was given all of the credit.

Carvers pasted the drawing on blocks of wood and carved away what was not to appear on the print. This was an incredibly tedious process. To depict rain, very fine raised lines are needed. Printers applied the correct color of ink to each block and pressed each onto the same sheet of paper. The lightest color was applied first. Usually 100-200 copies of the print were made. Color calendars, fans, etc. were also printed. These were very popular with the general public and, very lucrative for those involved. Artists and technicians were naturally happy with the trend and each advanced the medium. An 1803 print by Utamaro depicts a woodblock carving and printing scene of the time using pretty women instead of men. Safflowers provided a red dye called beni, which was extremely expensive. By weight, it was more precious than gold. Up to a dozen or so individual colors and combinations were used. Ukiyo-e pictorial art became very popular in Japan during the Edo period. It influenced western artists such as Van Gogh, Monet, Matisse, Whistler, and Bonnard among others. Depictions of beautiful, well-known women in fancy clothes became very popular and were subsequently eroticized. Later, landscapes, daily life, and even ghosts and goblins became suitable themes.

The Golden Age of Ukiyo-e

This period lasted about 50 years from the 1790s-1830s. As an Edo specialty, such prints were also known as azuma nishiki-e. After Japan was opened to foreign trade, especially during the 19th Century and later, many woodcuts were exported abroad, Western appreciation of the uniqueness of Japanese culture increased. Within Japan, nishiki-e brocade prints were used to make annual calendars more attractive. The months of the old lunar year consisted of "large" months of 30 days and "small" months of 29 days. Yearly competitions among interested artists resulted in many original, unique designs. Artistic and technical skills of many talented individuals contributed to a wealth of beautiful, original designs and prints. Depictions of contemporary living, manners, famous scenes from life and nature multiplied enormously.

Famous artists accepted young pupils who contributed their talents with instruction from their master teacher artists. Utagawa Hiroshige I is one example. When he died in 1858 his pupil married his daughter and changed his name to Hiroshige II. Hiroshige I depicted the Fifty-Three Stages of the Tōkaidō Road and One Hundred Famous Places of Edo, and many others. Hiroshige II painted Hundred Views of Famous Places in the Provinces. This series was not completed. After several years of marriage Hiroshige II and his much younger wife divorced. He then became known as Risshō or Kisai. His former wife remarried a young man of similar age who became known as Hiroshige III. He became a very famous artist of woodblock prints in Meiji. Two of the prints by Hiroshige III are # 84 and # 85 in this book.

Ukiyo-e Scenes

Cultured young women of the Edo period were very fashionable and dressed in lavish garments. The style, design, and multiple colors of their kimonos changed frequently. The garment with a narrow wrist type of opening was called a kosode. The kosodes were dyed in red, black, and white colors and worn as undergarments. Between 1596-1615, just prior to the Edo period, the kosode-type kimonos with delicate embroidery and designs with gold leaf imprints were made. By 1661-1673 beautiful motifs were added to fill blank spaces on what were called Kanbun kosode. Genroku kosode followed in 1688-1704 featuring literature motifs. The technique of yūzen dye developed during this era made pictorial designs possible.

Scenes of dress fashion patterns were dominated by kabuki actors and courtesans. Small patterns called Komon were favored by samurai, became popular among women. The popularity among common people of nishiki-e prints and an interest in clothing fashions established designs of the Edo period by the middle of the 17th Century. The themes of ukiyo-e also included birds, flowers, picture stories and landscapes.

It is very rare to see a woodblock scene with women showing their teeth. The practice of married Japanese women dying their teeth black (Ohaguro) existed well before the 17th Century. However, it became popular among aristocratic women prior to and during the Edo period. Even some male court nobles and samurai blackened their teeth. During the Edo period, it became fashionable among commoners but was restricted to married young women and about to be married young women about 17-18 years old. The practice of Ohaguro was abolished when the Edo period ended. Proper etiquette required women to cover their mouths when laughing or whenever their teeth were exposed. The black dye was an oxidized liquid formed by soaking iron fragments in tea or vinegar. Although it is exceedingly rare that ukiyo-e pictures show a female with blackened teeth, the woodblock print # 22 is such an example.

CHRONOLOGY OF SELECTED EVENTS RELATING TO UKIYO-E
(Modified from the descriptions of the Ōta Ukiyo-e Collection, Tokyo)

1600	-	The Battle of Sekigahara
1603	-	Tokugawa Ieyasu becomes Shogun. The beginning of the Edo Period
1617	-	Licensed quarters at Yoshiwara established
1629	-	Female impersonators prohibited in kabuki productions
1657	-	The great fire of Meireki destroys much of Edo Re-establishment of licensed quarters at Yoshiwara in Shin-Yoshiwara Hishikawa Moronobu moves to Edo
1700	-	Torii Kiyonobu publishes "Picturebook of Courtesans" Kaigetsudo School gains popularity
1765	-	Nishiki-e, multicolored prints developed
1783	-	Shiba Kōkan produces copperplate prints
1790	-	Strict censorship of Ukiyo-e under the Kansei Reform
1791	-	Kitagawa Utamaro publishes full face portraits of women
1794	-	Sharaku activity begins Utagawa Tokyokuni's "Portraits of Actors on Stage"
1822	-	Keisai Eisen's "Portraits of Women" Katsushika Hokusai's "Thirty-Six Views of Mt. Fuji"
1828	-	Utagawa Kuniyoshi "One Hundred Eight Heroes of the Water Margin"
1831	-	Utagawa Hiroshige's "Spots of the Eastern Capital"
1833	-	Utagawa Hiroshige's "Fifty-Three Stages of the Tōkaidō Road"
1842	-	Tenpō Reform restrictions on Ukiyo-e
1858	-	Parisians welcome Ukiyo-e exhibits
1868	-	Edo now called Tokyo

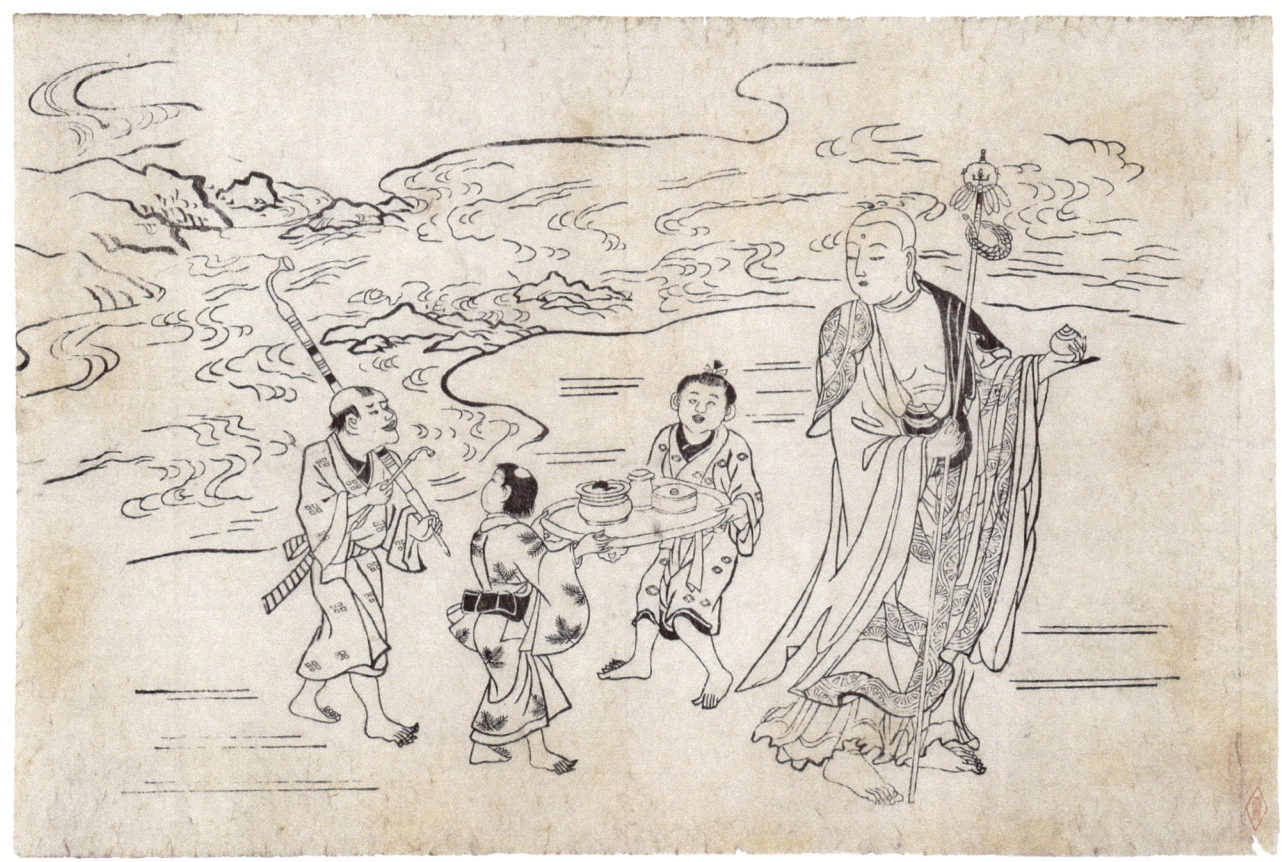

Mitate Yūkun Jizōson

A Parody of Jizōbosatsu Bodhisattva as a Courtesan

Artist: Unknown
Publisher: Unknown
ca. 1681-1684

1

This is an example of an early black on white print. It is called a sumizuri-e print. It shows three children who have been saved by Jizōbosatsu Bodhisattva (a disciple of Buddha). According to Buddhist mythology, children who die before their parents are sent to the sandy beach of the River Sanzu (the River Styx) for punishment. There they are condemned to build a memorial tomb for their parents with pebbles until Jizōbosatsu saves them.

In this print, Jizōbosatsu is shown as a courtesan wearing a feminine robe and holds a six-ring staff with a lighted rope. The two children in the center are carrying a tobacco tray. The child with a shaved head holds one very long and one short kiseru pipe. In the background is the rapidly flowing River Sanzu.

「見立遊君地蔵尊」
地蔵菩薩と賽の河原で受ける罰から救われた子どもたちが描かれている。親より先に世を去った子どもは、父母の供養塔を造るための石を、賽の河原で永遠に積み続けなければならないという罰を受け、それを地蔵菩薩が救うと考えられている。
この絵では、地蔵菩薩は遊女、子どもたちは禿や若い者として描かれている。地蔵菩薩は女性的で、手に火縄のついた錫杖を持ち、子どもたちはたばこ盆やきせるを運んでいる。

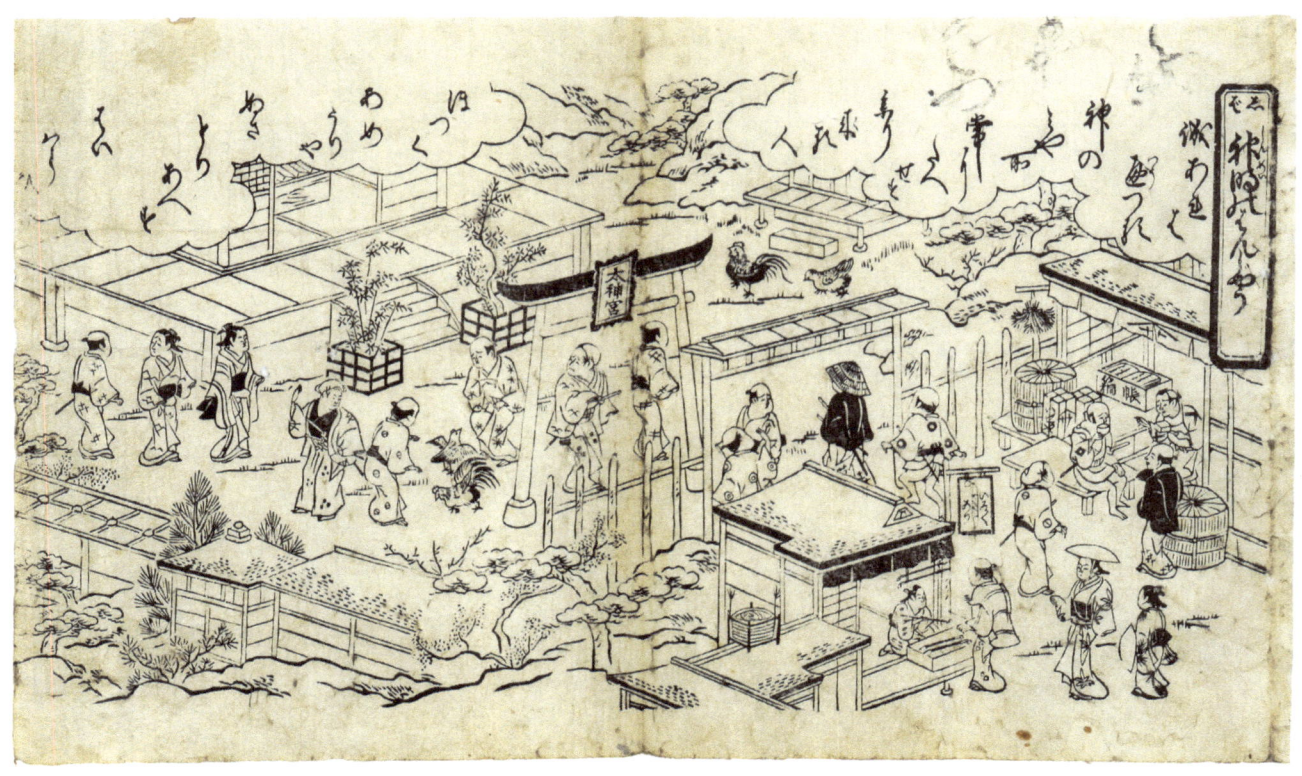

Shiba Shinmei no Hanjō

Lively Shiba Shinmei Shrine

Artist: Unknown
Publisher: Unknown
ca. 1716-1736

2

This is a simple sumizuri-e print black on white, depicting Shiba Shinmei Shrine with its surroundings. It attracted many visitors in the Edo period. There were many Samurai residences around the Shiba area. Note the samurai with a straw hat carrying two swords, followed by a servant.

In the center, there is a Torii Gate, the entrance to a Shintō shrine, with the "Great Shrine" tablet. To the right of the gate is a teahouse, and to the left, a kiseru pipe shop. Such shops were common near shrines and temples in those days. In the foreground on the roof is a large bucket of water for extinguishing fires.

「しば神明のはんじやう」
芝神明は多くの参詣者を集めたところで、この絵にもその様子が描かれている。芝の周囲には武家屋敷が多く、この絵にも、腰に刀を差す武士やその従者たちが描かれている。神明の門の手前、右手には水茶屋があり、左手にはきせる屋がある。当時、寺社の近くにはこのような店が数多くあった。

3

This is an example of the urushi-e print, using lacquer to brighten the black. The other colors are hand painted.

A woman is sitting on a porch with a printed fan in her left hand. On the fan is a picture quiz. She is concentrating on getting the correct answers. Beside her is an old type tobacco tray with smoking implements and two kiseru pipes. In days of old, it was considered proper to put two kiseru pipes, a charcoal pot, an ash receptacle, and a tobacco case on a tray as seen in this print.

Nōryō Bijin

A Beauty Sitting on the Porch in Summer

Artist: Okumura Toshinobu
Publisher: Komatsu-ya
ca. 1716-1736

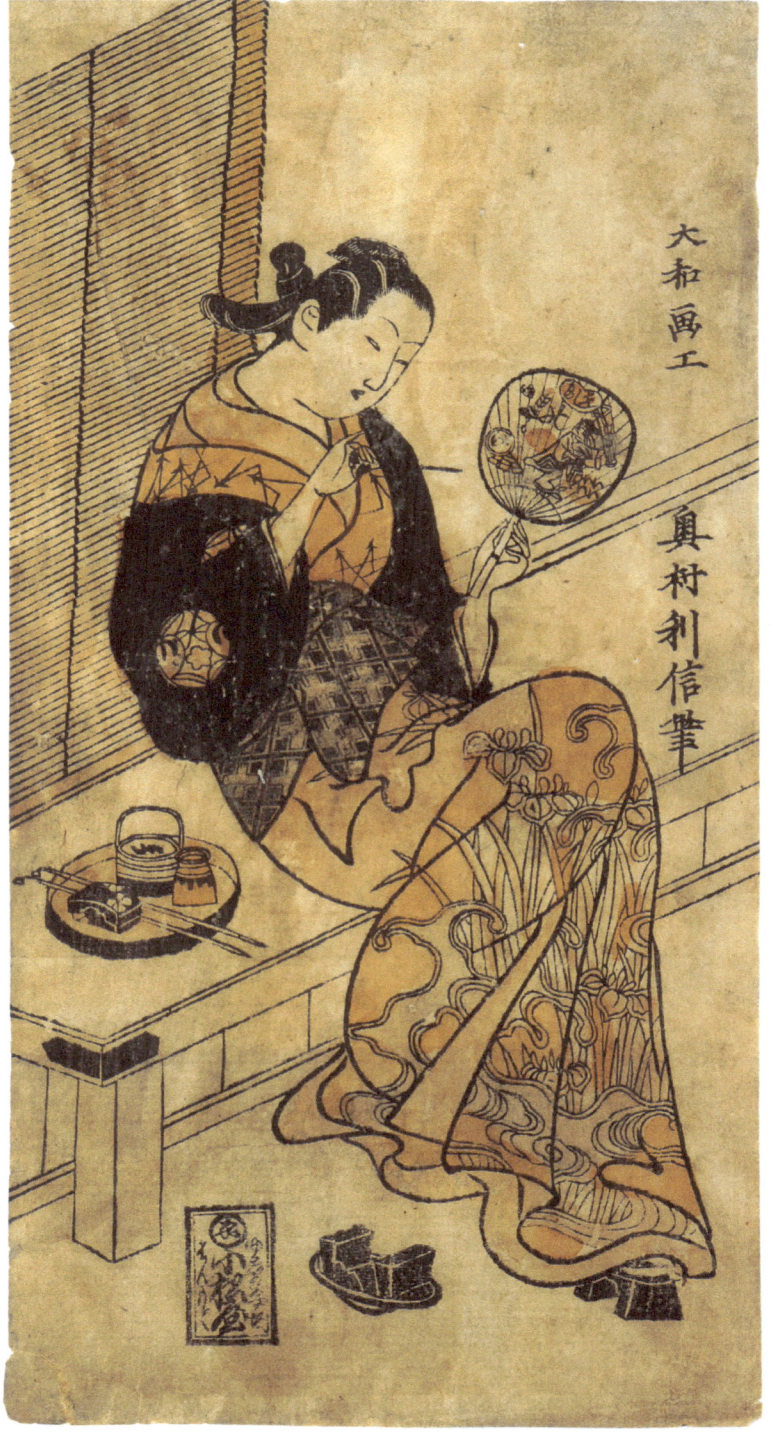

「納涼美人」
縁側で涼んでいる美女は、手にした団扇の判じ物を解くのに夢中になっている。彼女の傍らには、丸い盆のたばこ盆が置かれているが、これは古いタイプのたばこ盆で、きせるを２本備えるというのが、古い時代には正式であった。
この浮世絵は漆絵と呼ばれるもので、板で摺られているのは、絵の黒い輪郭部分のみである。その他の色は筆彩である。

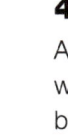

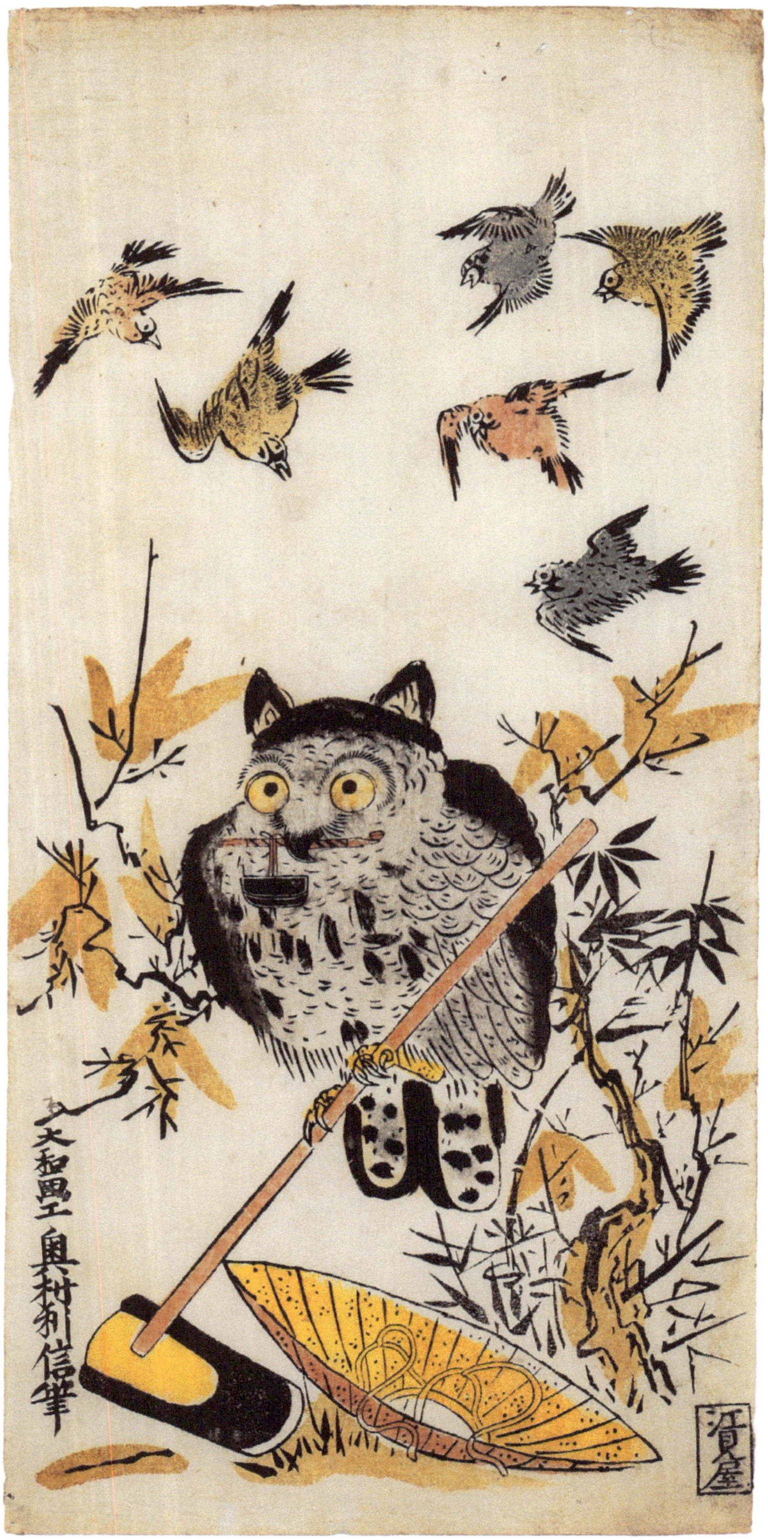

4

Another urushi-e print. After printing on a woodblock, other colors were added by brush.

An owl is holding a small kiseru pipe in its beak while perching on the handle of a hoe. Very large sparrows are flying above. The inverted straw hat at the bottom was left by a farmer. This scene is unusual because the subject may have a moral implication though its intention is unknown.

From the small kiseru pipe in the owl's beak hangs a small tobacco pouch. Note the tobacco pouch is without a pipe case. This type of tobacco pouch came into use soon after people started to carry tobacco with them. Later it became more common to use the tobacco pouch with a pipe case.

Mimizuku to Suzume

An Owl and Sparrows

Artist: Okumura Toshinobu
Publisher: Emi-ya Kichiemon
ca. 1716-1736

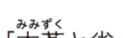

みみずく
「木菟と雀」
木菟が、きせるをくわえて鍬の柄に止まって
おり、その上には雀が飛んでいるという不思
議な図である。寓意画と思われるが、その意
味するところはわかっていない。木菟は、た
ばこ入れが結びつけられたきせるをくわえて
いるが、このたばこ入れにはきせるを入れる
筒が付属していないことがわかる。このよう
にきせる筒のないたばこ入れは、人々がたば
こを携帯しはじめてから後、比較的早い段階
で作られていた。

5

One more urushi-e print using lacquer to brighten the black on the man's jacket. The colors of yellow and orange are hand painted.

A scene from a kabuki drama is depicted. The topic of this kabuki drama is a quarrel by two chivalrous men. The man standing is the main character, Kurofune Chūemon in the play.

The print shows the front of a tobacco shop. The three diamond shaped plates in the middle indicate from top to down, the Japanese letters *ta*, *ba*, and *ko*, meaning tobacco. Parts of two boxes are depicted to the left of the man who is sitting. They are boxes for shredded tobacco. Different boxes were used for each brand.

Kurofune Deiri no Minato

From the Kabuki Drama,
Kurofune Deiri no Minato

Artist: Nishimura Shigenobu
Publisher: Urokogata-ya
1733

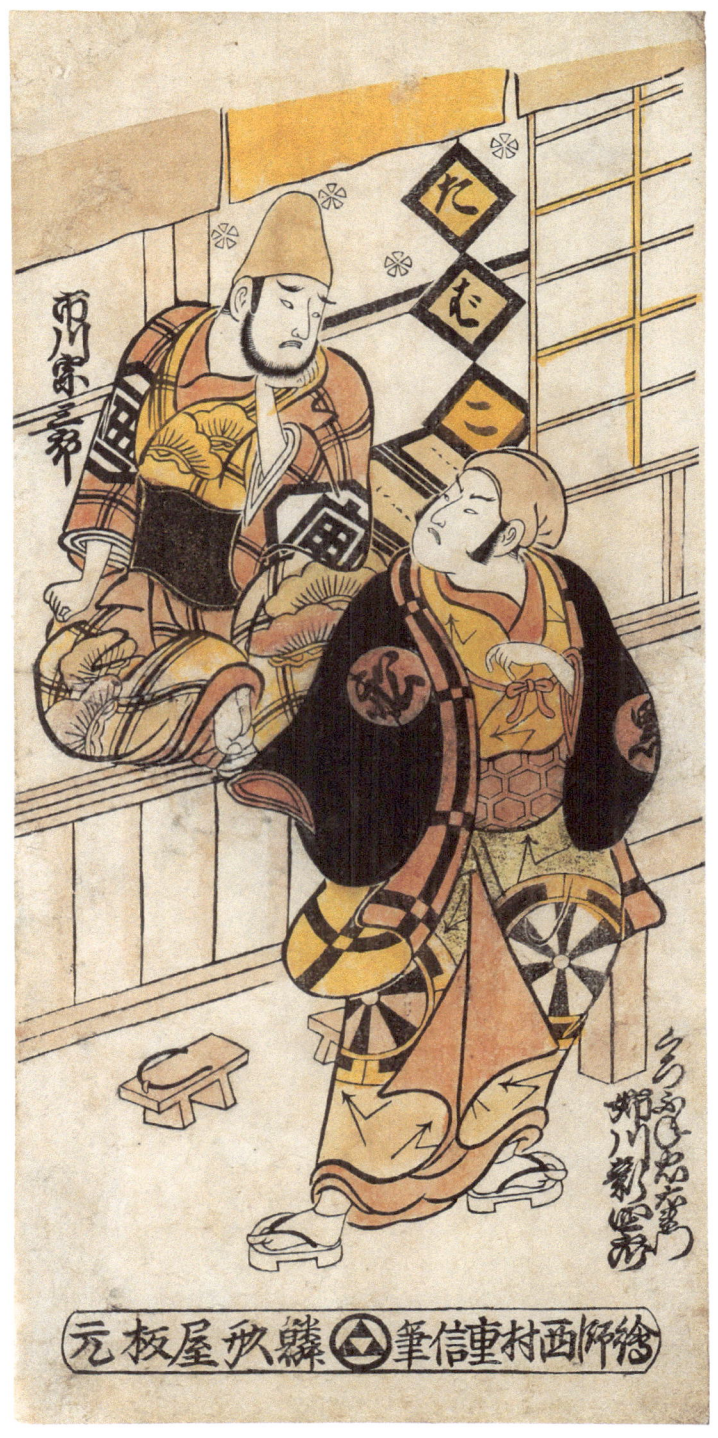

「黒船出入湊」
漆絵という、多色摺りの錦絵が創出される前に摺られた絵である。膠などで黒色を強調し、他の色は手で加えている。
描かれているのは歌舞伎狂言「黒船出入湊」の一場面で、主人公は右側に描かれている黒船忠右衛門である。
たばこ屋が描かれているが、菱形の板を三つ連ねた看板にはそれぞれ平仮名で「た」「ば」「こ」と書かれている。江戸時代、上方に多く見られた看板である。店の中に見える箱は、刻んだたばこの葉を収める箱で、当時は、葉の銘柄ごとに箱を用意し、客の希望で量り売りしていた。

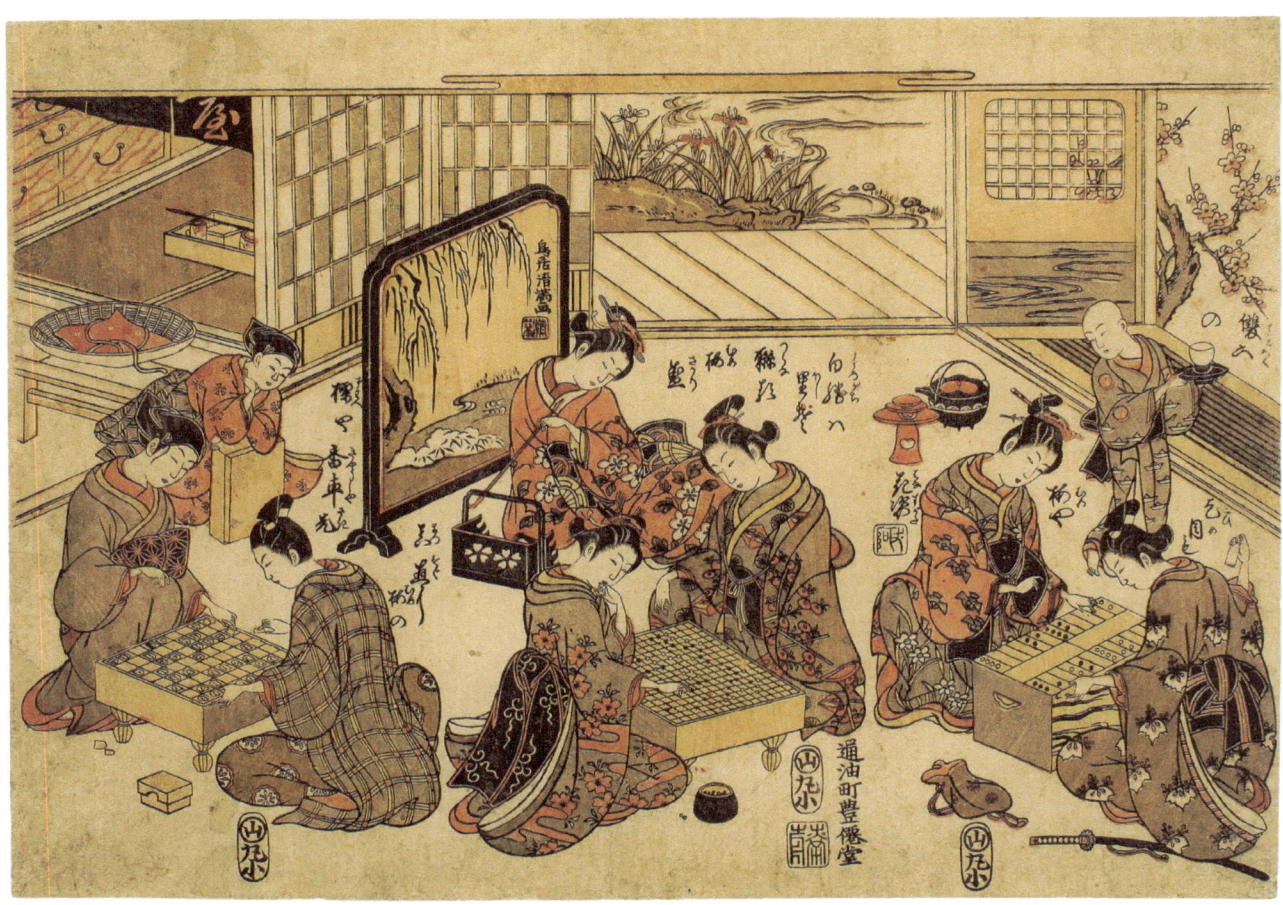

Shōgi, Go, Sugoroku

Three Tabletop Games

Artist: Torii Kiyomitsu
Publisher: Maru-ya Shōbē
ca. 1751-1764

6

People are enjoying three different Japanese games, called Shōgi, Go, and Sugoroku. Such games were very popular. Sugoroku is slowly going out of style, but both Shōgi and Go are still enjoyed and played today. In the Edo period, as now, there were professional players for Shōgi and Go.

The blooming plum tree on the right represents Spring. The iris blossoms in the upper middle represent Summer. A large framed screen shows a Winter scene of willow branches, bamboo leaves, and snow on the ground.

The boy watching the match is a tea server. The woman holding a thin long kiseru pipe in the center is a courtesan. A young woman at the far left wearing a hood is a bikuni, an itinerant entertainer. She is watching the games leaning over a box of her belongings.

「将棋　碁　双六」
三種の盤上遊戯が描かれている。盤双六はこののち廃れるが、将棋と碁は江戸時代から愛好者を増やしており、当時は、現在のように、プロの棋士たちもいた。

この絵では、それぞれのゲームについて、対戦する二人が描かれ、茶を運んだり、たばこを吸ったりしながら、対局を見守る一人が描かれている。

1枚の絵の中で季節が移っており、右から春（庭の梅の花）、夏（縁側の先に見える菖蒲）、冬（衝立の中に見える雪）となっている。

7

A famous kabuki actor Segawa Kikunojō II, with the nickname of Ōji Rokō, is depicted. He was an Oyama, a male actor playing a female role in kabuki dramas. He was very handsome and a favorite of young women. They followed his female styles of hair, combs and dress. This print portrays his graceful way of holding a kiseru pipe. He is wearing numerous ornamental hairpins. Note his crest, two of which are shown in a circular design on his robe on the left. He is wearing Japanese wooden clogs called geta. Above him is a Japanese haiku poem describing his dazzling female appearance. A haiku poem consists of five, seven, and five Japanese syllables.

Nidaime Segawa Kikunojō

Segawa Kikunojō II

Artist: Ishikawa Toyonobu
Publisher: Maru-ya Kyūzaemon
ca. 1756

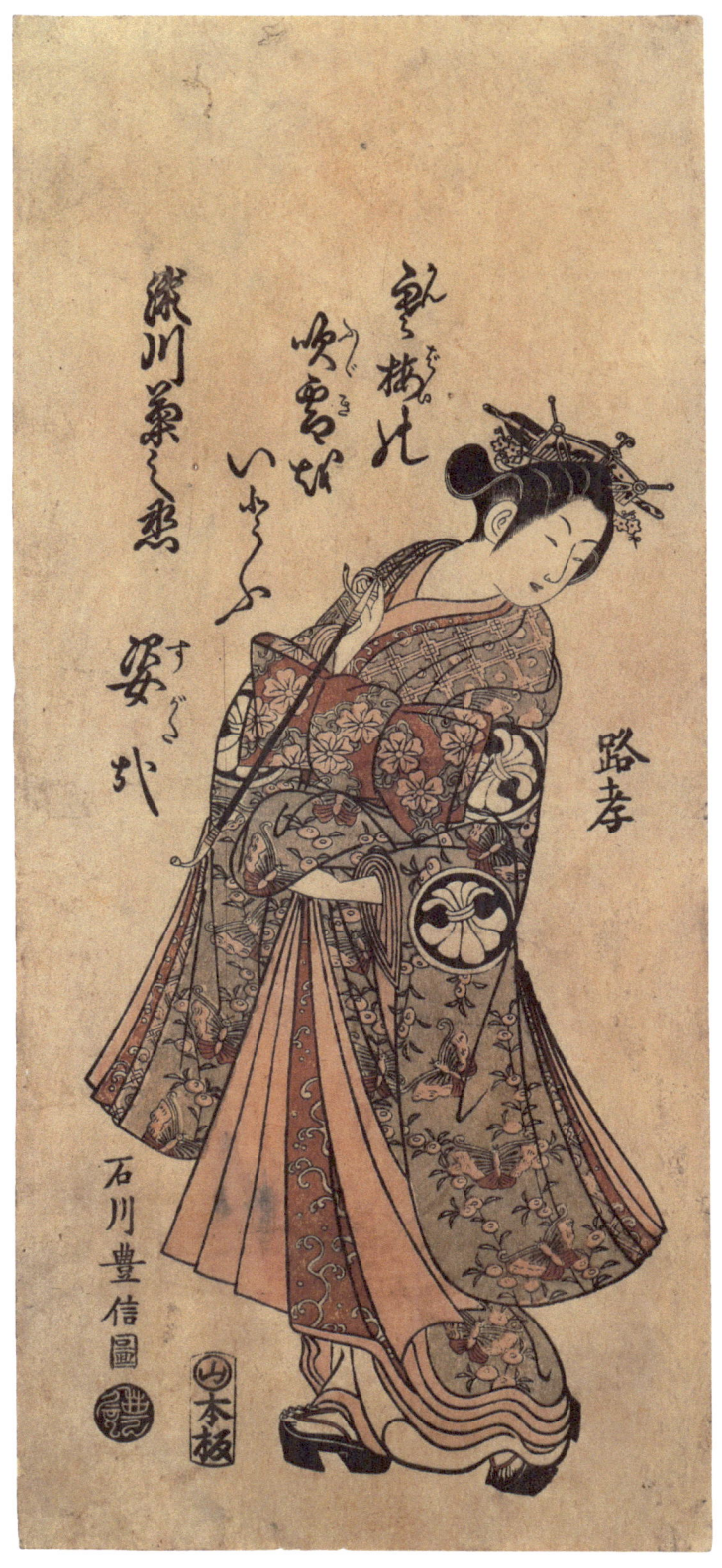

「二代目瀬川菊之丞」
王子路考（あるいは路孝）と呼ばれた二代目瀬川菊之丞は、美貌で有名な歌舞伎の女形であった。特に若い娘たちに絶大な人気があり、娘たちは彼の髪型や櫛、装いをこぞって真似た。この絵からも、きせるを手にする彼の優雅な仕草が見て取れる。

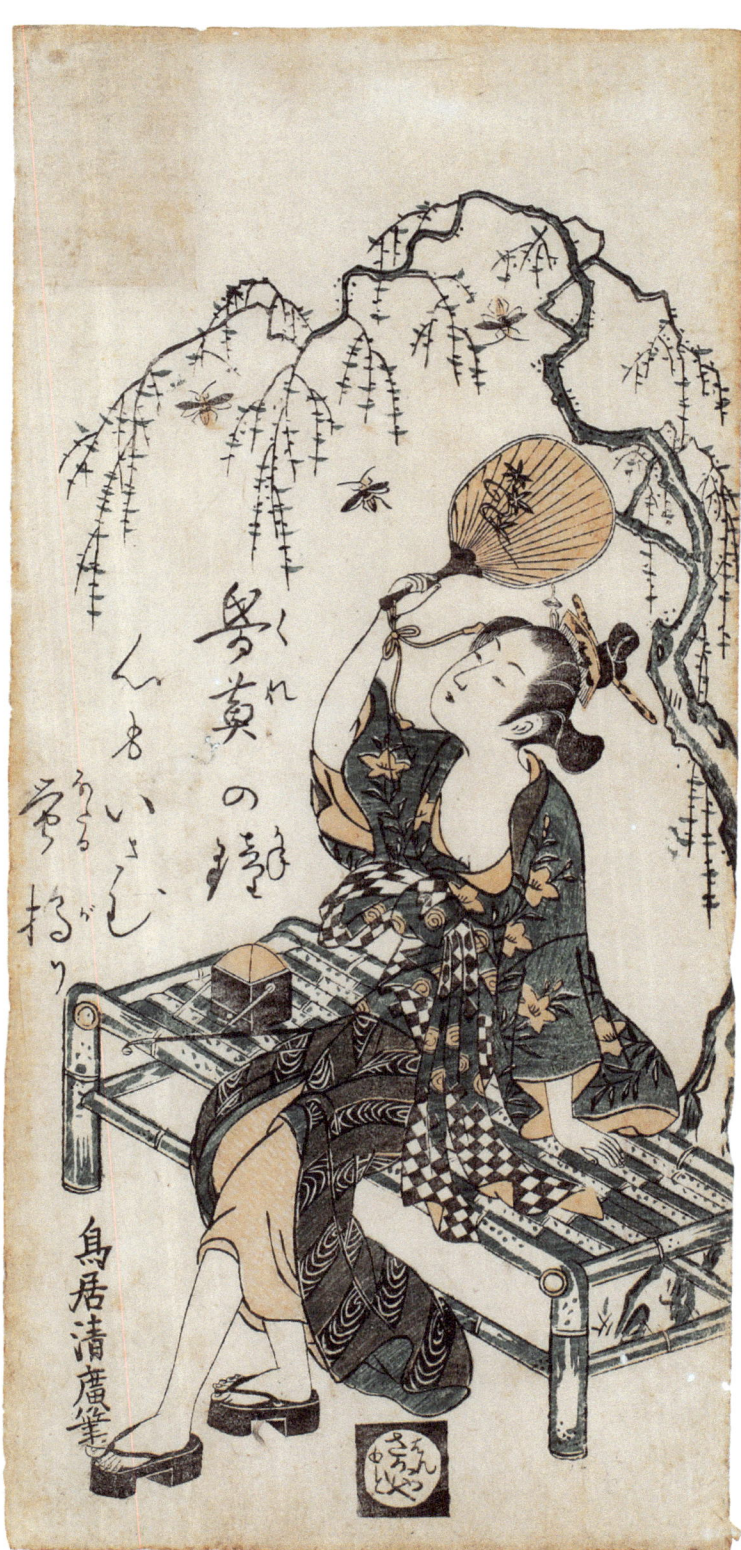

8

This print was made with a few woodblocks of the benisuri-e type before multiple color printing was invented. In 1765 full color woodblock printing was perfected by Suzuki Harunobu.

This is an interesting portrayal of a young woman using her fan to play with three huge fireflies. Fireflies were seen on the fringes of Edo. Sometimes people caught and placed them in insect cages to enjoy their dim light in their homes.

Hotaru Gari

Playing with Fireflies

Artist: Torii Kiyohiro
Publisher: Sakai-ya Kurobē
ca. 1751-1764

「蛍狩り」
団扇を手にした若い女性が、虫と戯れている。大きな虫に見えるが、この虫は蛍である。当時は、江戸の町はずれに行けば蛍を見ることができた。人々は、虫籠に蛍を入れ、そのほのかな灯りを家で楽しむこともあった。
この絵では、印刷に使用されている色板の数は、まだ少ない。多色摺りの錦絵は、明和2年（1765）に絵師の鈴木春信らによって創製された。

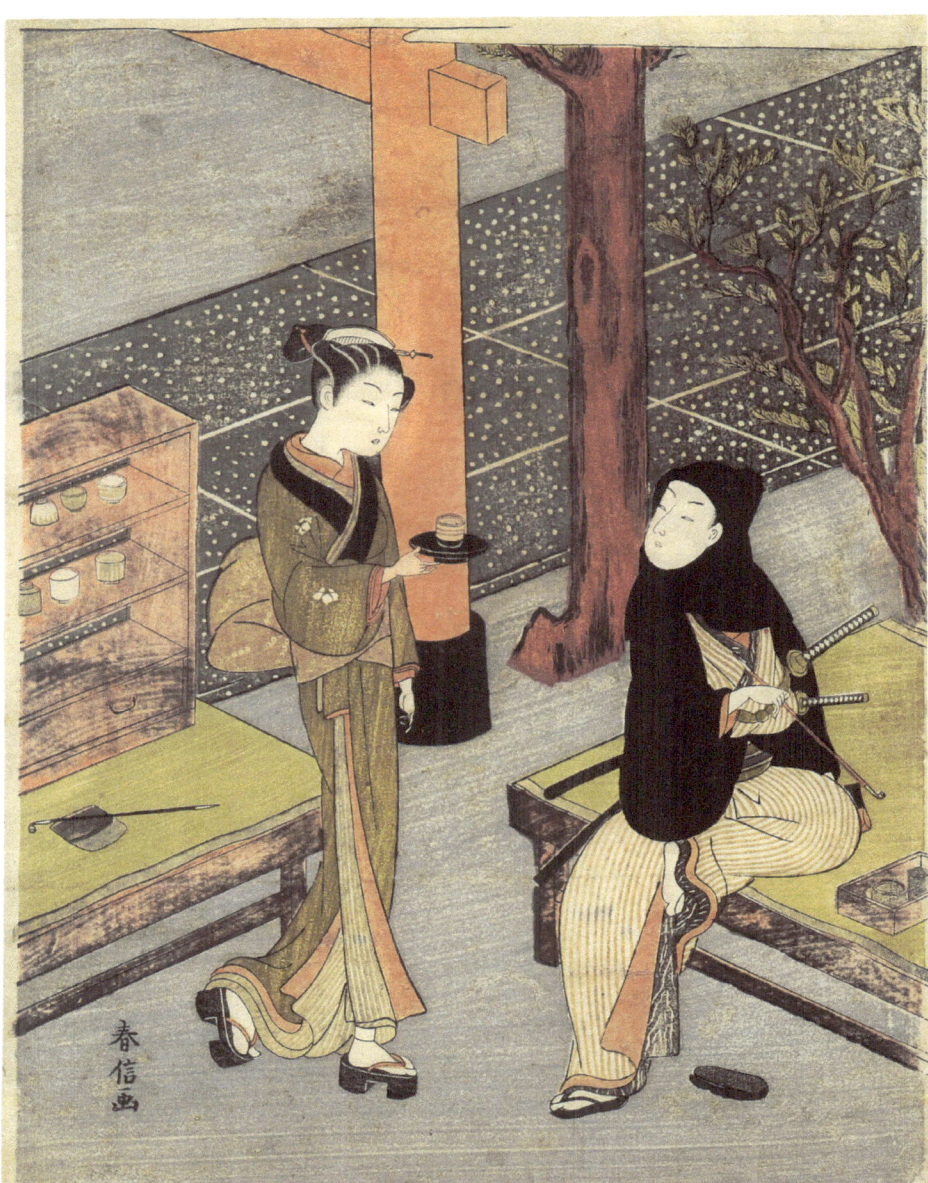

Osen Chaya

Kasamori Osen's Teahouse

Artist: Suzuki Harunobu
Publisher: Unknown
ca. 1765-1770

9

In this print, Kasamori Osen and a young samurai are depicted. Osen was very famous for her beauty, and the subject of many woodblock prints. She was the daughter of the owner of a popular teahouse located near the Kasamori Inari Shrine. Many men visited the shrine and then the teahouse to admire her. Here the samurai has a tobacco and tea break. He is gazing at Osen as she serves him tea. A portion of a Torii Gate can be seen on Osen's left. To her right is a row of shelves containing teacups. She is wearing geta clogs; the samurai, zōri sandals.

「お仙茶屋」
お仙と若い侍が描かれている。お仙は笠森稲荷にあった茶屋の娘で、当時、美貌で名高く、多くの浮世絵に描かれていた。毎日、大勢の男性がお仙を見るために、笠森稲荷を訪れていたという。この絵でも、侍はたばこを吸いながら、茶を運んできたお仙をじっと見つめている。
この絵では、色は、全て板木によって加えられている。多色摺り錦絵の技術は、本図の絵師、鈴木春信らによって創製された。

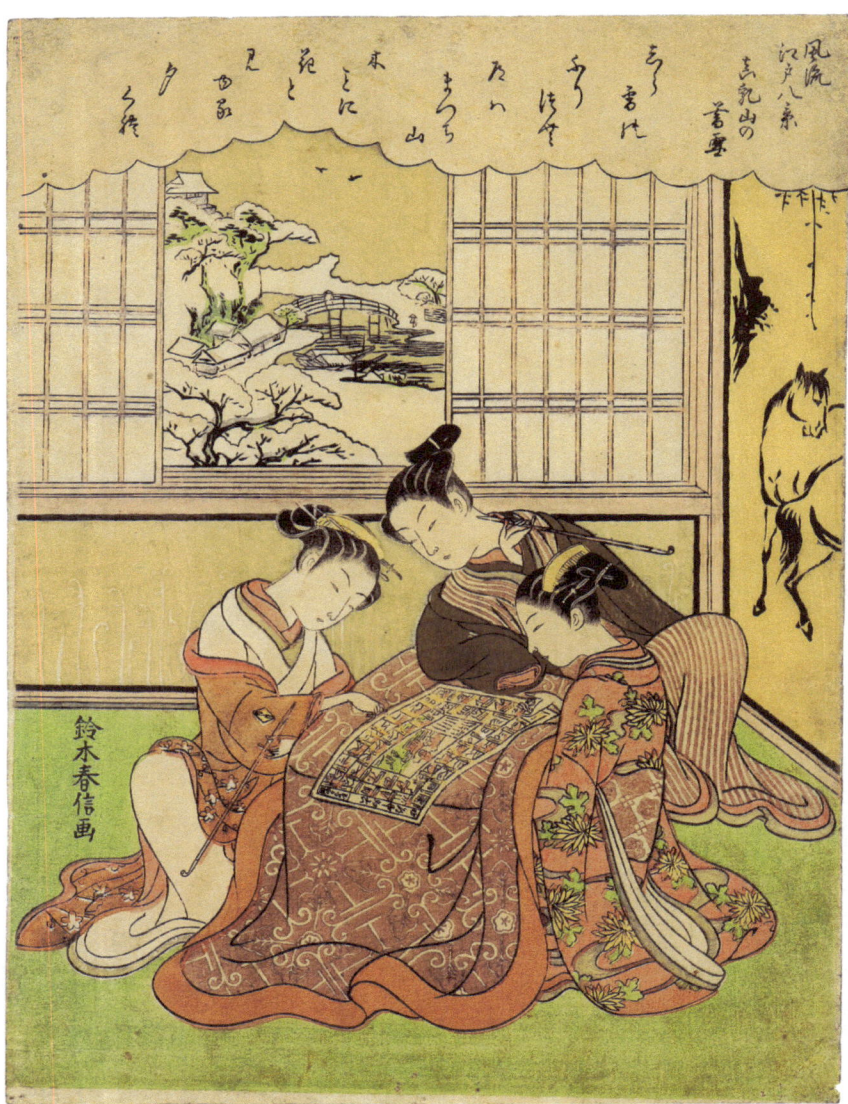

Fūryū Edo Hakkei Matsuchiyama no Bosetsu

Eight Sceneries of Elegant Edo Life, Snow at Dusk on Matsuchiyama Mountain

Artist: Suzuki Harunobu
Publisher: Unknown
ca. 1765-1770

10

Two women are playing a game called Dōchū Sugoroku. The game depicts on paper the landscape of the Fifty-Three Stages of the Tōkaidō Road from Edo to Kyoto. A single die is cast for the number of places one can move a piece called Koma along the stages of the Road. Koma is a general term for any piece used in a game such as this one, or Shōgi, Chess, etc.

A young man is observing the game and smoking. In the background through the open paper Shōji screens, one can see it has snowed. A blanket covering a charcoal heater keeps the players warm. The woman on the right is about to roll the die. To the right of the group is a framed sliding door showing a picture of a portion of a horse. This paper sliding door is called Fusuma and is used to partition the room. This scene depicts one of the ways of fūryū, which means enjoying an elegant life away from worldly affairs.

「風流江戸八景　真乳山の暮雪」
室内で二人の女性が絵双六で遊び、男性が一人、たばこを吸いながらそれを眺めている。窓の外では雪が降っており、彼らはコタツで暖を取っている。女性が遊んでいる双六は道中廻り双六で、江戸から京までの東海道中の名所が描かれている。サイコロとコマを使い、サイの目に従い、コマを進めていくという、現在でもよく行われるゲームである。

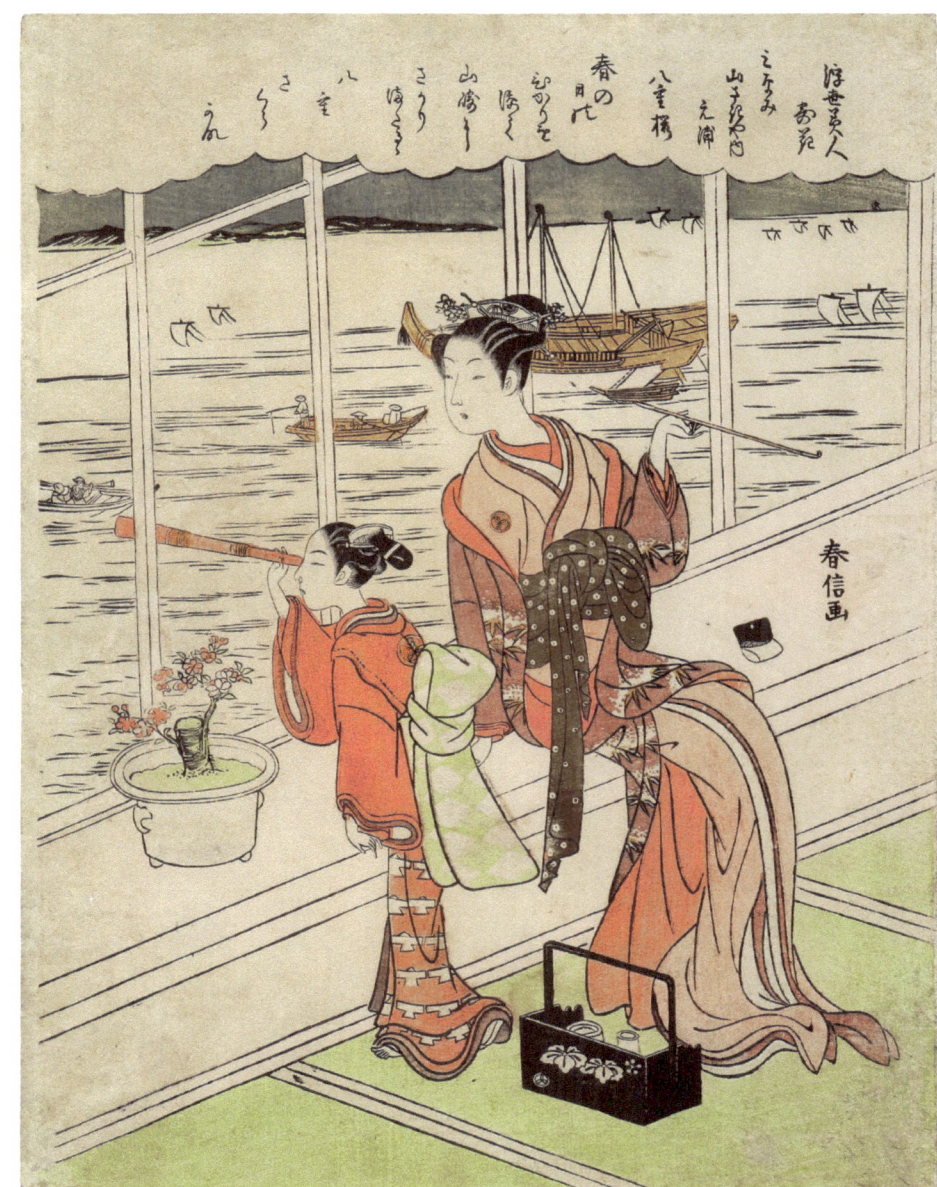

Ukiyo Bijin ni Yoseru Hana
Minami Yamasaki-ya uchi
Motoura Yaezakura

Comparing the Beautiful
Geisha Motoura to a Double-
Flowered Cherry Tree in a
Shinagawa Pleasure House

Artist: Suzuki Harunobu
Publisher: Unknown
ca. 1765-1770

11

In the Edo period there were many quarters of pleasure in Shinagawa near the sea. Unlike the quarters in the Yoshiwara district, the Shinagawa facilities were unauthorized by the government but were enjoyed by many for their casual atmosphere.

This print depicts a Shinagawa scene with a view of the sea. In the foreground are a geisha and a young apprentice. The geisha is smoking a kiseru pipe. The young girl is viewing the sea through a telescope. One large and some smaller boats can be seen. A tobacco tray is at the woman's feet. The flowering Bonsai cherry blossom tree is in the pot on the left of the young girl. The Japanese poem above them compares the beauty of the woman to that of the Bonsai cherry blossom tree.

「浮世美人寄花　ミなみ山さきや内　元浦　八重桜」
江戸時代、品川には多くの遊女がいた。幕府公認の吉原遊廓（北）は格式が高く、品川（南）は非公式ではあったが気軽に遊ぶことの出来る場所であった。品川の遊女を描く絵には、多くの場合、背景に海が描かれていた。この絵では、遊女とその見習いの子どもが描かれ、見習いの子どもは遠眼鏡で沖を見ている。
美人を花にたとえたシリーズで、ここでは、元浦という名の遊女が、傍らに置かれた盆栽の八重桜にたとえられている。

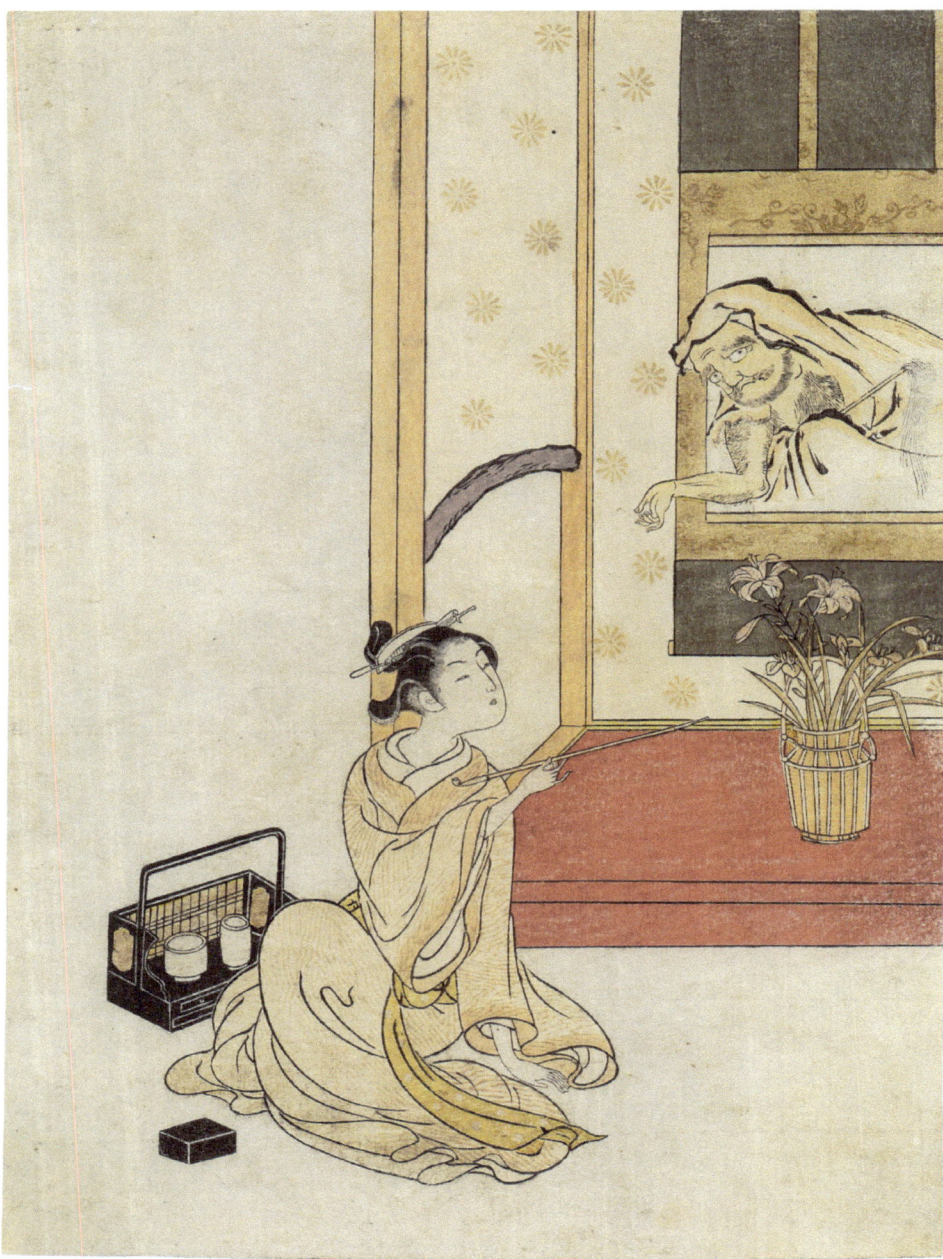

Daruma to Tabako

Bodhidharma and Tobacco

Artist: Unknown
Publisher: Unknown
ca. 1772-1781

12

This is a very humorous print with different possible interpretations. Daruma, Bodhidharma, is shown on the hanging scroll to the right. It is said that this Buddhist monk meditated for nine long years and that his arms and legs had shriveled into his body. In this print he is leaning out with a stretched arm, begging for the kiseru pipe of the young lady. The print may simply show that the enlightened monk wants to smoke. Or does it imply that receiving her pipe means accepting her offer of courtship? It shows that the pleasure of smoking and the beauty of a woman are hard to contend with, even for the enlightened, ascetic Daruma. Note her beauty as symbolized by the flowering lily decoration.

「だるまとたばこ」
掛軸の中の達磨がきせるを受け取ろうとしている、たいへん楽しい絵である。達磨は、厳しい修行を積んだことで知られているが、この絵が言っているのは、達磨でさえも、たばこを吸わずに掛軸に納まっていられないということであろうか。あるいは、吸い付けきせるを女性から受け取るのは、女性からの好意を受け入れるということを意味するため、禁欲的な達磨でさえも、女性になびくということであろうか。

13

This is a hashira-e print. Hashira means a column. In those days people hung simply mounted hashira-e as hanging scrolls on columns to decorate the house interior. In this print, the monk Saigyō (1118-1190) is looking at Mt. Fuji, exhaling smoke from his long kiseru pipe. In the Edo period, he was often the subject of woodblock prints. Although tobacco was still unknown in Japan in the 12th century, he is shown smoking in some prints.

Saigyō is well known for his mastery of tanka poems. In contrast to haiku poems of 5-7-5 syllables, tanka poems consist of 5-7-5-7-7, a total of 31 syllables. In this print, the poem above Saigyō is a haiku with the theme of Saigyō and Mt. Fuji. On the top is Mt. Fuji. His stable boy walking Saigyō's horse is at the bottom.

Fujimi Saigyō

Saigyō, Viewing Mt. Fuji and Smoking

Artist: Unknown
Publisher: Unknown
ca. 1772-1781

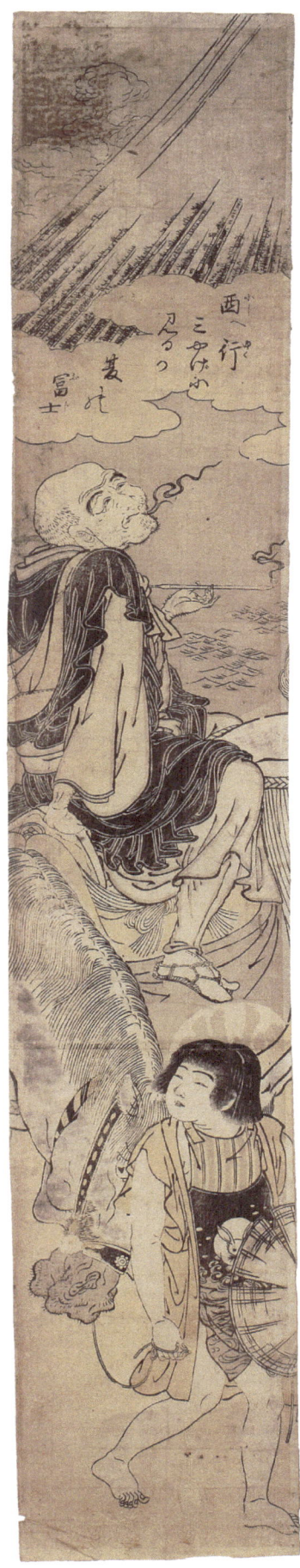

「富士見西行」
この絵は、柱絵と呼ばれている。当時の人々は、このような絵を柱の節隠しとして使い、あるいは紙などで表装し、簡易な掛軸として家に飾ったりもした。
この絵には西行が描かれている。西行は 12 世紀に実在していた人物で、多くの優れた和歌を残したことで知られているが、江戸時代には、浮世絵にもよく描かれた。西行のいた時代、当然たばこはまだ日本にはなかったが、この絵のように、たばこを吸いながら富士山をながめる西行も描かれている。

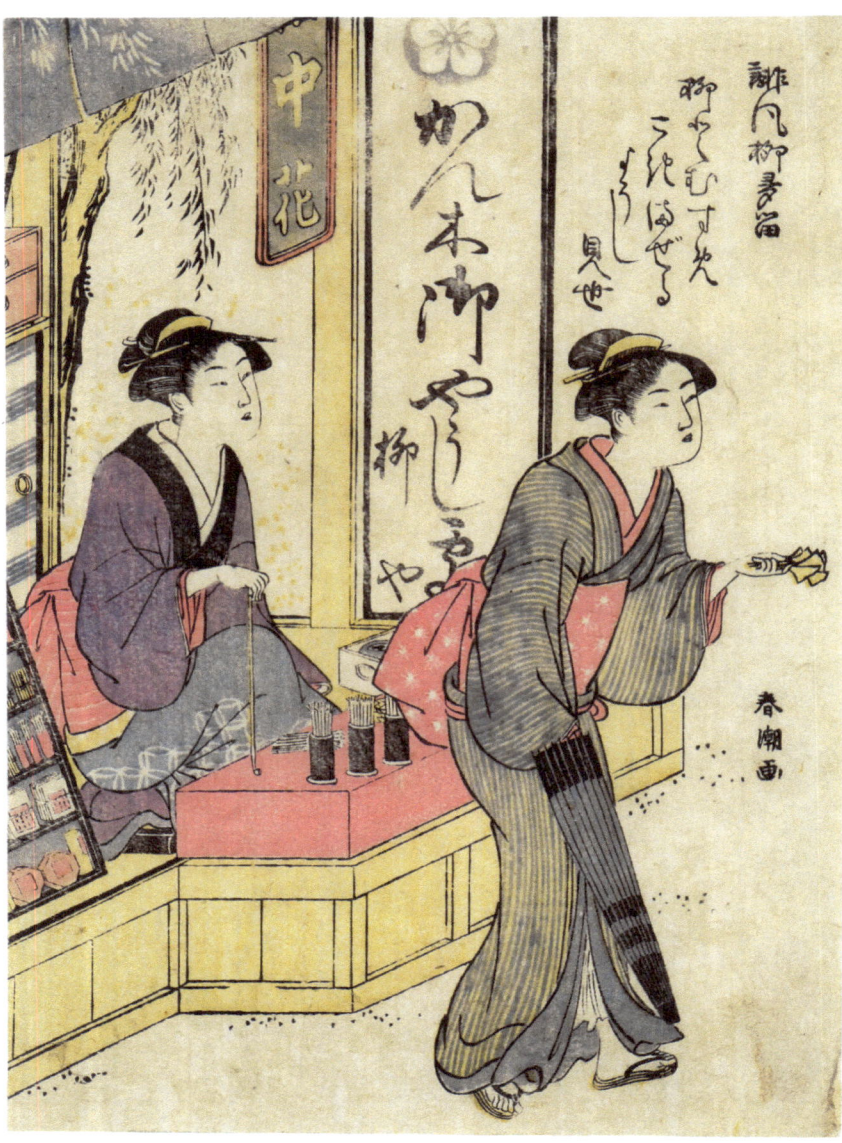

Yōji Mise to Kanban Musume

A Tooth Stick Shop and Two Beauties

Artist: Katsukawa Shunchō
Publisher: Unknown
ca. 1781-1789

14

A tooth stick shop is depicted. Note the long tooth sticks in the three containers in front of the shop. These sticks were made of willow. The tip of each stick was beaten to form a tuft to be used like a toothbrush. To the far left a part of the display shelf is shown.

There were many such shops in the premises of shrines and temples in the Edo period. Tooth stick stores were famous for having beautiful women to lure customers into the store. The most famous was the Hon-Yanagi-ya's Ofuji of the 1760s. It was said that she was one of the three most beautiful young women in Edo. Her father's shop Hon-Yanagi-ya was near the Sensō-ji Temple in Asakusa right next to a big Ginkgo tree.

The name of the shop in this print is Yanagi-ya as seen in the store signboard in the center of the print. Because the print was made between 1781-1789, the woman sitting with a kiseru pipe is not Ofuji. The standing woman has Ginkgo leaves in her left hand. It seems the name of Ofuji was always associated with Ginkgo trees and inseparable from tooth stick shops.

「楊枝店と看板娘」

楊枝店が描かれている。江戸時代、多くの寺社の境内にはこのような店があった。楊枝店には美女の看板娘がつきものだが、特に、明和（1764-1772）頃には本柳屋のお藤が有名で、お藤は明和の三美人の一人に数えられていた。本柳屋は浅草寺の本堂の裏にあり、店の周りには銀杏の樹があった。

画中の店は「柳屋」で、絵の出版は天明（1781-1789）頃であると思われるため、ここに描かれている看板娘はお藤ではない。しかし、描かれたもう一人の娘が銀杏の葉を手にしていることからも、お藤に関連づけて描かれたと考えられる。

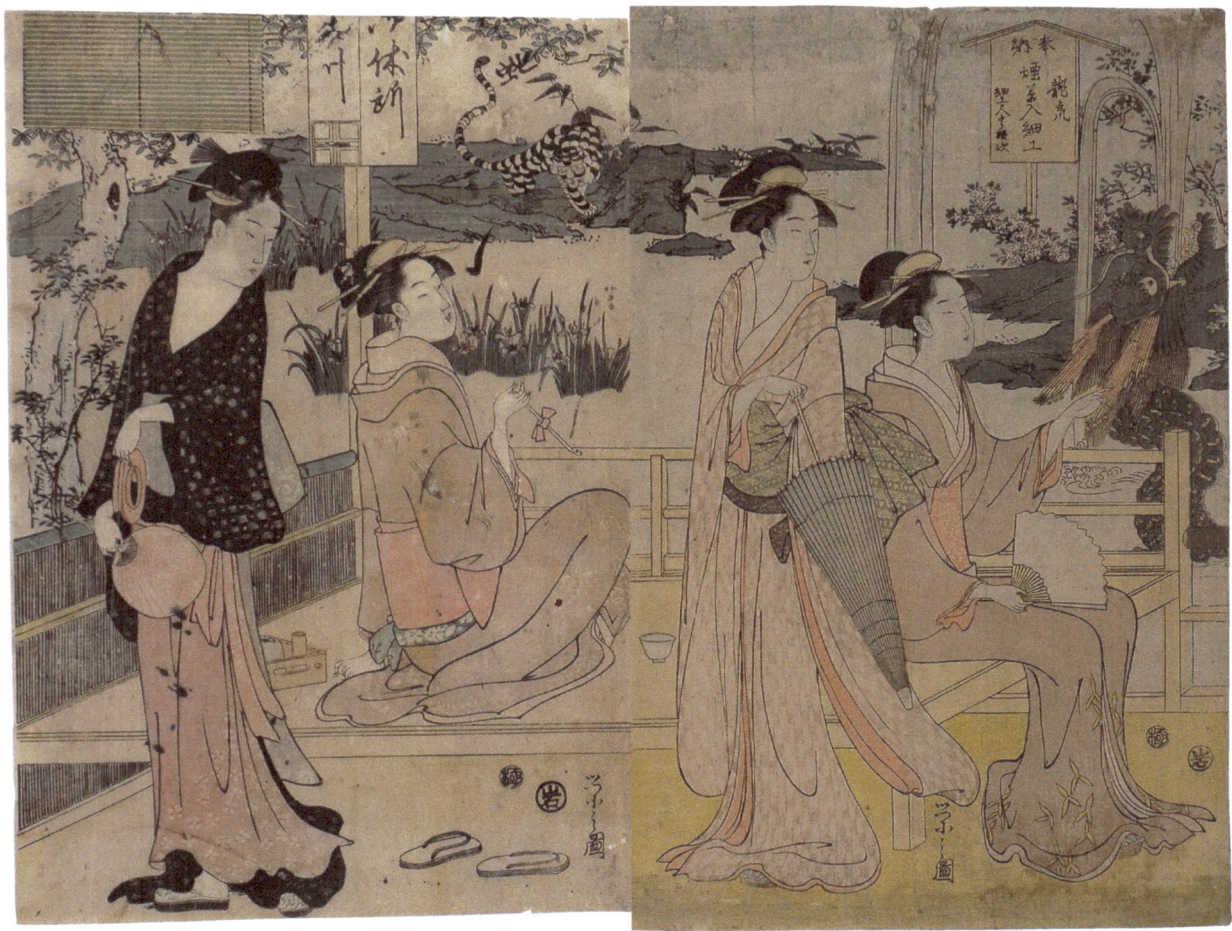

Tabakoire Saiku Ryū-ko

A Teahouse with a Dragon and Tiger Motif

Artist: Chōbunsai Eishi
Publisher: Iwato-ya Genpachi
ca. 1789-1801

15

This print illustrates an Edo period teahouse in the 1790s with a dragon and tiger motif. Originally, there were three panels. Unfortunately, the third panel on the right side was lost. A dragon and a tiger are depicted behind four women. The dragon's head and part of his tail are on the far right. The rest of his long tail was on the lost panel. Above the dragon is a sign explaining that the dragon and tiger were made from many tobacco pouches, kiseru pipes, and their containers. Black and yellow tobacco pouches were used for the tiger, and kiseru pipes and green containers were used for the dragon.
In the Edo period, objects like these were made from shells, baskets, straw, string, etc. They were very popular among ordinary people. Some teahouses exhibited them to attract visitors to drink tea and enjoy the surroundings. Three of the four women are visitors. The one on the left wearing a Japanese apron is a teahouse waitress.

「煙草入細工　龍虎」
寛政（1789-1801）頃の見世物茶屋の様子。ここでは、たばこ入れで造られた龍と虎が飾られている。退色しているが、虎は黒と黄のたばこ入れ、龍は、緑のきせる入れとその中に収められたきせるで造られていたことがわかる。3枚続きの右1枚が欠けており、残念ながら龍の長い尾は見ることができない。
江戸時代後期には、貝や籠、麦わら、糸などで人形などを造る細工物の見世物が大流行していた。このように、茶屋にも、造り物や珍しい鳥などを見せたりするところがあった。

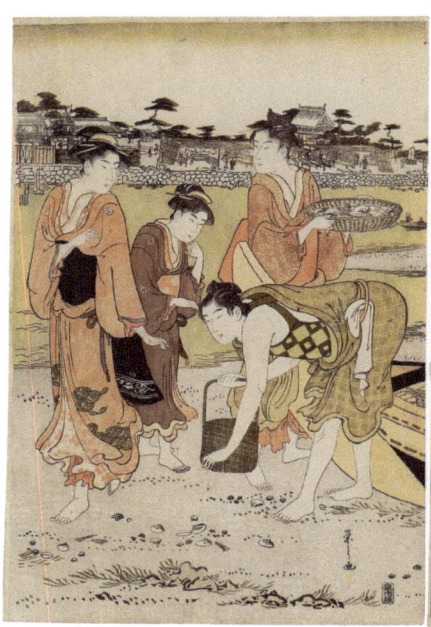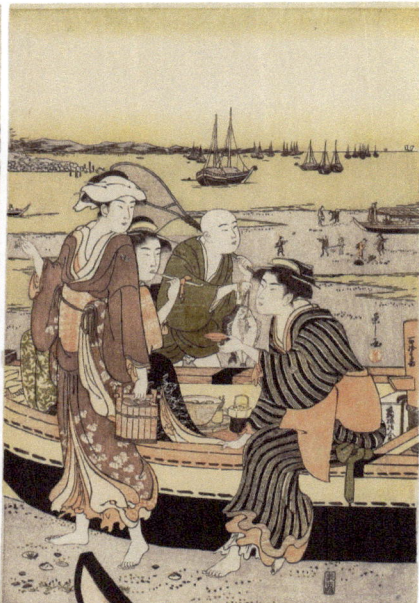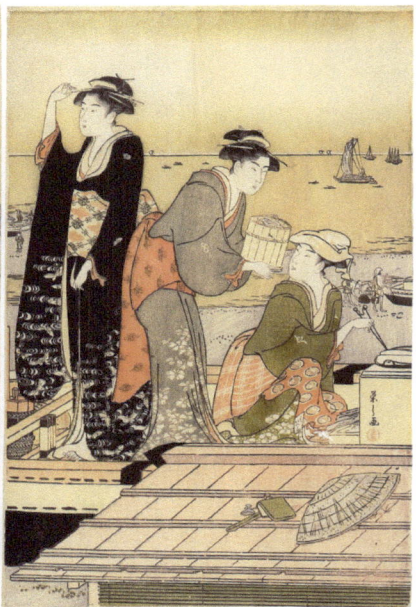

Shiohigari

Gathering Shellfish

Artist: Chōbunsai Eishi
Publisher: Izumi-ya Ichibē
ca. 1789-1801

16

People are enjoying gathering shellfish. In the Edo period it was a popular activity for people to go to seashores for shellfish gathering in Spring. Some well-to-do chartered boats to go out on the sea in shallow places like Suzaki or Shinagawa. They went there before daylight. During low tide the boats would be grounded as shown. Many enjoyed spending the day gathering shellfish, as well as eating, drinking, and smoking. The food and drinks one consumes for pleasure, such as tea, alcohol, and tobacco, are called Shikōhin in Japanese, as described in Dr. Ohkawa's Introduction on page *v*.

「潮干狩り」
江戸の人々にとって、春の潮干狩りは毎年恒例の楽しみであった。中には、船を借り、大勢で出かける人もいたが、そのような人たちは、夜明け前から船に乗り込み、遠浅の海に出て干潮を待ち、干上がった海から貝や小魚を拾い集めた。貝を拾うたけでなく、飲んだり食べたりしながら一日を楽しんだ。

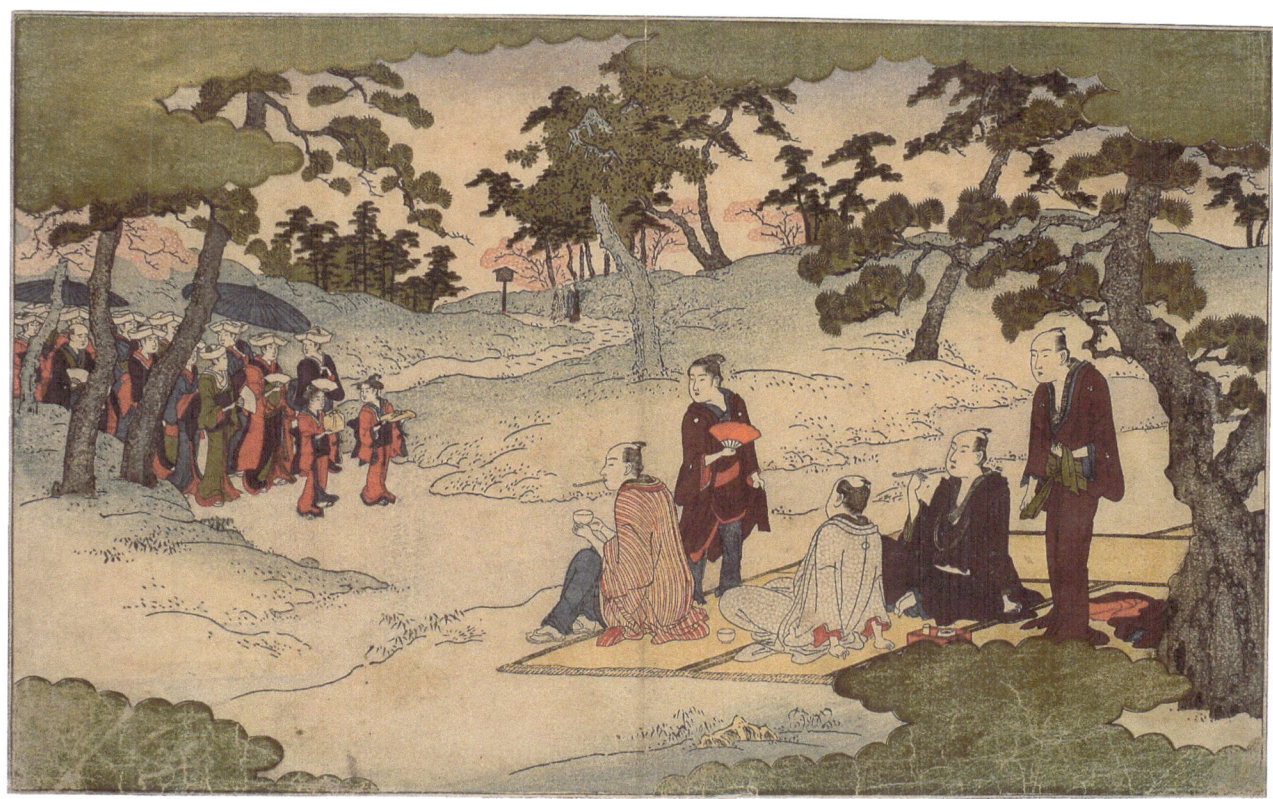

Fugen-zō

Fugen-zō Kyōka Poem Book

Artist: Kitagawa Utamaro
Publisher: Tsuta-ya Jūzaburō
1790

17

This is one of the prints by Utamaro inserted into the gorgeous kyōka poem book called Fugen-zō. The kyōka is the tanka form poem with a humorous theme. Fugen-zō is a variety of cherry blossoms. All of the five prints in the Fugen-zō kyōka poem book depict famous cherry blossom regions.

This print shows different people enjoying the cherry blossoms on the hills of Ueno. To the right are a group of five men. To the left are mostly women belonging to the aristocracy. In the Edo period, the tombs of the Tokugawa shogunate were in the Kan'eiji Temple in Ueno. Hence, it was prohibited to drink alcohol or sing there. The people in this print are not drinking alcohol. They are sitting under the trees, drinking tea, or smoking their kiseru pipes.

「普賢像」
この絵本の書名は「普賢像」であるが、それは桜の品種名「普賢象」に由来する。この狂歌絵本には歌麿の絵が５点挿入されていて、すべてが桜の名所の画となっている。ここで描かれているのは上野山内であるが、上野寛永寺には将軍家の霊廟があり、しかも住職は宮家出身であったため、ここでの花見は、飲酒や鳴り物が禁じられていた。この絵にも、桜の間を静かに歩く御殿女中らしい一団と、敷物を広げて酒は飲まず、茶を飲み、たばこを吸うだけの男性たちが描かれている。

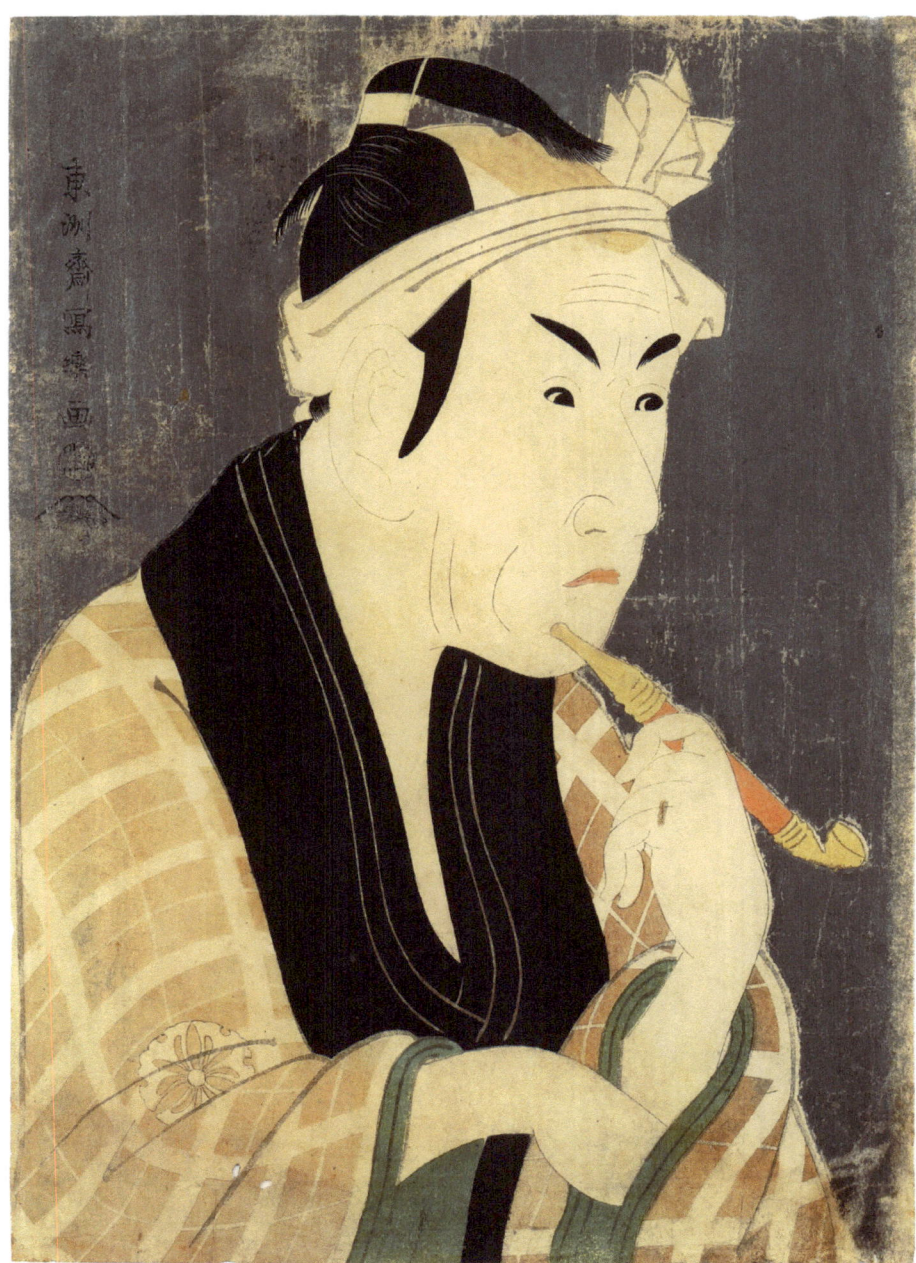

Matsumoto Kōshirō no
Sakana-ya Gorobē

Matsumoto Kōshirō IV, as the
Fish Vendor Gorobē

Artist: Tōshūsai Sharaku
Publisher: Tsuta-ya Jūzaburō
1794

18

A well-known Edo period kabuki actor, Matsumoto Kōshirō IV, is depicted. He performed in May 1794 the gallant role of Sakana-ya Gorobē, the fish vendor in a play titled *"Katakiuchi Noriaibanashi"*. He looks very stern holding a short-stemmed red kiseru pipe.

The artist, Tōshūsai Sharaku, produced more than 100 different prints and dozens of other works in less than two years. This is one of his earlier works. The color of Kōshirō's shaved head and the Kōshirō Gōshi, checkered pattern of his costume, were originally indigo blue. Although the indigo color faded away, the background mica is still well preserved.

「松本幸四郎の肴屋五郎兵衛」
寛政6年（1794）に上演された「敵討乗
合噺」の登場人物、仁侠の肴屋五郎兵衛に
扮した四代目の松本幸四郎が描かれてい
る。幸四郎の肴屋五郎兵衛は、頑固そうな
顔をして、朱色の短い羅宇のきせるを持っ
ている。
この絵は有名な東洲斎写楽によって描かれ
たもので、彼の初期の作品の一つである。
月代の色や、衣装の左右の肩の色の違いか
らもわかるように藍色が退色しているが、
背景の雲母はたいへんよく残っている。

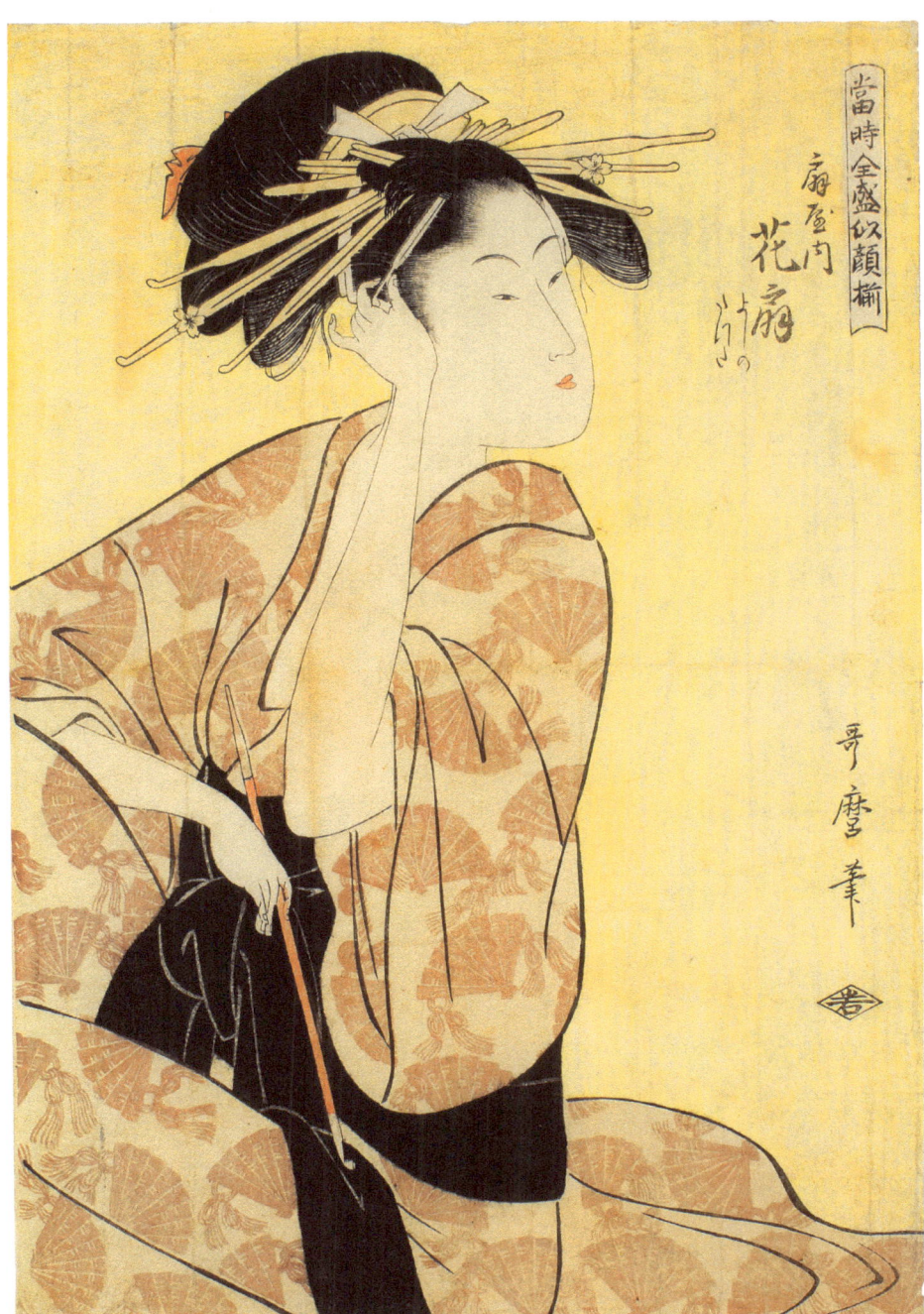

Tōji Zensei Nigao Zoroe
Hanaōgi

A Portrait of the Highest Rank
Courtesan, Hanaōgi

Artist: Kitagawa Utamaro
Publisher: Wakasa-ya Yoichi
1794

19

The artist Utamaro depicted Hanaōgi IV, one of the highest rank courtesans of the Edo period. She belonged to the Ōgi-ya pleasure quarter of Yoshiwara. She is holding a kiseru pipe with a long red stem in her right hand, which symbolizes her high status. Note the many ornamental hairpins in Hanaōgi's hair. She is wearing a casual cotton kimono called yukata with the pattern of fans. There are also embossed cherry blossoms, flowers, underneath the fans on her yukata. Hana means a flower; Ōgi means a fan. Her yukata symborizes her name, Hanaōgi.

「当時全盛似顔揃　扇屋内花扇　よしの　たつた」
ここに描かれた花扇は、四代目の花扇である。吉原の大見世扇屋の遊女で、この当時「呼出」という最高位にあった。この絵が描かれた直後、なじみの客と駆け落ち事件を起こしたことが知られている。この駆け落ちに関係してか、同じ絵でありながら、花扇の名が「花」とされ、シリーズ名まで変えられた絵も確認されている。
花扇が手にするのは、朱羅宇のきせるで、遊女のシンボルであった。なお、何代目の花扇のものであるかは不明であるが、たばこと塩の博物館は、花扇の所有と伝えられるたばこ盆と、朱羅宇のきせるを所蔵している。

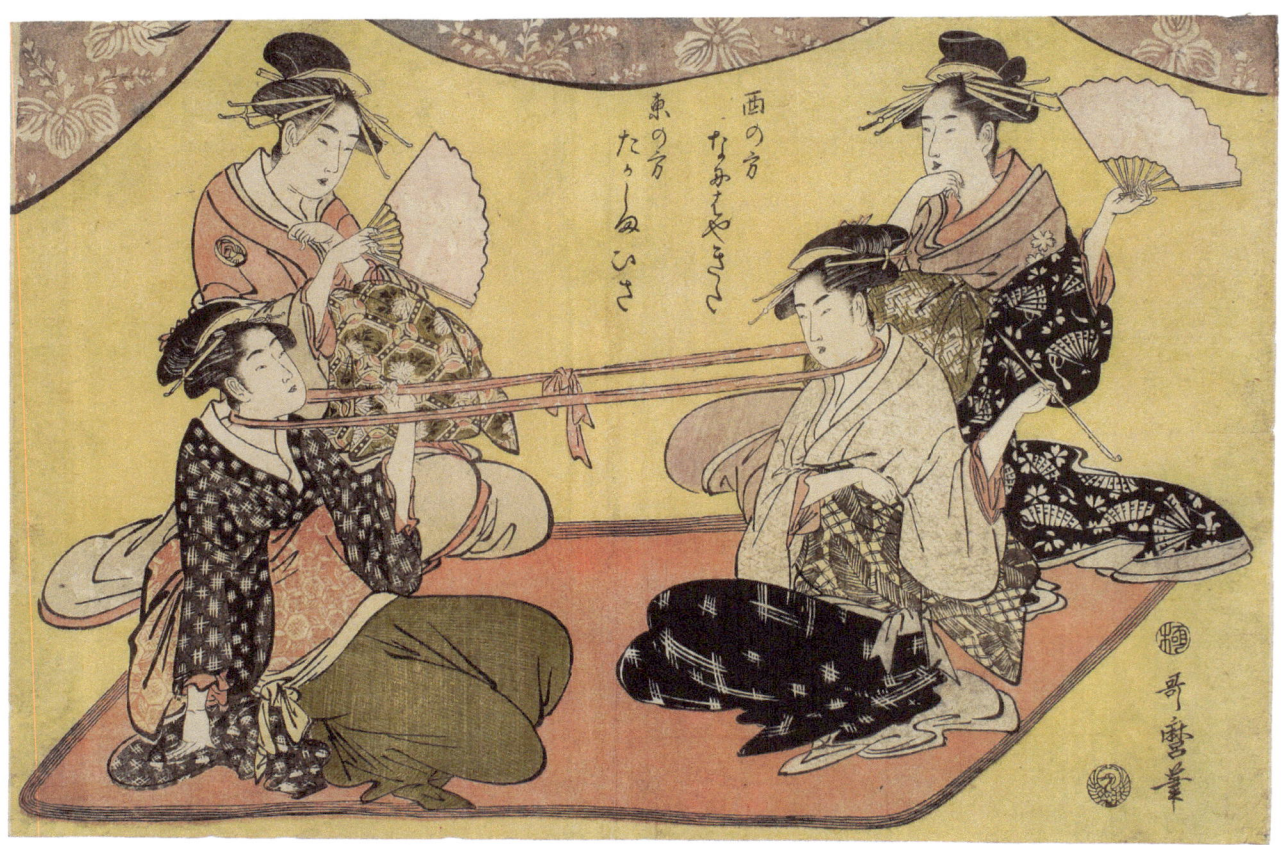

Nibijin Kubihiki

Playing the Sash Game

Artist: Kitagawa Utamaro
Publisher: Tsuru-ya Kiemon
ca. 1793-1794

20

Four beautiful women are depicted in this print by the artist Utamaro. Two of them are enjoying a game called kubihiki. A sash is tied in a loop. It is thrown behind the neck of each contestant. Both lean backwards. The winner is the one who can pull her opponent forward. The two contestants are Takashima Hisa and Naniwa-ya Kita. They were waitresses from two competing teahouses and were famous beauties in Edo. The two women with fans cheering each player are Chōji-ya Hinazuru and Ōgi-ya Hanaōgi. Both were members of the highest rank courtesans in Yoshiwara. It is interesting to note that one of the contestants has a kiseru pipe in her left hand even while playing the strenuous game.

「二美人首引き」
高島ひさと難波屋きたが首引きを行い、丁字屋の雛鶴と扇屋の花扇が、扇を手に応援している。高島ひさと難波屋きたは、共にお茶屋の看板娘で、寛政の美人として名高かった。また丁字屋と扇屋は吉原の大見世で、雛鶴と花扇は、それぞれの最高位の遊女であった。
首引きの最中にも、難波屋のきたがきせるを手にしているのがおもしろい。
なお、この絵については、四人の女性全ての名が入っているもの、ここに掲げたもののように「きた」「ひさ」の名だけが記されたもの、そして全ての名が削られたものの三種が知られている。

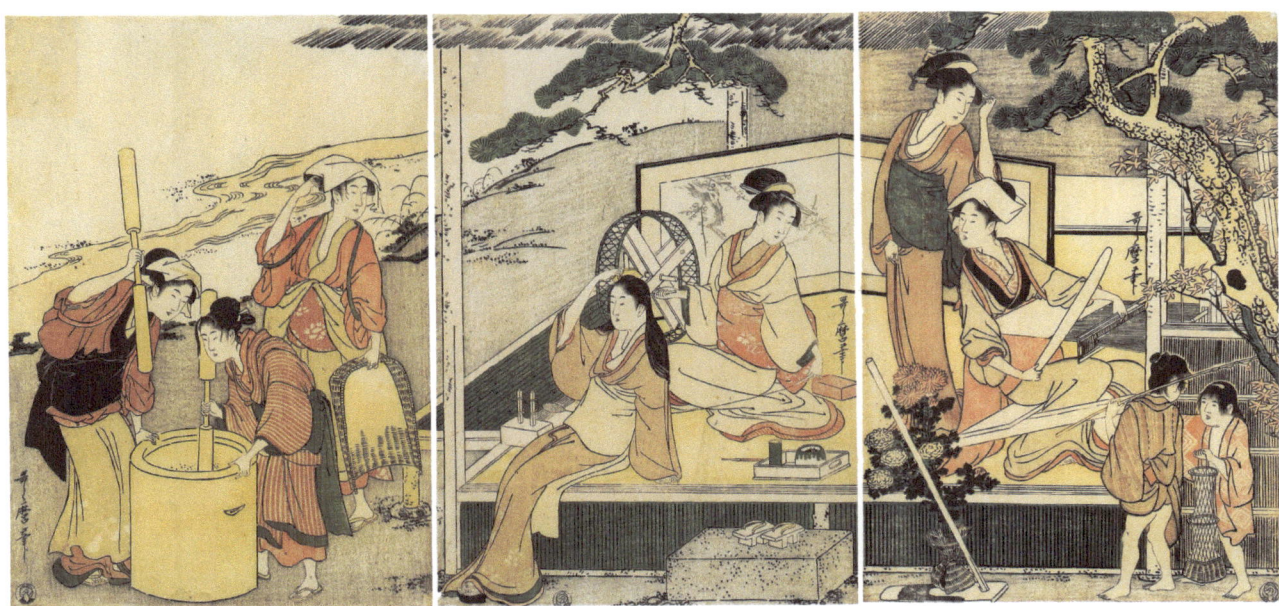

Nōka no Aki

Farmer's House in Autumn

Artist: Kitagawa Utamaro
Publisher: Tsuru-ya Kiemon
ca. 1801-1804

21

This woodblock print, nishiki-e, shows different tasks performed by the women of farm families. They are depicted as hard working and beautiful women.

From right to left they are weaving, spinning, and milling cereal. In the left panel, the woman standing holds the rim of a basket. The woman in the background of the middle panel is spinning thread. In the right panel, the woman sitting is working on a loom. One of the children has a fishing pole. The other is carrying a basket. They just returned from fishing.

Note there are no men. Obviously the artist did not try to depict a real farm village scene where adults of both genders would be working.

「農家の秋」
この絵には、農家の女性たちの働く姿が描かれている。右から、機織、紡績、製粉となっている。子どもたちは、釣り竿と魚籠を持っており、釣りから帰ってきたものと思われる。部屋には、ひと休みするためのたばこ盆が置かれている。素朴な農家の女性たちが描かれているが、男性の姿は見えない。農村の現実ではないが、長閑な田園風景を伝えている。

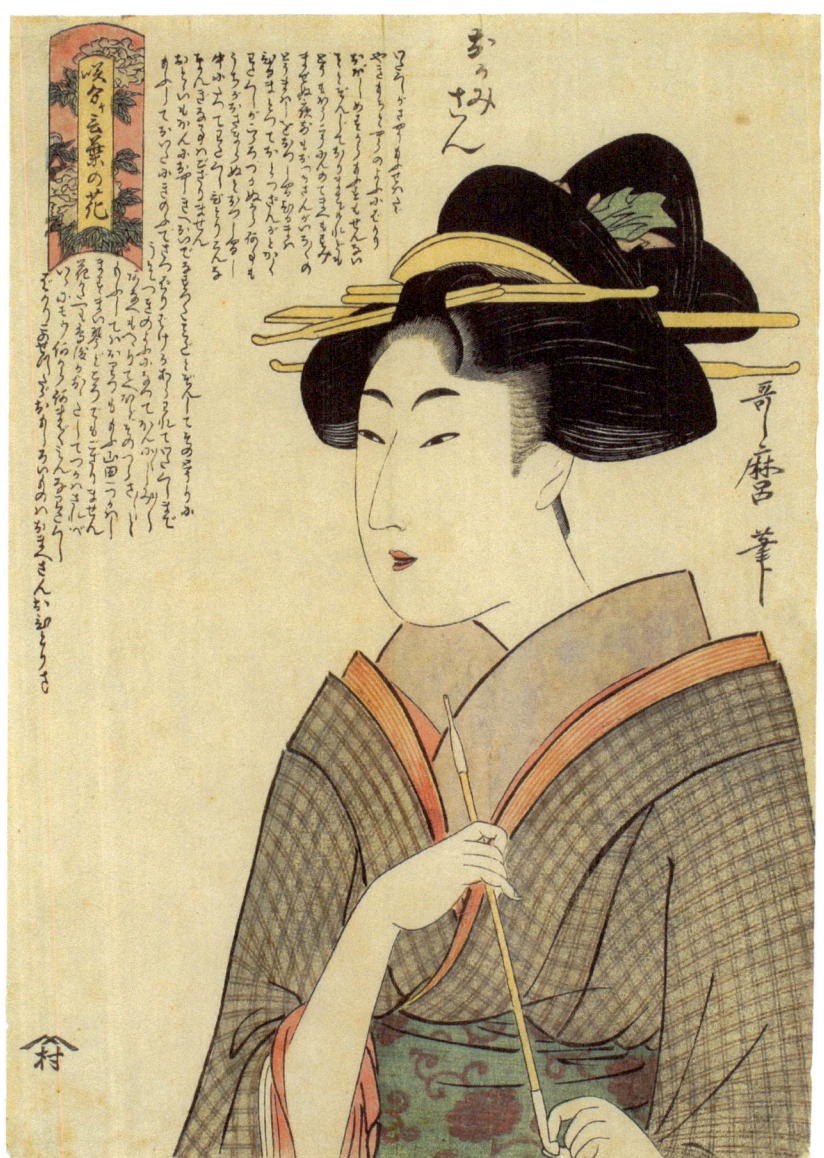

Sakiwake Kotoba no Hana, Okamisan

Verbal Story Series: A Merchant's Wife

Artist: Kitagawa Utamaro
Publisher: Yamamura
1802

22

This print is from the Ukiyo-e series involving variations in verbal stories. The written text called Variation of Blooms is shown above the beautiful lady. The text described a merchant's wife complaining to her husband that her parents-in-law chided her for something.

Note that her teeth look black. During the Edo period, married women dyed their teeth. They believed that tobacco oil would make their black teeth shimmer. Hence the smoking rate of women was quite high in those days. The merchant's wife is putting shredded tobacco leaf in a kiseru pipe with her left forefinger. Note the modest pattern of her kimono in contrast to the many long ornamental pins in her hair.

「咲分ケ言葉の花　おかみさん」
描かれているのは商家のおかみさんで、義理の両親に小言を言われたことを旦那に愚痴っている。彼女の歯は黒く見えるが、江戸時代は、既婚女性は歯を黒く染めて（お歯黒）いた。お歯黒は、たばこの脂で美しく見えると信じられていたこともあり、当時の女性の喫煙率は大変高かった。

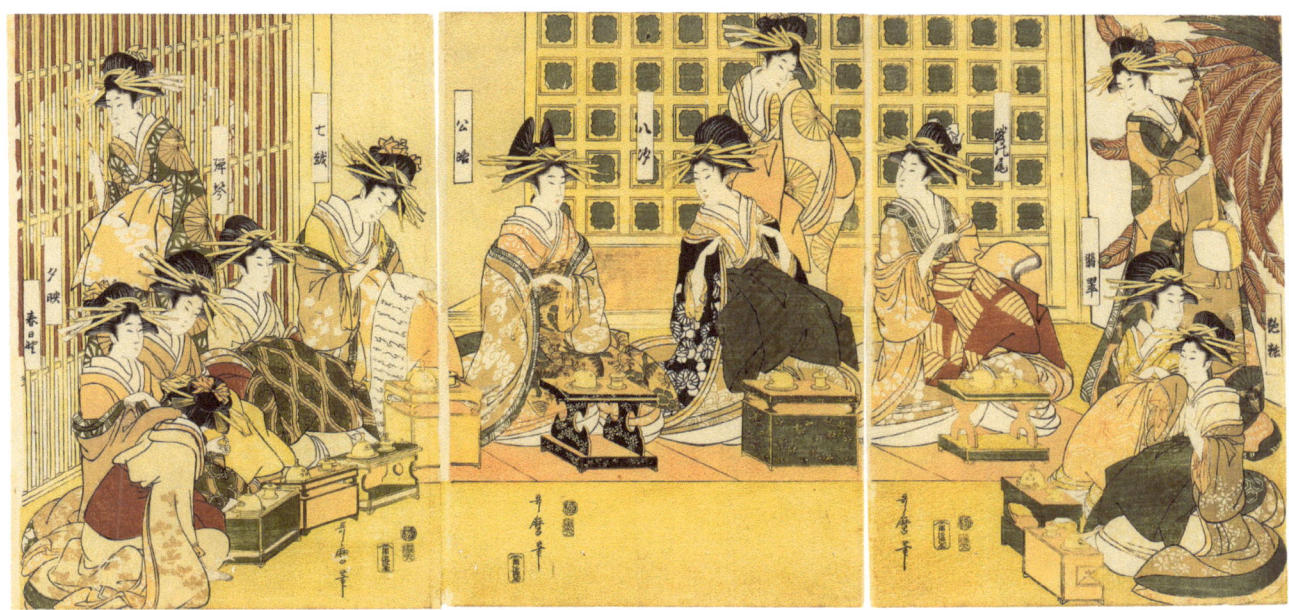

Harimise

Waiting for Guests in Front of Ōgi-ya

Artist: Kitagawa Utamaro
Publisher: Ōmi-ya Gonkurō
1806

23

This print depicts a large room inside of Ōgi-ya in Yoshiwara. The title, Harimise, indicates that the women sitting in the front are waiting for guests.

There are three standing women in the back. They are of the highest rank courtesan and need not participate in harimise because they can afford to wait for guests in their own rooms. They were put in this print only as the symbols of Ōgi-ya. Of the nine women sitting, four of them are seated on the red carpet, indicating their higher rank. Their tobacco trays in front of them are also more elaborate than those of the five other women sitting on the floor. The woman at the left front kneeling down is a servant.

「張見世」
扇屋の遊女十二人が描かれている。座っている遊女九人は店先に並び、格子越しに客の指名を待っている最中で、これを張見世といった。九人の遊女のうち、緋毛氈の上に座っている四人は、他の五人より格が上であった。一人一人の前に置かれたたばこ盆も、緋毛氈上の四人の方が大きく立派である。
なお、立ち姿で描かれているのは、当時扇屋で最も位の高かった「呼出」の遊女三人と思われるが、実際には「呼出」は張見世を行わなかったため、ここでは扇屋の代表的遊女として象徴的に描かれたと考えられる。

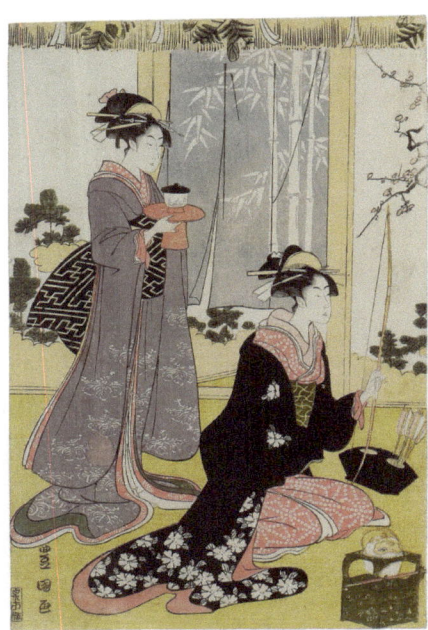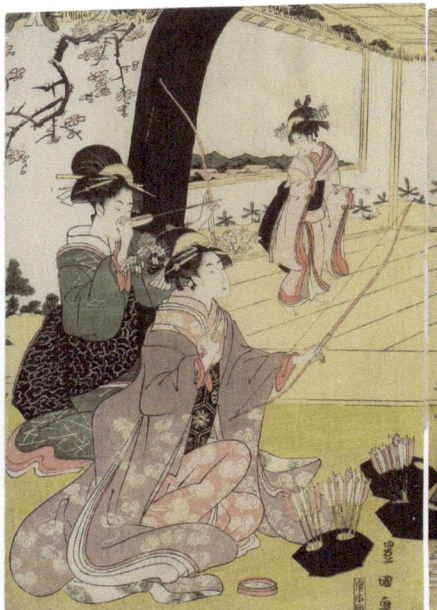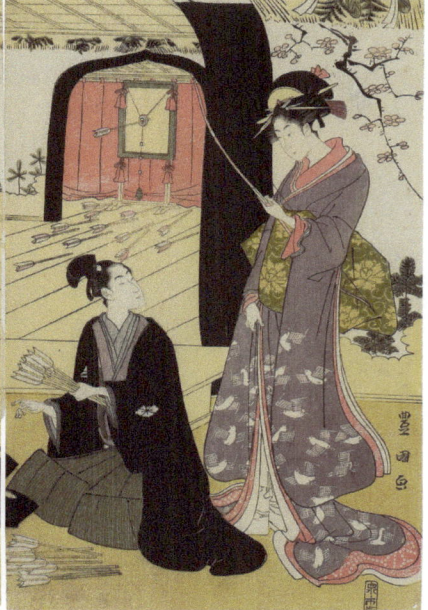

Yōkyū

Yōkyū at a Nobleman's Residence

Artist: Utagawa Toyokuni I
Publisher: Izumi-ya Ichibē
ca. 1789-1801

24

A nobleman's daughter is playing an archery game called yōkyū as a New Year's recreation. Yōkyū is a small bow made just for this game. In the Edo period, there were many archery fields in popular places such as Ryōgoku and Asakusa. Many common people played this game. The scene in this print, however, is not a public yōkyū playing field.

This print shows a spacious area of a nobleman's residence where his daughter can play. There are many valets near her. A maid is serving her tea during a break. The background of each of these three panels has New Year's decorations. In the center panel one can see through the window the roofs of various houses in the distance. This indicates that the scene depicted in the print is on the second floor of this elaborate residence.

「楊弓」
楊弓は遊戯用の小形の弓である。江戸時代は盛り場などには楊弓場がつきもので、誰でもが気軽に楽しめる遊びであった。しかし、ここに描かれているのは、そのような楊弓場ではなく、大きな屋敷の一室であろうと思われる。ここは当時めずらしかった二階家らしく、奥の窓からは、町の家々の屋根が見える。
高貴な家の娘が楊弓で遊び、女中たちが世話をしている。娘の側にはたばこ盆が置かれ、お茶を用意している女中もいる。

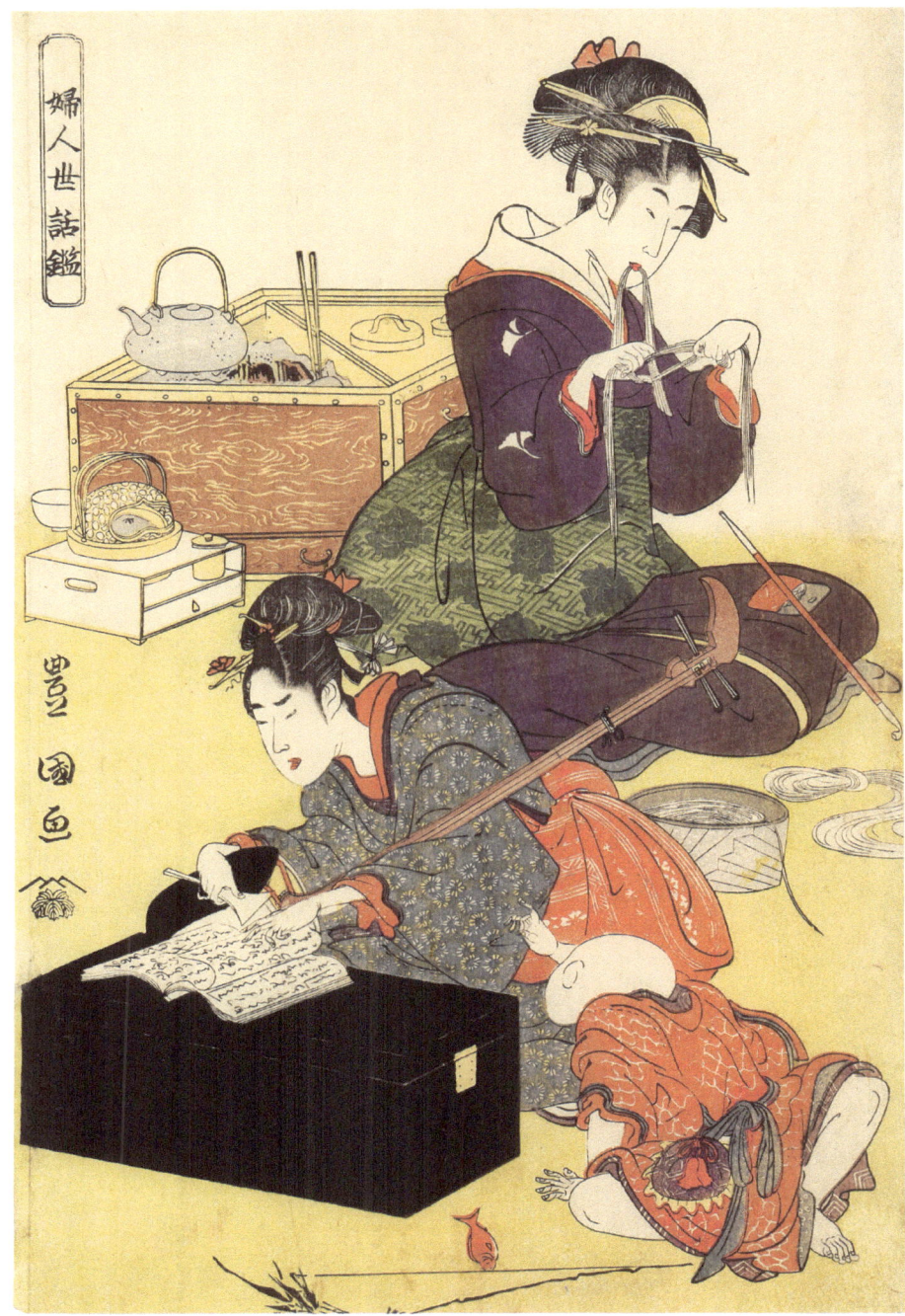

Fujin Sewa Kagami

A Scene from an Ordinary Family's Life in Edo

Artist: Utagawa Toyokuni I
Publisher: Tsuta-ya Jūzaburō
ca. 1789-1801

25

A room of an ordinary family's house is shown. The mother is twining hemp thread. Her daughter is practicing a shamisen and singing a song. In the Edo period, many girls learned how to play the shamisen and sing in accompaniment so that they could be hired by a samurai family. A small child is pulling his sister's sleeve, trying to get her attention.
A big brazier with a tea-kettle and a tobacco tray can be seen behind the mother. In front of the daughter, the music score book is on top of the black shamisen case. A little clay fish toy named yumi-tai is for the child.

「婦人世話鑑」
商家と思われる家の一室が描かれている。母は苧を績っており、娘が三味線と浄瑠璃をおさらいしている。当時は、武家に奉公するため、娘たちは浄瑠璃を学ぶことが多かった。幼児は姉の袖を引き、気を引こうとしている。
母の膝にはきせるとたばこ入れが乗っており、背後には火鉢やたばこ盆も見える。

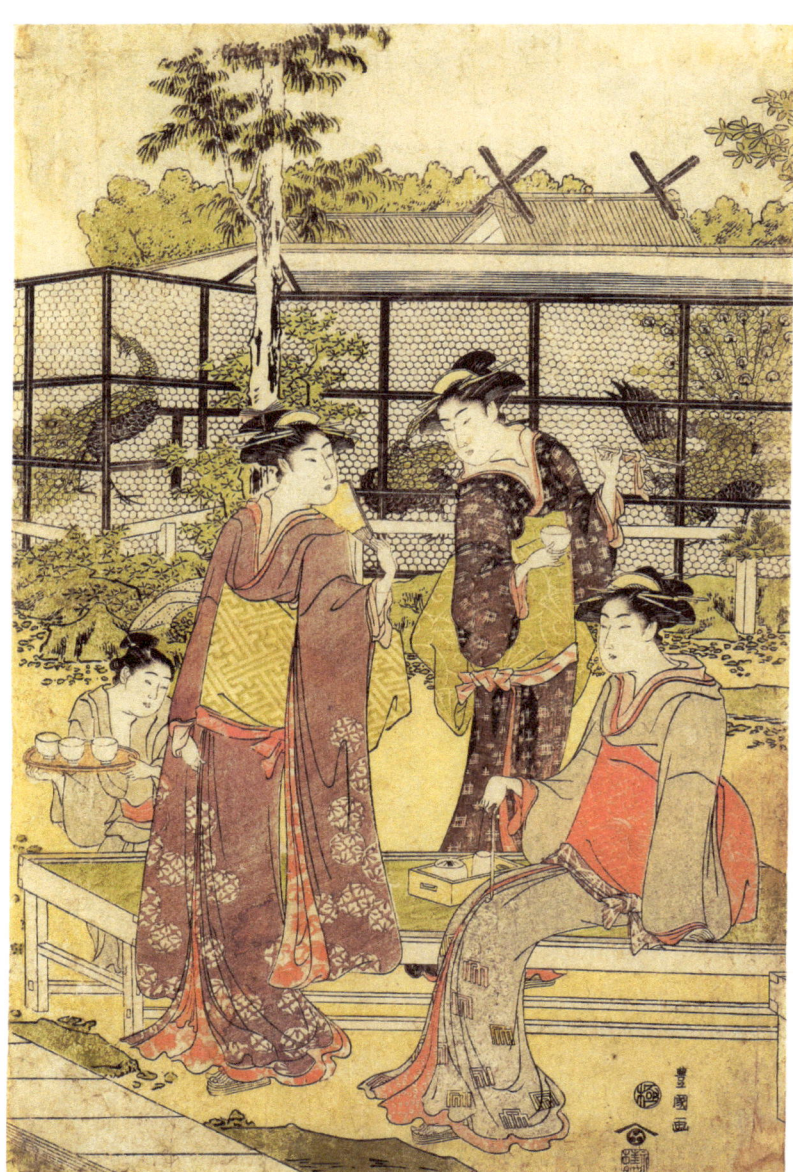

Kachō Chaya

A Teahouse with Rare Birds

Artist: Utagawa Toyokuni I
Publisher: Nishimura-ya Yohachi
ca. 1789-1801

26

This is a scene of a teahouse with its special attraction. Three women and a little boy servant are present. The three are enjoying the teahouse area, where peacocks are seen in a cage behind them. Peacocks are not native to Japan and were very rare. In the Edo period there were no zoos. Some teahouses exhibited rare birds to attract customers. Some panels from this collection were lost. This print shows only a portion of the cage. This teahouse was near Shiba Shinmei Shrine. Its characteristic roof can be seen in the distance.

「花鳥茶屋」
江戸時代には、外国渡来の珍しい鳥や造り物などで人寄せをする茶屋があった。神明造りの屋根が見えるため、この絵は、芝神明近辺の花鳥茶屋を描いたと考えられる。美人の後ろに描かれた大きな鳥かごには、孔雀が三羽いるのがわかる。この絵は続きものの一部であるため、他にも鳥が描かれていたと考えられる。

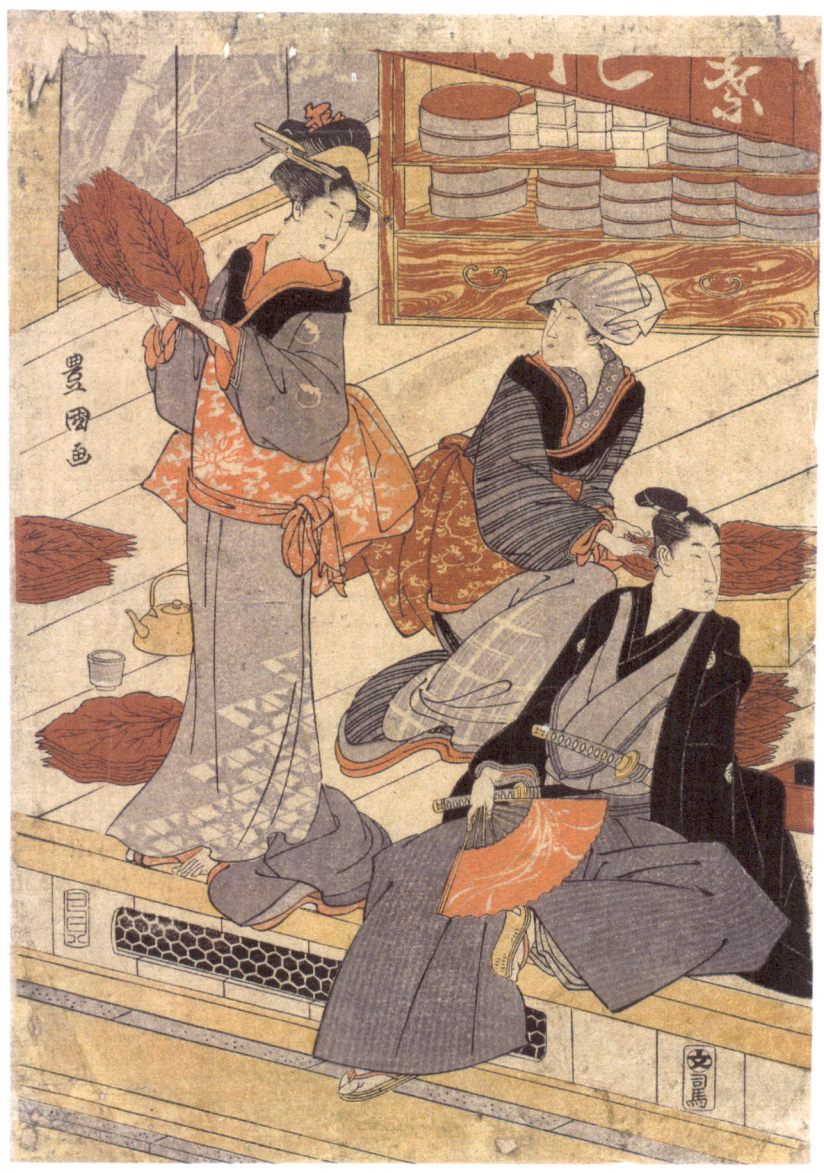

Tabako Mise

A Tobacco Shop

Artist: Utagawa Toyokuni I
Publisher: Maru-ya Bun'emon
1800

27

An Edo period tobacco shop is depicted. In those days, people smoked tobacco leaves shredded as thin as hair. Shredding tobacco so thin took great skill. A skilled worker shredded tobacco leaves in front of the shop.

This is a very big shop. The samurai is the customer, and the two women are clerks. The one sitting is binding tobacco leaves to be shredded. A skilled worker was probably depicted next to her in the part of the print that was lost. In the back of the tobacco shop are many bundles of shredded tobacco wrapped with paper. Note the fan in the Samurai's right hand and the two swords by his belt.

「たばこ店」
この絵は続き物の一部と考えられ、江戸時代のたばこ屋が描かれている。江戸時代、人々は髪の毛ほどの細さに刻まれたたばこを吸っていたが、当時、たばこの刻みは店で行われていた。この絵では、武士は店の客で、二人の女性が店の者である。座っている女性は、刻むために葉を小さく巻こうとしており、本来は、この隣に、刻み職人が描かれている部分があると思われる。

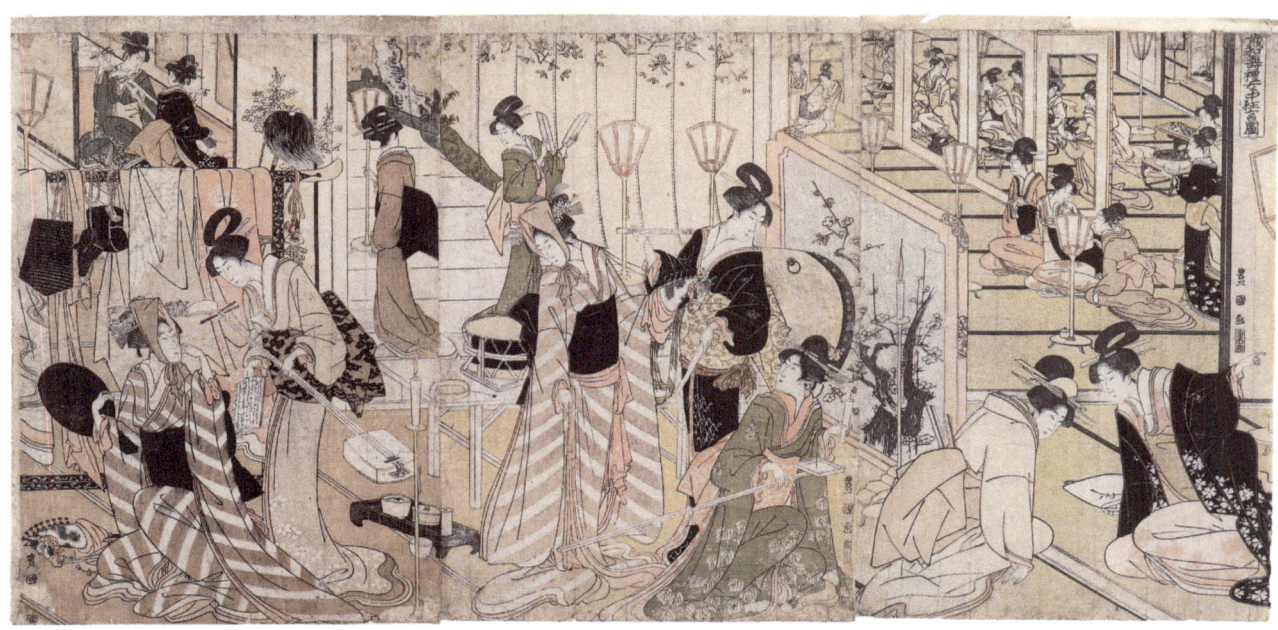

Toshiwasure Jochū Kyōgen Zu

The Year-End Amateur Play by the Maids

Artist: Utagawa Toyokuni I
Publisher: Izumi-ya Ichibē
ca. 1801-1804

28

The maids of a very wealthy family are preparing for an amateur comedy play for a year-end party. This print depicts the maids preparing for the stage. Their costumes, instruments, and accessories are in the foreground. An audience of many more maids are waiting in the upper right background. The left front is a dressing room with a tobacco tray. A woman in the middle with a drumstick is about to beat the large drum. The woman in the background is clapping two wooden blocks together to announce the beginning of the play. A very busy scene indeed!

「歳和寿礼女中狂言図」
お屋敷の女中たちが忘年会を開き、芝居を披露しようとしている。描かれているのは、手前がその楽屋で、衣装や楽器、小道具などが見える。右奥には、芝居が始まるのを待つ女中たちも描かれている。

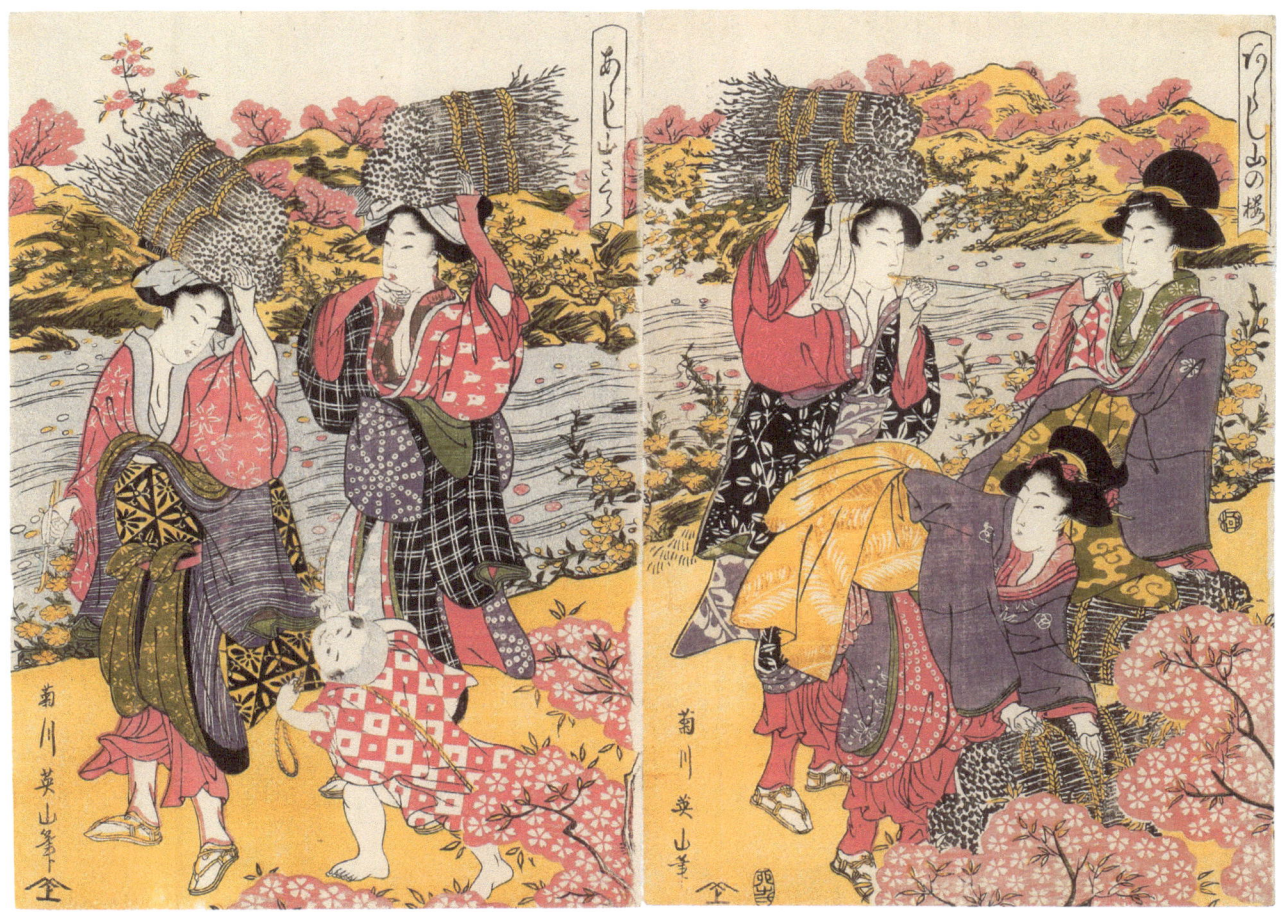

Arashiyama no Sakura

Cherry Blossoms in Arashiyama, Kyoto

Artist: Kikukawa Eisan
Publisher: Unknown
1807

29

This print depicts a Spring scene during cherry blossom time in Arashi-yama in the city of Kyoto. Unfortunatelly, the middle panel is lost.

Five women are carrying firewood from the mountains to sell. On the left panel the two women and a little boy pulling a rope are shown. On the right panel three of them are taking a break by the riverside. One of them is setting down her firewood. Another, already sitting on her stack of firewood, is smoking. The woman carrying the firewood on top of her head is trying to get a light from another woman's kiseru pipe. In the Edo period, of course, there were no lighters or matches. Getting a light from another's kiseru pipe was a common practice.

「あらし山の桜」
桜の名所として知られる京の嵐山で柴を運ぶ五人の女性が描かれている。三人は一休みしようとしており、すでに一人は降ろした柴に腰掛け、たばこを吸いはじめている。そのたばこを吸い始めている女性から、もう一人の女性がもらい火をしているが、ライターやマッチのない当時、もらい火はよく見られる光景であった。
なお、本図は、本来3枚続きであったと考えられ、残念ながら中央の1枚が欠けている。

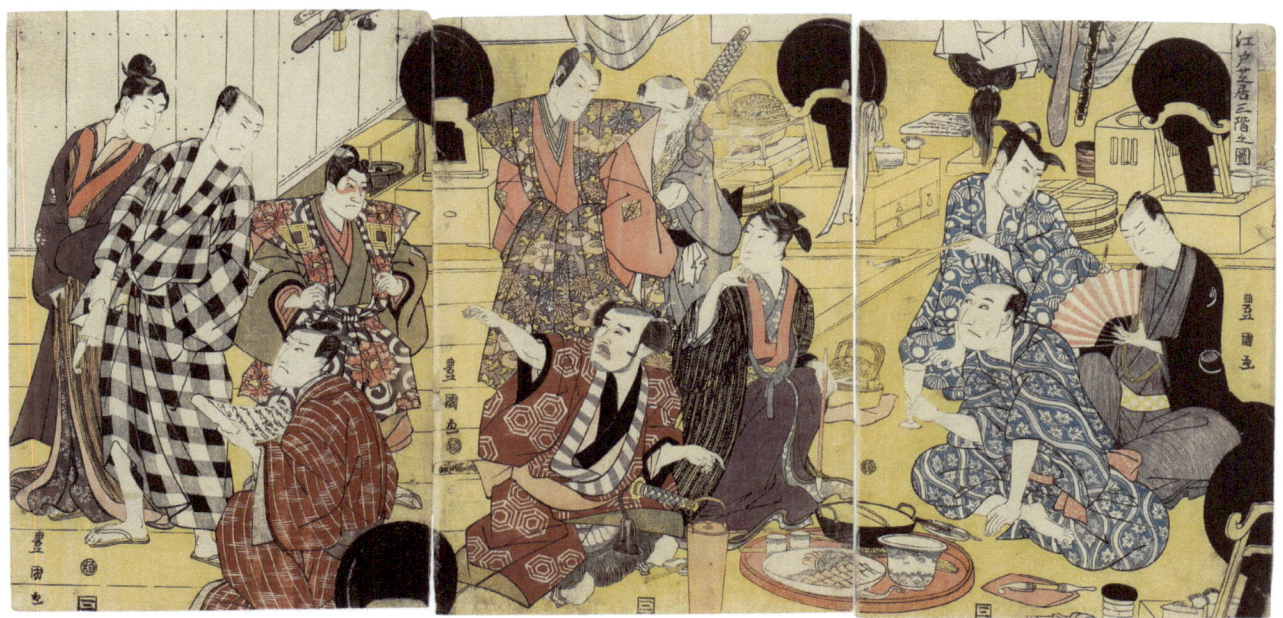

Edo Shibai Sangai no Zu

Kabuki Actors' Dressing Room

Artist: Utagawa Toyokuni I
Publisher: Shimizu
ca. 1801-1804

30

A dressing room is shown with a group of kabuki actors. Some of the actors are already dressed and others are resting in their casual cotton yukatas. They do as they wish: eating, smoking, and drinking.

As one scans the scene, one sees many interesting objects such as a tall sake glass and a very tall sake vessel with the handle. On the right panel there is a kiseru pipe and a tobacco pouch on the floor. In the background three dressers, each with a large round mirror, are seen. Also, a black wig is hanging on the wall.

「江戸芝居三階之図」
歌舞伎役者たちの楽屋が描かれている。役者の背後には化粧台や大きな鏡もある。出番を控えて身支度が済んでいる役者もいるが、まだ浴衣でくつろいでいる役者もいる。休憩している役者は、食べたり、飲んだり、たばこを吸ったり、好きなようにして過ごしている。

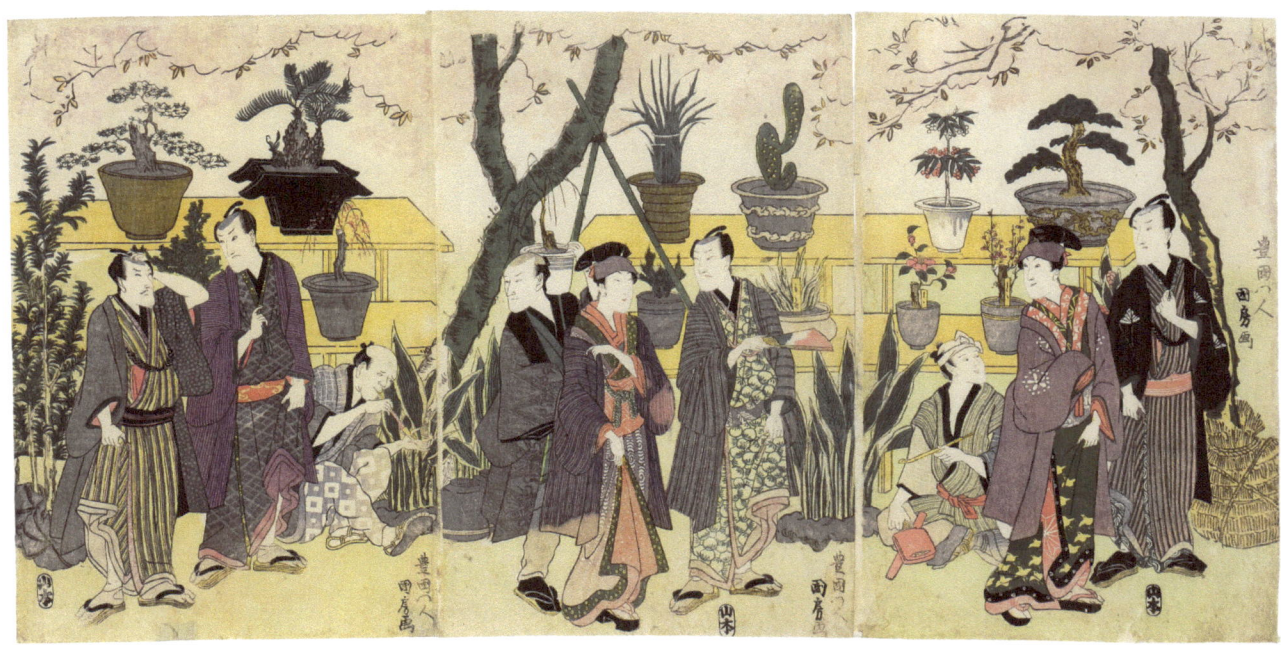

Yakusha to Ueki Uri

Two Gardeners and Kabuki Actors in a Nursery

Artist: Utagawa Kunifusa
Publisher: Yamamoto
ca. 1811

31

Then as well as now it is very popular to grow plants and bonsai among many ordinary Japanese. In the Edo period people loved particular varieties of plants so that the price of such plants became very inflated. They also loved rare plants not native to Japan.

In this print, two gardeners and seven kabuki actors are depicted. The gardeners are selling bonsai, and even cacti and cycads that do not grow in the Edo area. Both are smoking kiseru pipes. One is removing some of the burnt tobacco from his pipe. He is catching the tobacco ashes in his left hand and fluffing it up so that the residual tobacco will burn and be able to be smoked again. This was a common practice among working-class men. They could smoke repeatedly with only a small amount of shredded tobacco leaves.

「役者地顔見立　植木市」
江戸時代、庶民の間では、小さな植物を育てることが流行していた。特に変種が好まれ、価格が高騰することもあり、また、日本原産ではない植物も好まれていた。この絵には、二人の植木売りと七人の歌舞伎役者が描かれているが、サボテンやソテツなど、江戸近辺の産ではない植物も売られているのがわかる。
植木売りは二人ともたばこを吸っているが、そのうち一人はたばこの灰を手のひらに吹き出している。職人や物売りは、このようにして灰になりかけた刻みに空気を送りこんで、再び吸ったり、あるいはそこから、次の一服のための火種を取ったりした。

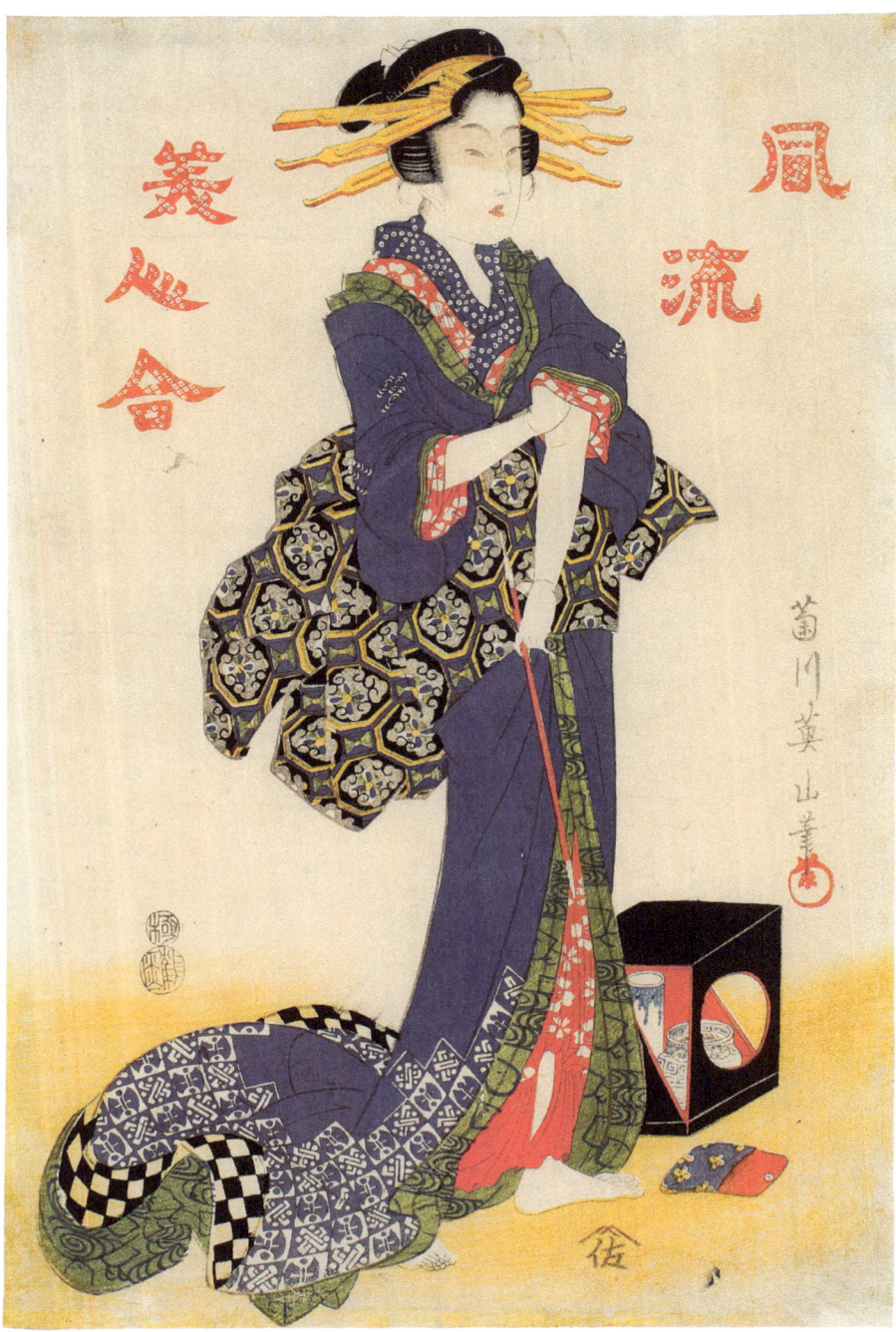

Fūryū Bijin Awase

Elegant Beauty Collection

Artist: Kikukawa Eisan
Publisher: Sensa
1811

32

This is a standing portrait of a beautiful woman in her room. The many ornamental hairpins emphasize her status as a courtesan and her beauty. She has a long red stemmed kiseru pipe and a tobacco pouch made of cloth. A tobacco tray is by her left foot. The box type tobacco tray is black. Inside are two items. One is a pot for the burning charcoal. The other, a tall cylindrical container, is for ashes. The five Japanese letters give the title of this print from the Elegant Beauty Collection.

「風流美人合」
遊女の立ち姿を描いている。遊女は朱羅宇のきせるを手に持ち、その足下にはたばこ入れと箱形のたばこ盆が見える。たばこ入れは懐中物で布製らしく、黒く塗られた箱形のたばこ盆の中には、灰入れと灰落しがある。

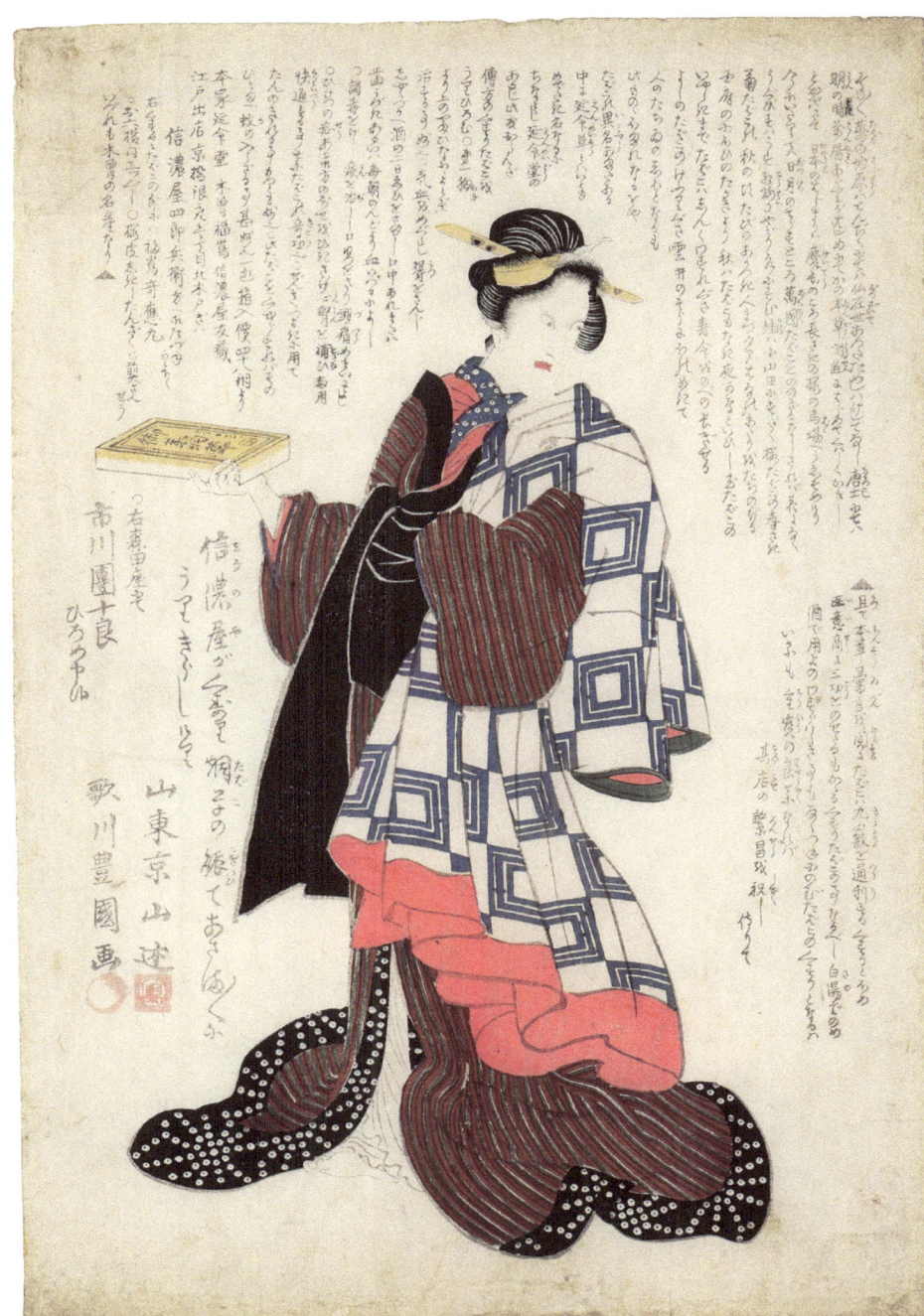

Kusuri-tabako no Uri Hirome

Promoting a Medicinal Tobacco

Artist: Utagawa Toyokuni I
Publisher: Unknown
1813

33

This print was originally an advertising leaflet. The well-known kabuki actor Ichikawa Danjūrō VII is promoting Kusuri-tabako on stage. The Kusuri-tabako was a special medicinal tobacco. Danjūrō's long promotional speech is written in Japanese above him. It reads that the Kusuri-tabako is effective against depression, hangover, cough, fever, headache, and so on. It was said to be very popular because it could be smoked with a pipe kiseru just like any ordinary tobacco for pleasure.

「薬たばこの売り弘め」
七代目市川団十郎が舞台上で薬たばこを宣伝している場面を描いている。画面上部の宣伝文によれば、薬たばこは、欝や二日酔い、咳、発熱、頭痛などに効用があり、普通のたばこのように、きせるで吸うというタイプであったという。

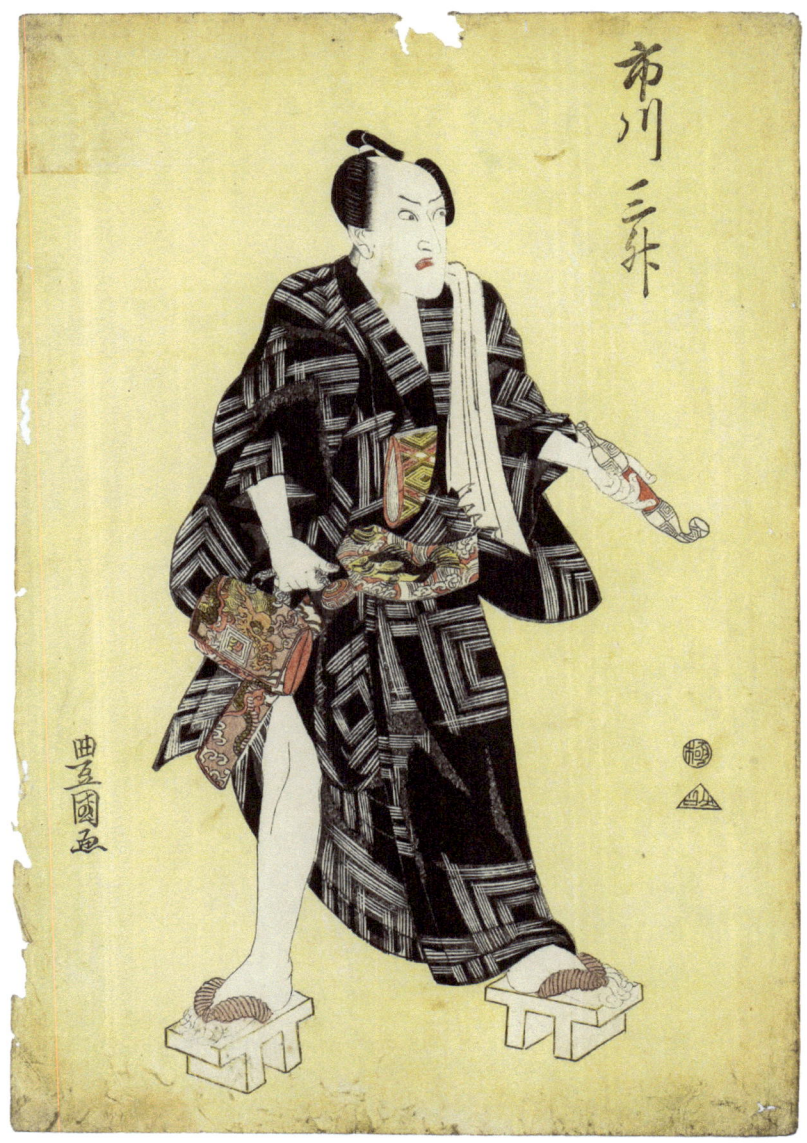

Shichidaime Ichikawa Danjūrō

Ichikawa Danjūrō VII

Artist: Utagawa Toyokuni I
Publisher: Unknown
1812

34

This is a portrait of the young kabuki actor, Ichikawa Danjūrō VII. He was famous for his huge bulging eyes.

In this print he is in a casual wear called a yukata and is enjoying his free time. He is standing on wooden geta clogs. The partly-shown rectangular purse on his chest is for carrying paper. There is a fine kiseru pipe in his left hand and a big tobacco pouch in his right hand. Note that the bowl and mouthpiece of the kiseru pipe, his yukata, his paper holder, and his tobacco pouch all have a triple square pattern. It was his crest.

「七代目市川団十郎」
若かりし頃の七代目市川団十郎が描かれている。団十郎は浴衣姿で、立派なきせるとたばこ入れを手にしている。団十郎のきせるやたばこ入れ、浴衣には、三重の枡の紋様があるが、これは「三升」といい、団十郎が使用していた紋である。

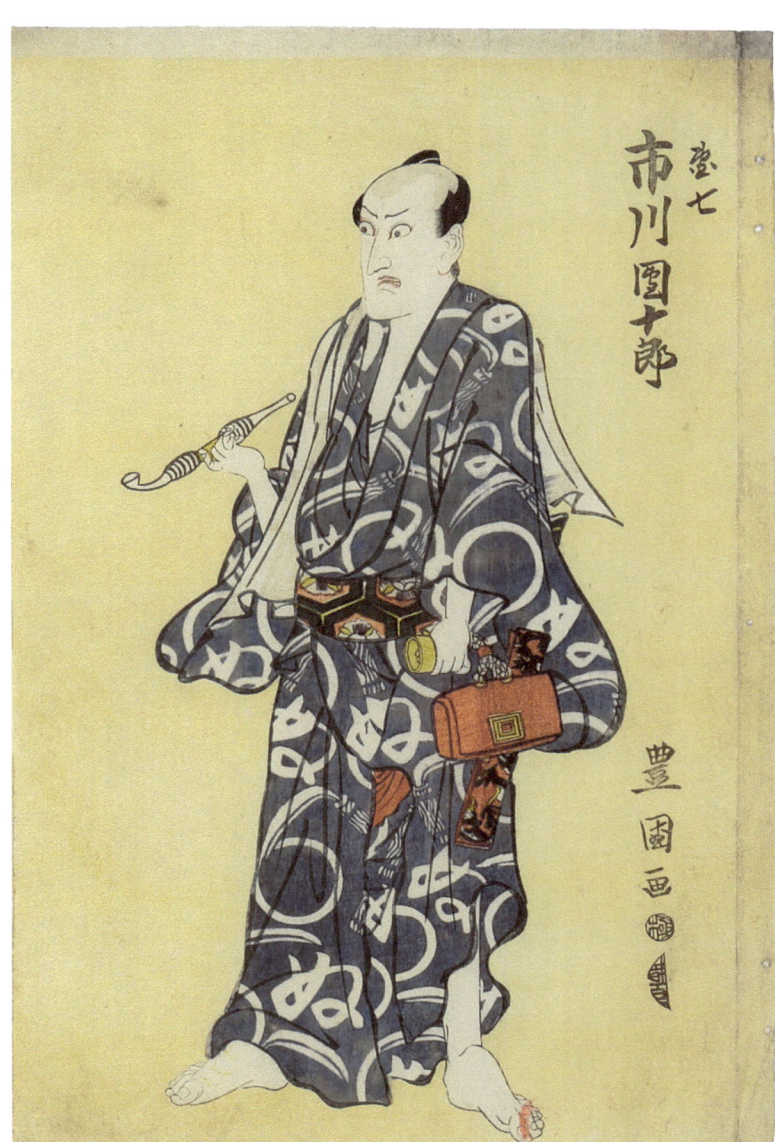

Shichidaime Ichikawa Danjūrō

Ichikawa Danjūrō VII

Artist: Utagawa Toyokuni I
Publisher: Unknown
1812

35

This is a scene from a kabuki drama. The kabuki actor, Ichikawa Danjūrō VII, is playing a homeless character named Danshichi. He is wearing a casual yukata with a pattern of many sickles, rings and the Japanese letter Nu. The Japanese word for sickle is *kama*. The word for ring is *wa*. The letter Nu is *nu*. When all three are put together forming a word "*kama-wa-nu*," it means do not worry. The pattern was famous as a favorite of Danjūrō's. His yukata was dyed indigo, but now has faded. He carries a big red tobacco pouch. As a tobacco pouch was an important decorative accessory for men in those days, men often carried very fine tobacco pouches.

「曽我祭侠競　市川団十郎の団七」
舞台のワンシーンに取材している。団十郎が身にまとっている浴衣には、「鎌」の絵と「輪」と「ぬ」の字の模様がある。これは「かまわぬ」の判じ物になっていて、当時は、団十郎好みの紋様として知られていた。団十郎が手にしている赤いたばこ入れが、藍色の浴衣に映えているが、当時は、たばこ入れは男性が身を飾るアイテムであったため、立派なたばこ入れを使用することも多かった。

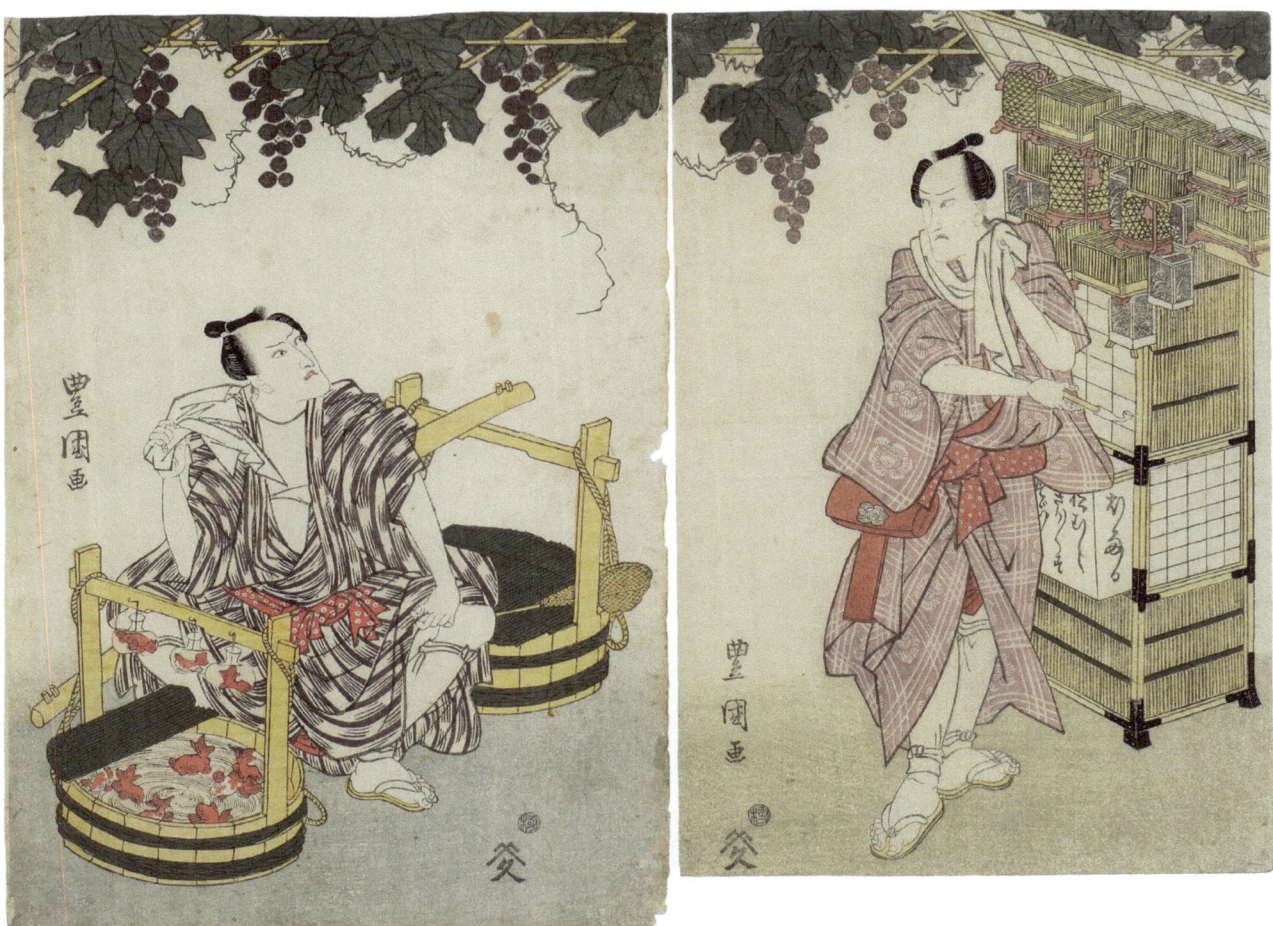

Mushiuri to Kingyouri

Venders in the Street of Edo

Artist: Utagawa Toyokuni I
Publisher: Yamamoto Heikichi
ca. 1818

36

Two kabuki actors, Nakamura Utaemon III and Ichikawa Danjūrō VII, are shown. This is probably not a scene from a real kabuki drama. It gives the impression of a summer day. In the left panel, Nakamura Utaemon is selling goldfish. In the Edo period, people would buy goldfish in glass containers. Goldfish and their glass containers can be seen hanging from the handle of the pail. In the right panel, Ichikawa Danjūrō is a vendor of insects. He sells fireflies, crickets, and grasshoppers in their cages. Many Japanese kept such insects to enjoy their lights and sounds. Both actors are portrayed as typical of such vendors. Ichikawa Danjūrō is smoking a kiseru pipe. A big red tobacco pouch hangs from his sash. Above both actors there are grapes hanging from the vines.

「虫売りと金魚売り」
三代目中村歌右衛門と七代目市川団十郎が描かれている。この絵は芝居に取材したものではなく、人気役者を当世風の物売りとして描いており、歌右衛門は金魚売り、団十郎は虫売りになっている。金魚売りのガラスの金魚入れや虫売りの虫籠なども描かれていて、当時の物売りの様子がよく分かる。団十郎はたばこを吸っており、腰には大きな赤いたばこ入れが提がっている。

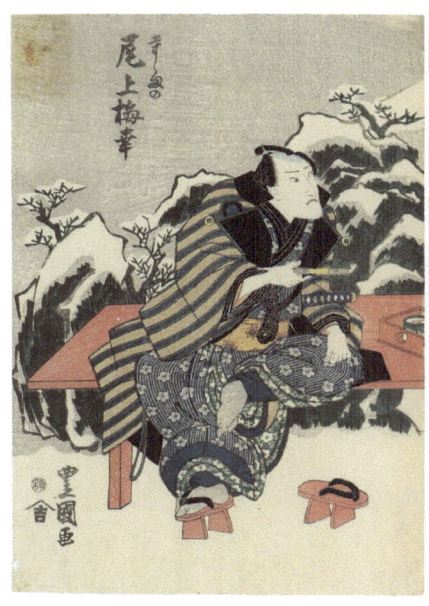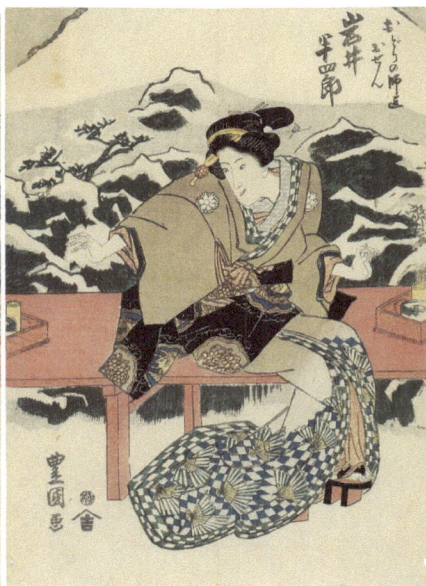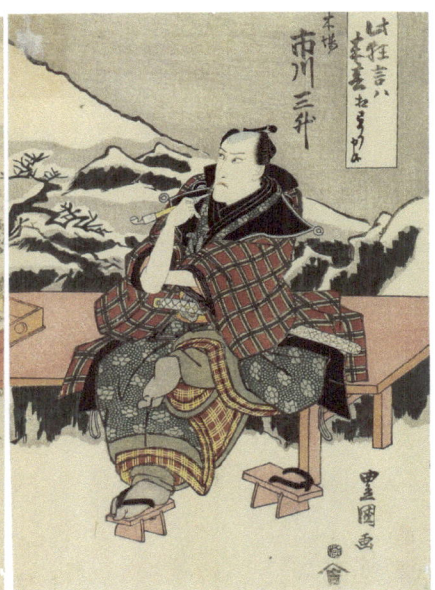

Kono Kyōgen wa Raishun Aiwakari Mōshisōrō

A Playbill for the Forthcoming Spring Show

Artist: Utagawa Toyokuni I
Publisher: Enomoto-ya Kichibē
ca. 1821

37

The Japanese writing in the upper right hand corner states that this drama will be presented next Spring. Hence the print was an advertisement to promote a kabuki play. Three very popular actors are depicted. From the left they are Onoe Kikugorō III, Iwai Hanshirō V, and Ichikawa Danjūrō VII. Many people in Edo were looking forward to attending this play. In March 1819, Ichikawa Danjūrō VII and Onoe Kikugorō III quarreled. Since then they did not appear on the same stage for three years. Subsequently, Iwai Hanshirō V settled the quarrel between the two, and they agreed to perform together in 1822. In this print Hanshirō is shown in the middle, negotiating between Danjūrō and Kikugorō. It appears that both Danjūrō and Kikugorō kept their cool by smoking their kiseru pipes. Note the base portion of Mt. Fuji in the distance.

「此狂言ハ来春相わかり申候」
タイトルにもある通り、この絵は芝居の予告として出版されたと考えられる。左から三代目尾上菊五郎、五代目岩井半四郎、七代目市川団十郎という、歌舞伎界の大スターが描かれている。実は、団十郎と菊五郎は、文政2年（1819）3月に不仲となり、長い間同じ舞台には上がっていなかった。半四郎の仲裁で和解し、実際に二人は、文政5年11月に共演した。岩井半四郎をはさんで腰掛ける二人は、たばこで気持ちを落ち着かせているようにも見える。

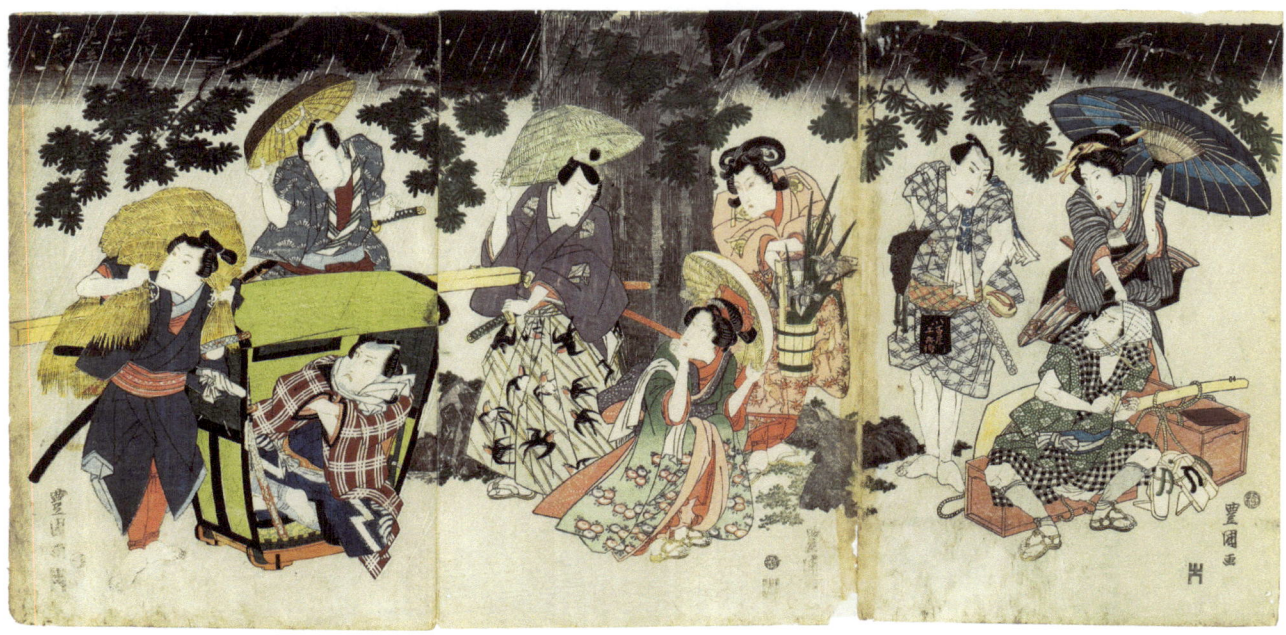

Jidai Sewa Mitate Amayadori

Nine Kabuki Actors Taking Shelter from the Rain

Artist: Utagawa Toyokuni I
Publisher: Imari-ya Ushizō
ca. 1823-1824

38

These are three panels depicting nine people taking shelter from the rain. They are waiting under a large tree, wishing for the rain to stop. Although their social statuses are obviously different, they are in the same predicament. The varied characters depicted here are all kabuki actors.

In the right panel the man sitting is a repairman of wooden geta clogs. He is trying to smoke and is striking a flint stone and metal together to obtain a spark. A woman standing behind him holding an oil-paper umbrella is a geisha. The man standing next to her is a vegetable vendor. Note he is barefooted. He is holding his sandals in his hand so that they will not get wet and dirty.

In the middle panel a boy named Hakoōmaru is holding a bucket of irises. The girl sitting is a common country girl. The samurai wearing a hakama, Japanese pleated trousers, with swallows and rain pattern, is Nagoya Sanza. Both Hakoōmaru and Nagoya Sanza were extremely popular characters in kabuki dramas in the Edo period.

In the left panel the man sitting in a kago, palanquin, is Banzuiin Chōbē, a famous character in kabuki plays. A young samurai is standing behind the kago and holding his hat. The Samurai Shirai Gonpachi, a popular hero of kabuki dramas, is standing by the kago.

「時代世ハ見立雨やとり」
九人の人物が大木の下で雨宿りしている。彼等はさまざまな身分の人々で、このような時には、社会的な身分にかかわらず、皆平等であることがわかる。実は、描かれているのは歌舞伎役者たちで、白井権八、幡随院長兵衛など、よく知られた狂言の登場人物に扮しているものもいる。右端で座っている男性は足駄の歯入れで、彼はたばこを吸おうと、火打金と火打石を打ち付けている。

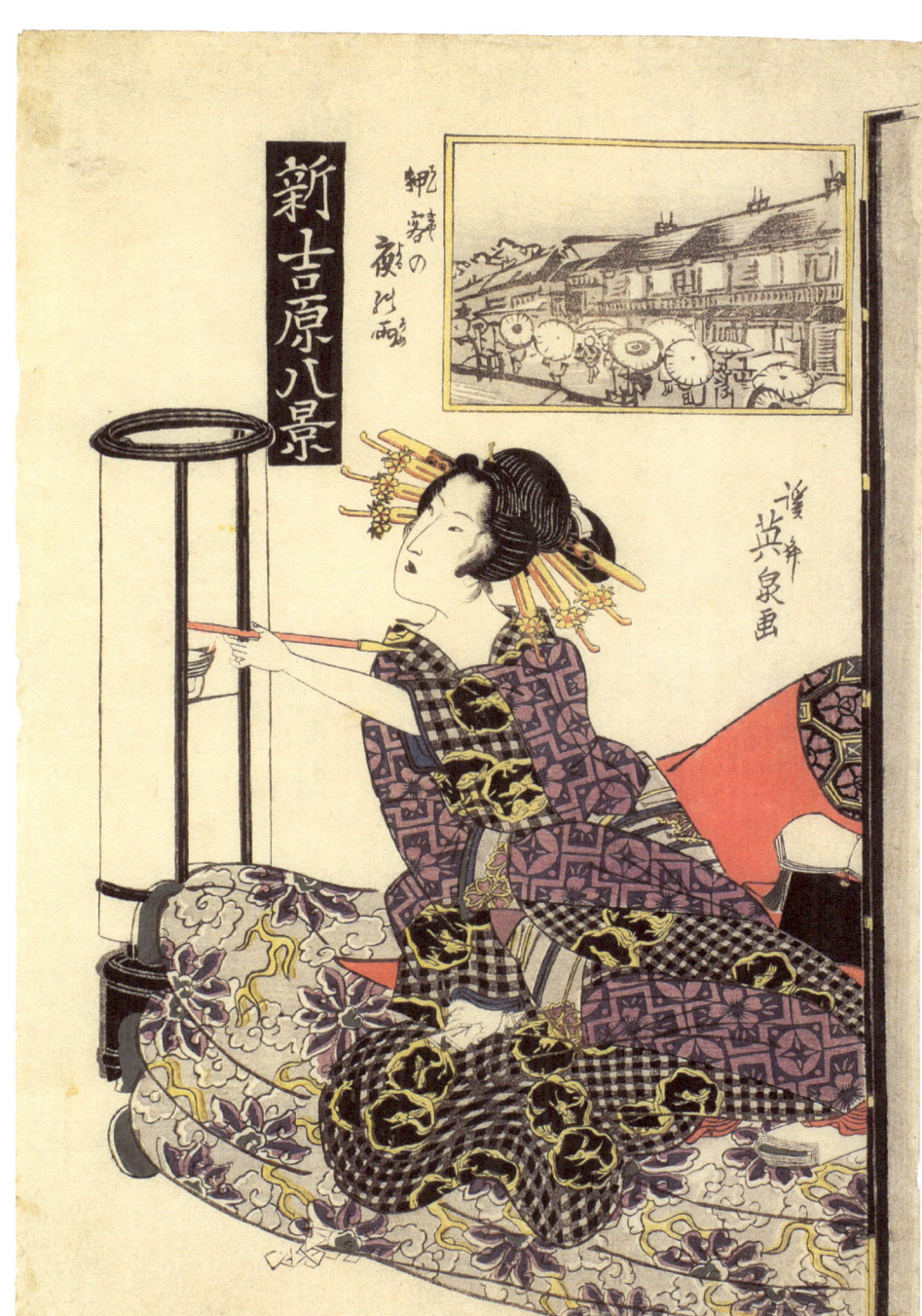

Shin Yoshiwara Hakkei,
Konkyaku no Yoru no Ame

Eight Scenes from
Yoshiwara

Artist: Keisai Eisen
Publisher: Unknown
1818-1830

39

This woman, still in her bed clothes, is starting to smoke. She is getting a light for her kiseru pipe from a burning lamp called an andon. Usually, people would get a light for smoking from charcoal burning in a fire pot on a tobacco tray placed near the bed. The fact that she is obtaining a light from the burning lamp seems to be a sign of her quick temperament.

The upper framed inset is a scene from the main street of Yoshiwara. This is not a picture hanging on the wall. Framed inset pictures such as this are sometimes placed in the woodblock prints which depicted beautiful women or kabuki actors.

「新吉原八景　狎客の夜の雨」
遊女の床の傍らにはたばこ盆が備えられていることも多かったが、この遊女はたばこの火を行灯から取ろうとしている。仕草を見ると、この遊女の気性は少し荒そうにも見える。
右上のコマ絵には、雨が降る吉原の様子が描かれている。

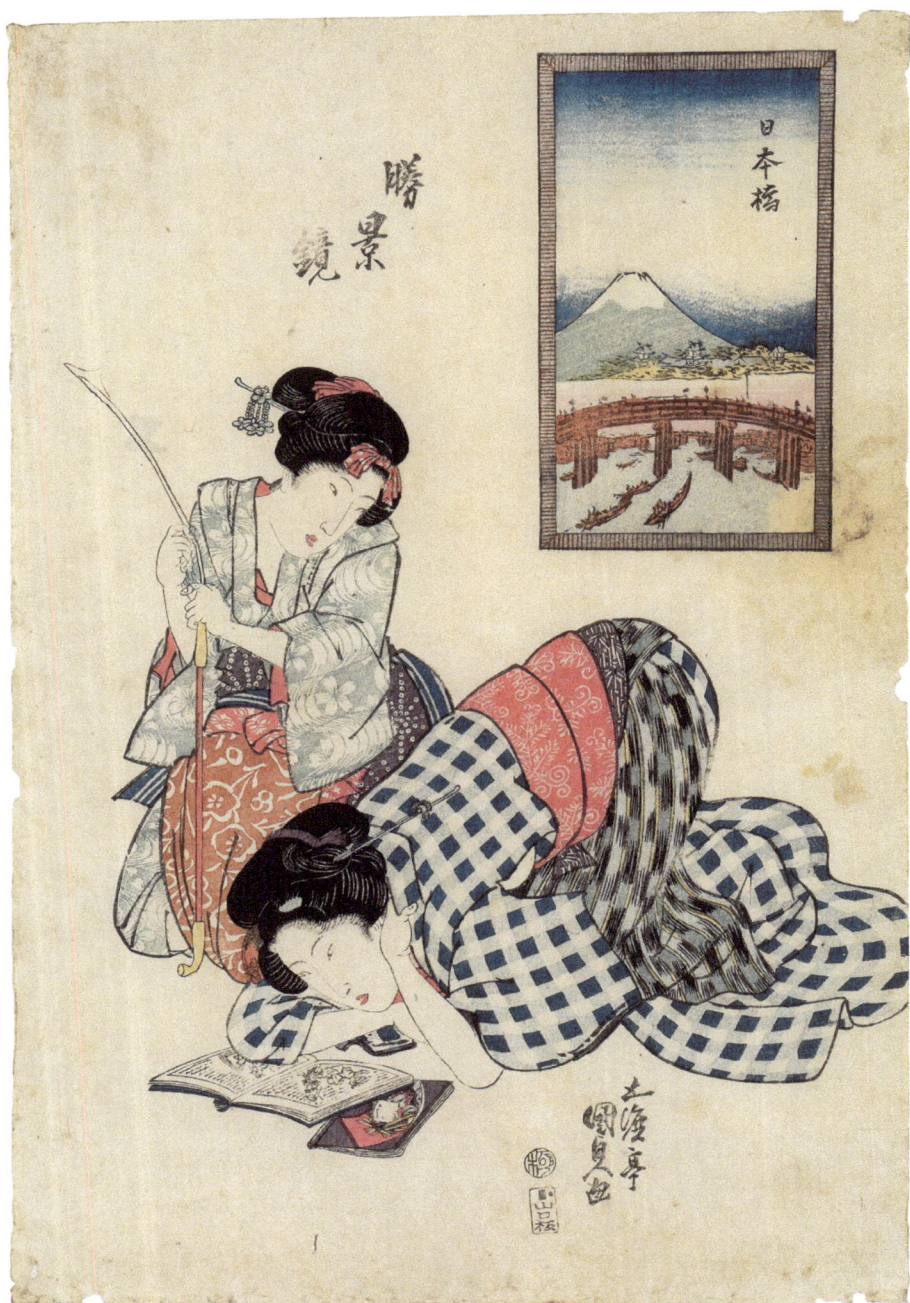

Shōkei Kagami Nihonbashi

A Series of Beautiful Places:
Nihonbashi Bridge

Artist: Utagawa Kunisada
(Toyokuni III)
Publisher: Yamaguchi-ya Tōbē
ca. 1818-1830

40

This print depicts a mother and a daughter scene. The daughter is cleaning a long kiseru pipe with a twisted, stiff paper string. Perhaps the kiseru pipe belongs to the mother who asked her daughter to clean it. The mother is kneeling down on the floor, preoccupied with reading a popular novel. Such printed amusement was popular among ordinary people in the Edo era. They enjoyed collecting woodblock prints and reading popular novels. The inset framed picture above is that of Mt. Fuji, Edojō Castle, and the Nihonbashi Bridge. In those days, Mt. Fuji could be easily seen from the Nihonbashi Bridge.

「勝景鏡　日本橋」
娘が紙縒できせる掃除をする間、母は草双紙を読むのに夢中になっている。おそらく、このきせるは母のもので、母が娘に掃除を頼んだのであろう。この絵のように、江戸時代、特に都市江戸では、印刷物が普及しており、一般の人々が浮世絵や草双紙を手にして、楽しんでいた。
上部のコマ絵には、手前から、日本橋、江戸城、富士山が描かれている。

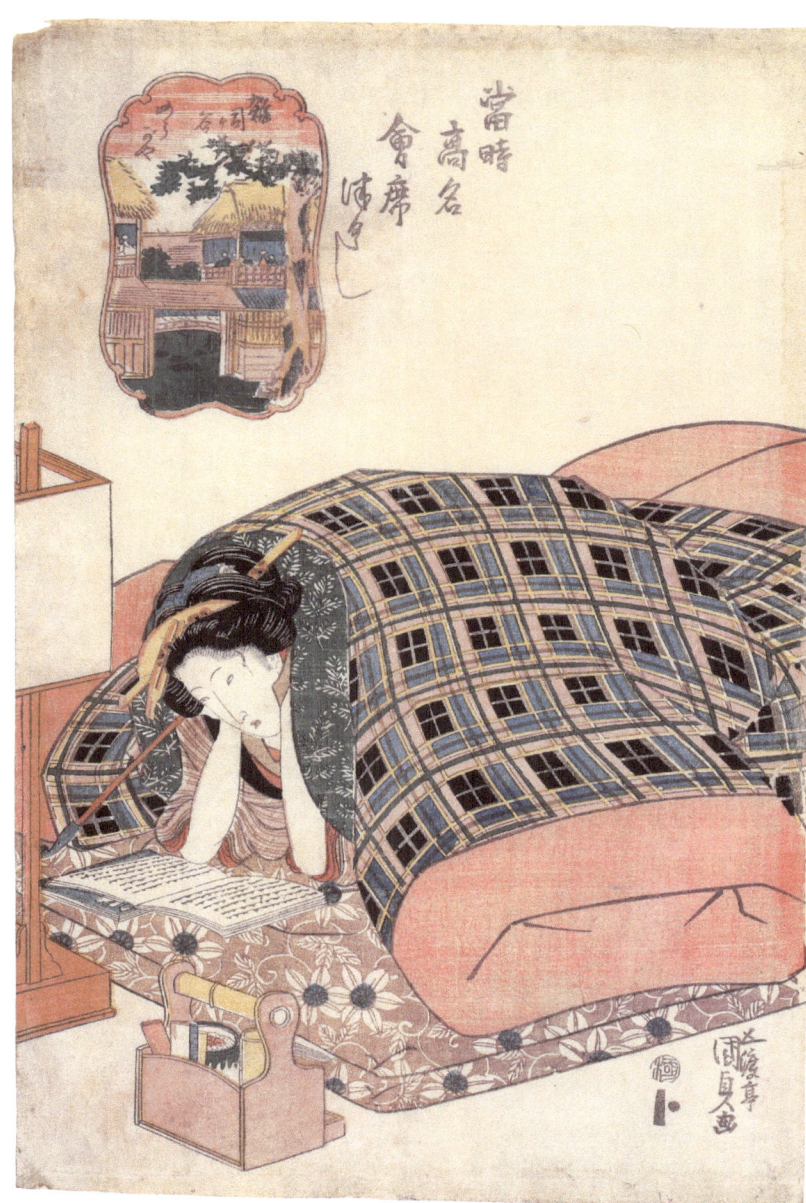

Tōji Kōmei Kaiseki Tsukushi:
Zōshigaya Myōga-ya

A Series of Celebrated Restaurants:
Zōshigaya Myōga-ya

Artist: Utagawa Kunisada
(Toyokuni III)
Publisher: Yamaguchi-ya Tōbē
ca. 1818-1830

41

A young woman is lying and reading a book by the dim light of a lamp called an andon. She is covered by a heavy quilt, shaped like a kimono. It is called a Yogi or Kaimaki. A kiseru pipe is by her side. The scene is of a winter night.

The print is one of a series in which a celebrated restaurant is depicted in the small inset space near the top of each print. The famous restaurant in this print is Myōga-ya.

「当時高名会席つくし　雑司ヶ谷　めうがや」
蒲団にもぐりこんだ女性が、行灯のほのかな明かりの下で、たばこを吸いながら本を読んでいる。彼女の蒲団は綿入りで着物のような形をしており、このようなものは、夜着またはかい巻きと呼ばれている。冬の夜の情景であることがわかる。
このシリーズには、上部のコマ絵に料亭の名が入っているが、この絵には、雑司ヶ谷にあった茗荷屋の名が記されている。

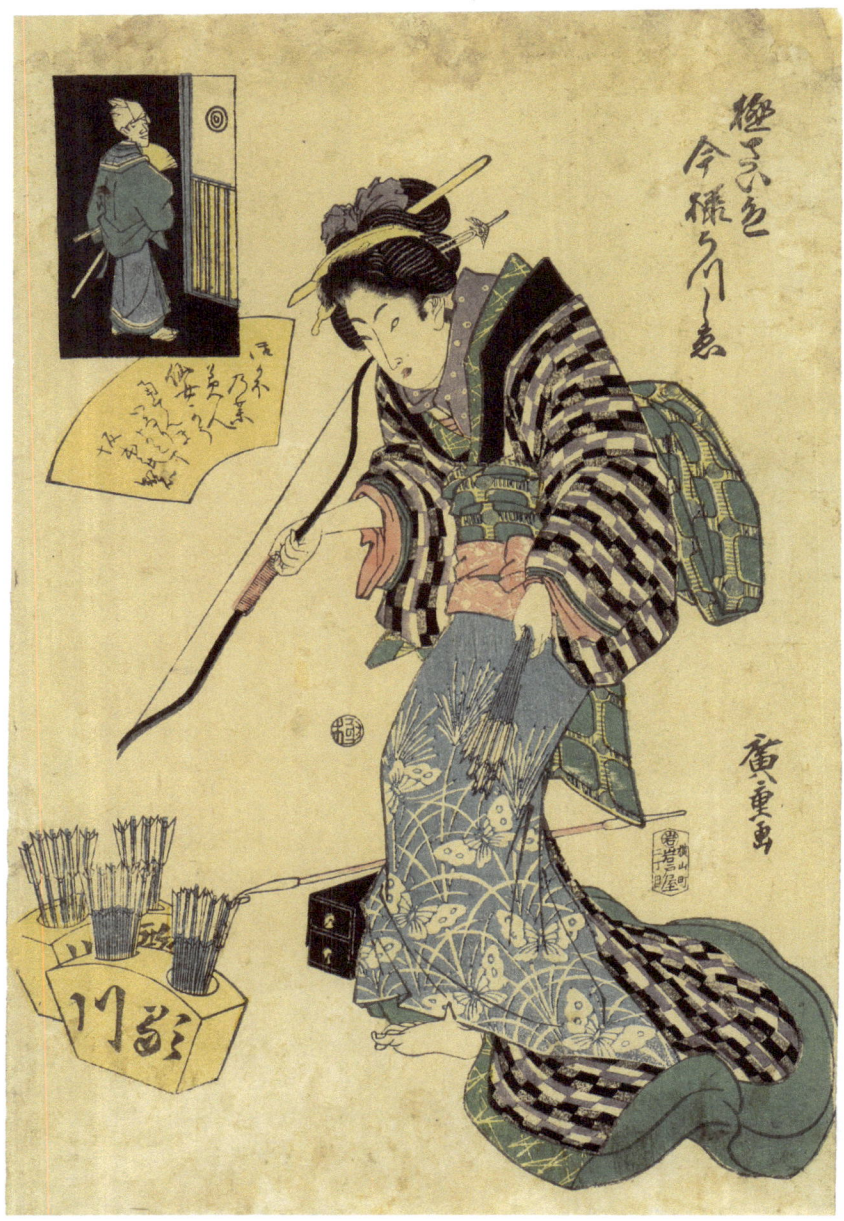

Gokusaishiki Imayō Utsushi-e

A Colorful Scene of the Modern Life

Artist: Utagawa Hiroshige I
Publisher: Iwato-ya Kisaburō
ca. 1818-1830

42

As described in print #24, there were many places in the Edo period where one could play yōkyū, the Japanese archery game. It was available in many popular amusement areas.

In this print a woman who assists players at the public yōkyū places is depicted. She was called Yaba-onna or Yatori-onna. After the Tenpō Reforms from 1841 following social upheavals, women were no longer allowed to work in such places.

A very long kiseru pipe lies on the floor for her to smoke while waiting for the archery players. Note the two small containers, each containing two groups of short arrows. Above the Yabaonna's head is a framed inset picture of the entrance to the establishment. The writing below is an unrelated advertisement for face powder called Senjo-kō cosmetics.

「極さい色今様うつしゑ」
江戸時代、盛り場には楊弓場があり、人々は楊弓を楽しんでいた。ここに描かれているのは、矢場女あるいは矢取女と呼ばれる女性で、楊弓場で人々の世話をしていた。
弓と矢を用意する女の傍らには長いきせるが置かれている。彼女は、たばこを吸いながら客を待っていたのだろう。
この作品は、後に東海道五十三次シリーズなどの風景画で著名になる初代歌川広重の極初期の作品である。

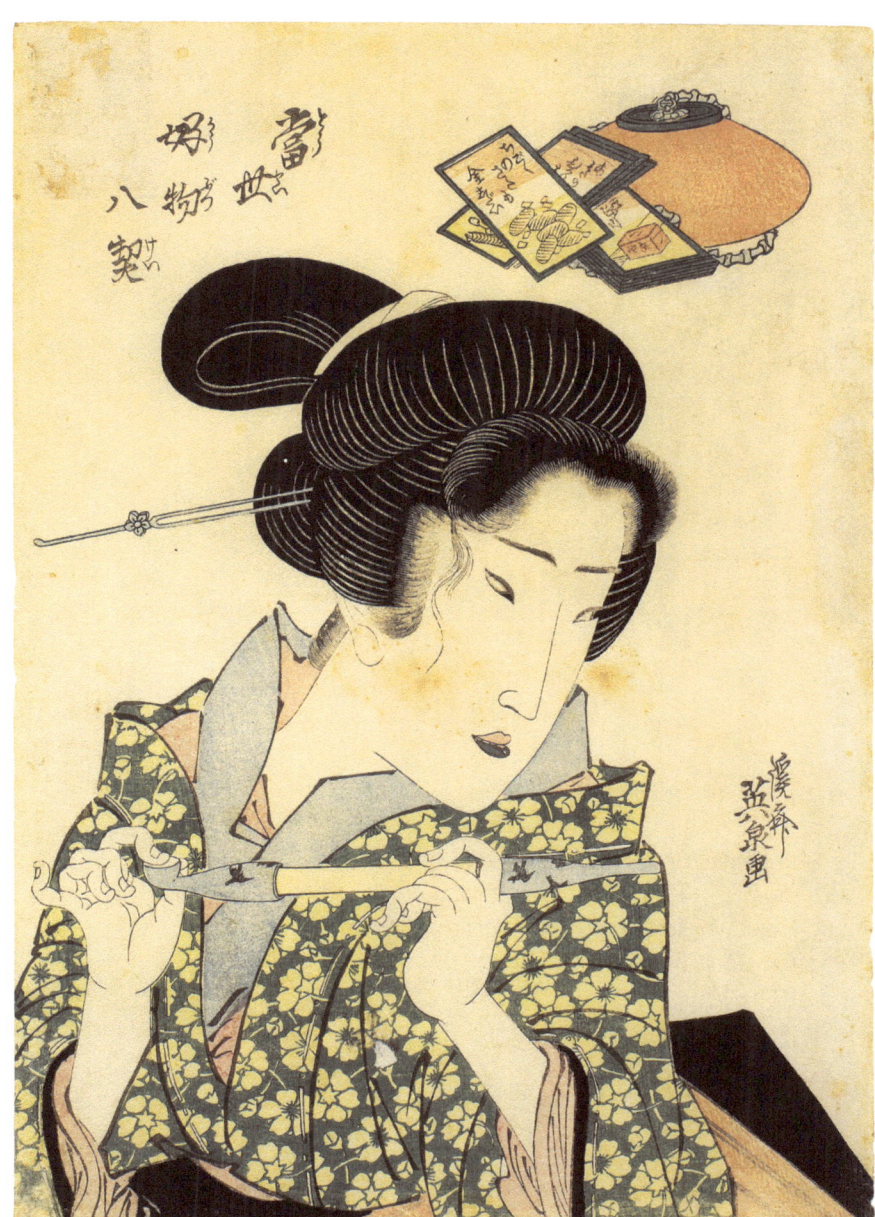

Tōsei Kōbutsu Hakkei

The Eight Patterns of the Latest Mode

Artist: Keisai Eisen
Publisher: Unkown
ca. 1823

43

A fashionable woman is preparing to smoke her large pipe. Her right forefinger is used to press shredded tobacco leaf into the kiseru pipe bowl. Birds are engraved on the bowl and mouthpiece of the pipe. Note that the color of her lips looks a little strange. This style of painting lips was called Sasabeni. It was very popular in the first half of the 19th century. The lower lip had an iridescent golden green shimmer. There were two methods to create this effect. One was to use a lot of rouge on the lower lip. The other was to use black ink first and then cover the lip with rouge.

There are assorted cards and a Japanese lantern depicted behind the woman's head. The Japanese letters describe the title of this print.

「当世好物八契」
女性がたばこを吸おうと、刻みたばこをきせるの火皿に詰めている。彼女の下唇の色は緑色をしているが、この唇の色は文化文政（1804-1830）頃に流行していたもので、笹紅と呼ばれていた。笹紅は、紅を濃く塗り重ねることで出したというが、紅が高価であったため、墨を紅の下に塗ることもあったという。

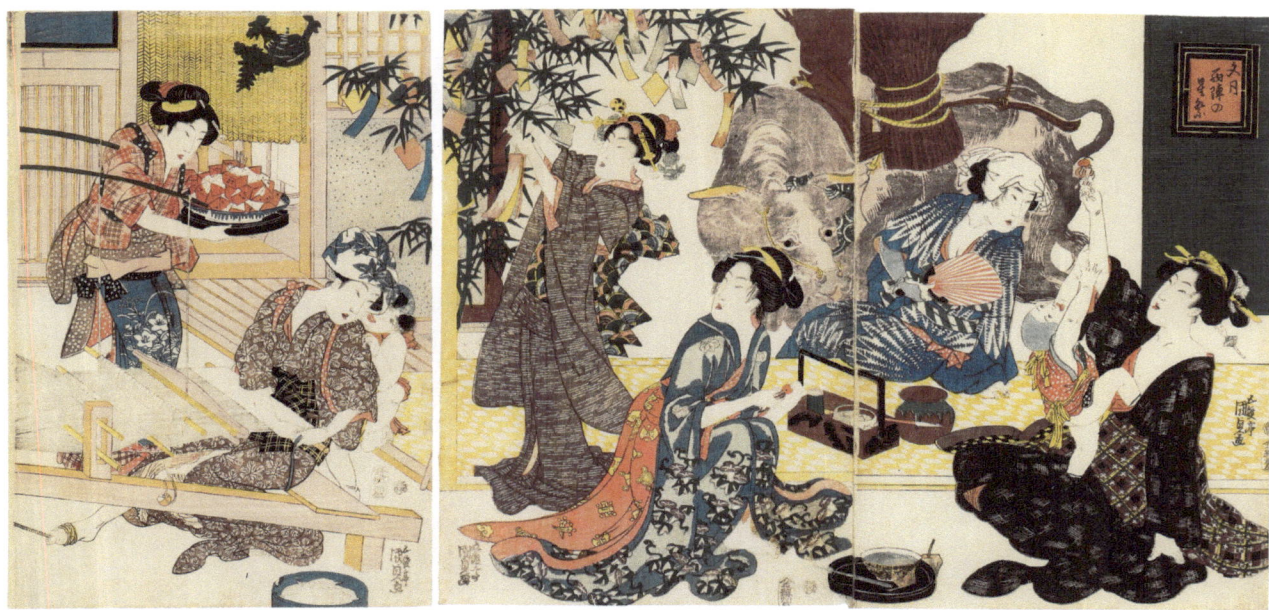

Fumizuki Nishijin no Hoshimatsuri

The Star Festival in July of Nishijin, Kyoto

Artist: Utagawa Kunisada (Toyokuni III)
Publisher: Sōshū-ya Yohē
ca. 1818-1830

44

An image of the myth of the Star Festival is depicted. The Star Festival was held annually on July 7th. On the day of the Star Festival, as shown in the middle panel, ordinary people decorated a bamboo tree with rectangular or lozenge shaped cards of five different colors. They wrote on them calligraphy or poems and prayed for their progress in composition, calligraphy, needlework, etc.

According to the myth, the Princess Orihime and Prince Hikoboshi could meet only once a year on this date. In the nighttime sky Orihime is the star Vega, and Hikoboshi is the star Altair. The two are separated by the Milky Way. The Chinese name for Vega is Shokujo which means a weaving lady. The Chinese name of Altair is Kengyū, a man who can handle cattle.

In this print Orihime is depicted in the left panel as a weaving mother. Hikoboshi, a male, is depicted in the middle and the right panels as a woman leading a cow to carry firewood. In the left panel a young woman is bringing some watermelon to Orihime. The two women and a baby in the front are playing with Japanese ground cherries.

「文月西陣の星祭」
この絵は七夕を描いたものであるが、織姫と彦星を、それぞれ、機を織る母親と牛に荷を運ばせる柴売りの女性として描き替えている。日本では、江戸時代の頃から、葉竹に五色の短冊を飾り、そこに文字や歌を記し、書道や裁縫の上達を願う風習が一般の人々の間にも広まった。この絵にも、葉竹を飾る女性が描かれている。スイカやほおずきなども、七夕を彩っている。

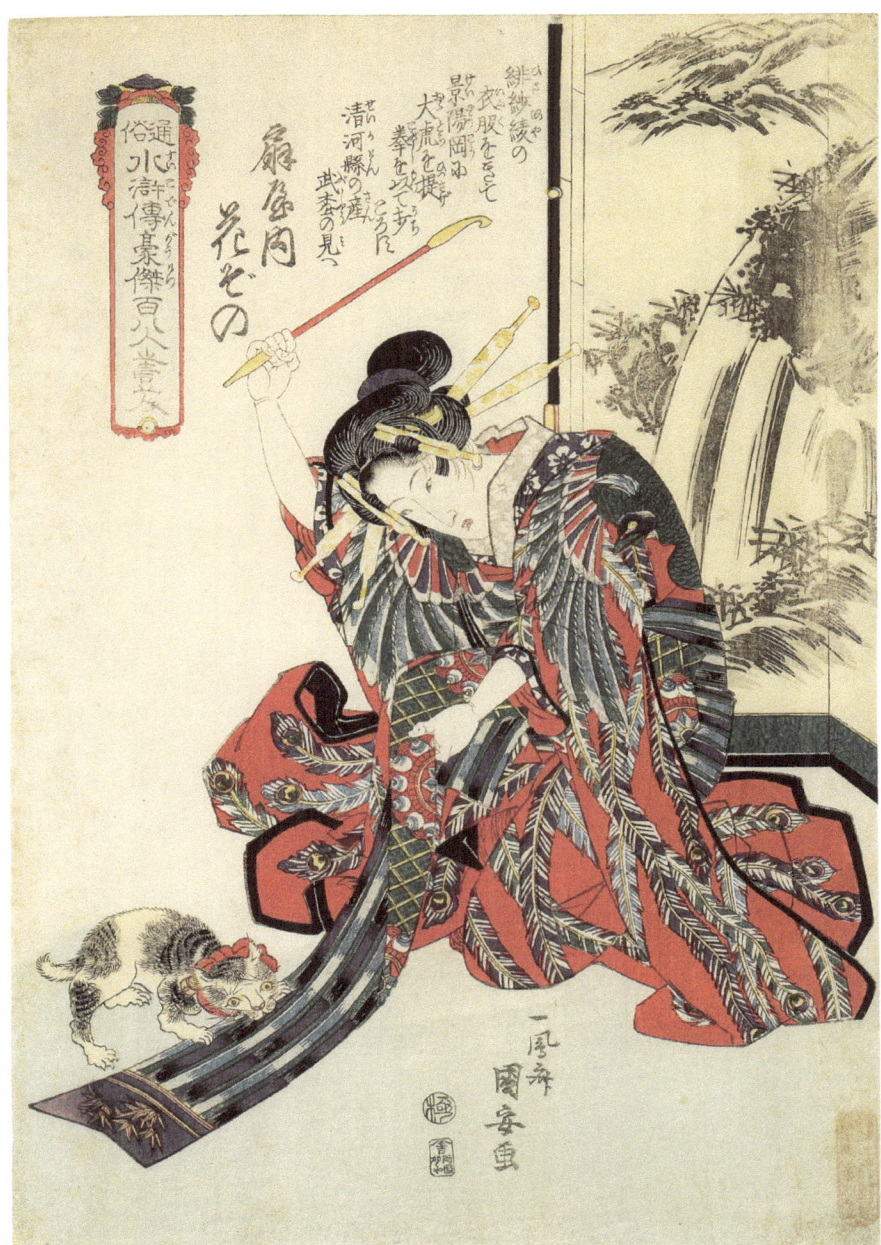

Tsūzoku Suikoden Gōketsu
Hyakuhachi-nin no Hitori,
Ōgi-ya Hanazono

Ōgi-ya Hanazono as one of
the One Hundred and Eight
Heroines

Artist: Utagawa Kuniyasu
Publisher: Kaga-ya Kichibē
ca. 1830-1844

45

This very well dressed lady is trying to scare away a cat with
her kiseru pipe in a threatening manner. The cat is playing with
her gorgeous sash. It was not uncommon in Japan for adults
to scold children by holding their kiseru pipes over their heads.
Now most people are cigarette smokers. Very few have kiseru
pipes.

Note the mountains and waterfall pictured on the screen
behind the woman. The Japanese writing above her compares
her to a Chinese hero Bushō, a character in an old story called
Suiko-den. Bushō is famous for fighting a big tiger with his
bare hands. In this print, the brave hero is depicted as the
woman, and a big tiger as the small cat. Note that this series
involving heroines is different from the series of heroes with a
similar title by Utagawa Kuniyoshi printed in 1828.

「通俗水滸伝豪傑百八人之壹人　扇屋内花ぞの」
天保（1830-1844）頃、江戸では水滸伝が人
気で、歌川国芳は同じタイトルで水滸伝の豪
傑のシリーズ物を描いているが、国安はそれ
を遊女として描き替えた。ここでは、素手で
虎退治をした武松が、帯にじゃれる猫をきせ
るで叱る遊女として、描き替えられている。
なお、花ぞのは、きせるを手に、猫を追い払
おうとしているが、昔は、このように、きせ
るを手に子どもなどを叱るという光景はよく
見られた。

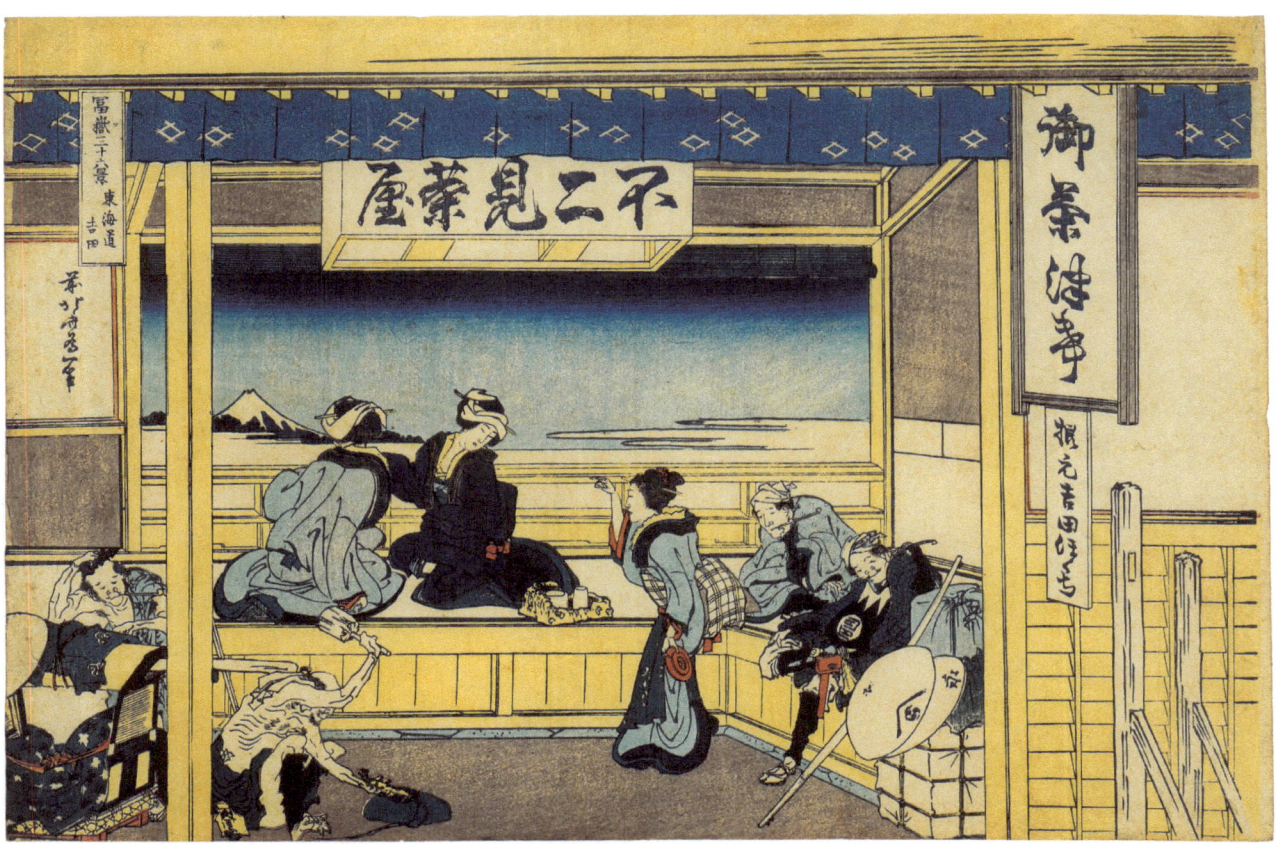

Fugaku Sanjū Rokkei Tōkaidō Yoshida

Thirty-Six Views of Mt. Fuji, Tōkaidō Yoshida

Artist: Katsushika Hokusai
Publisher: Nishimura-ya Yohachi
ca. 1831

46

This is one of the famous scenes of Katsushika Hokusai's Thirty-Six Views of Mt. Fuji. The place is Yoshida on the Tōkaidō Road near Nagoya. The people are enjoying the view of Mt. Fuji while taking a break at the Fujimi Chaya. Its name means a teahouse with a view of Mt. Fuji.

Two men on the right are smoking. One on the earth floor is repairing a straw sandal, and still another on the far left is wiping sweat off his head. In front of the woman in the middle, there is a tobacco tray made from a large natural tree stump. She is listening to the woman who is pointing with her finger in the direction of Mt. Fuji. The other woman sitting down is looking at Mt. Fuji in the far distance. The sign above is the name of the teahouse. The signs on the right describe the main menu of Ocha-zuke, a simple rice dish, and the souvenirs that can be purchased. Note the straw hats on the lower right.

「冨嶽三十六景　東海道吉田」
有名な葛飾北斎画の冨嶽三十六景シリーズの1枚。
ここでは、不二見茶屋という茶屋から人々が富士山を眺めている。たばこを吸い、あるいは草鞋を直し、旅の途中の身体を休めている。女性たちの前には置かれているたばこ盆は、樹木の根や幹をそのまま使って作られたたばこ盆である。右手には、吉田名物の火口の看板が見える。当時、人々は、火打石と火打金で火花を起こし、その火花を火口に移し、火種とした。

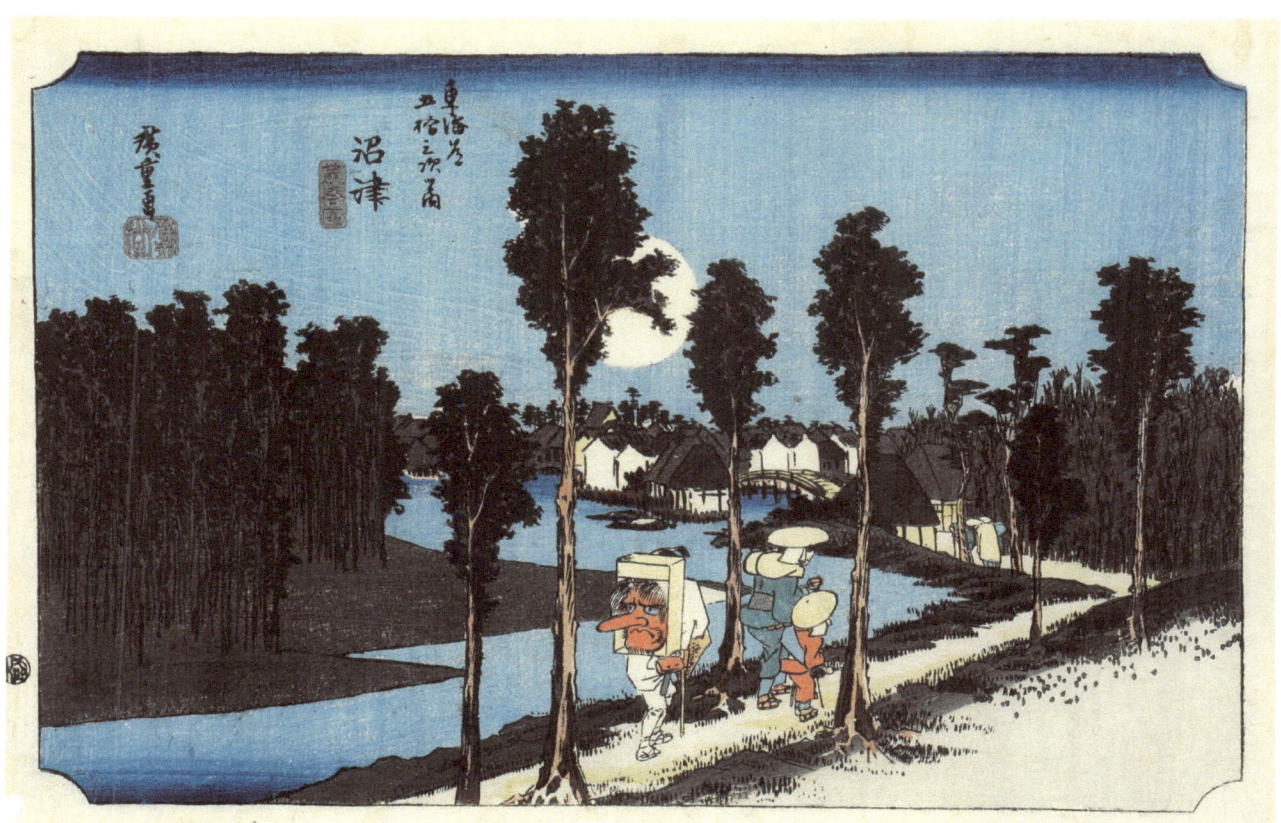

Tōkaidō Gojūsan Tsugi no Uchi, Numazu

One of the Fifty-Three Stages of the Tōkaidō Road: Numazu

Artist: Utagawa Hiroshige I
Publisher: Takeuchi Magohachi
ca. 1833-1835

47

This famous print is one of the Fifty-Three Stages of the Tōkaidō Road. The scene is the stage of Numazu and its surrounding landscapes.

At dusk three travelers are hurrying to the next Stage. The woman and a girl are Bikuni entertainers. The man behind them is carrying on his back a large red mask of Tengu, a long-nosed goblin of Japanese folklore. He is on a pilgrimage to the Kotohira Shrine in the town of Sanuki.

Note the lovely scene with a moon at dusk. A grove of trees is seen on the right as well as on the opposite bank. Some dwellings can be seen in the distance with a waterway and a bridge over it. A few people are ahead of the three travelers in this pleasant scene.

「東海道五拾三次之内　沼津　黄昏図」
初代広重の著名な東海道シリーズの内、沼津の図。
黄昏時、三人の旅人が道を急いでいる。先方の二人の女性は、旅芸人の比丘尼と考えられており、後の男性は、天狗の面を背負っていることから、金比羅詣と考えられている。

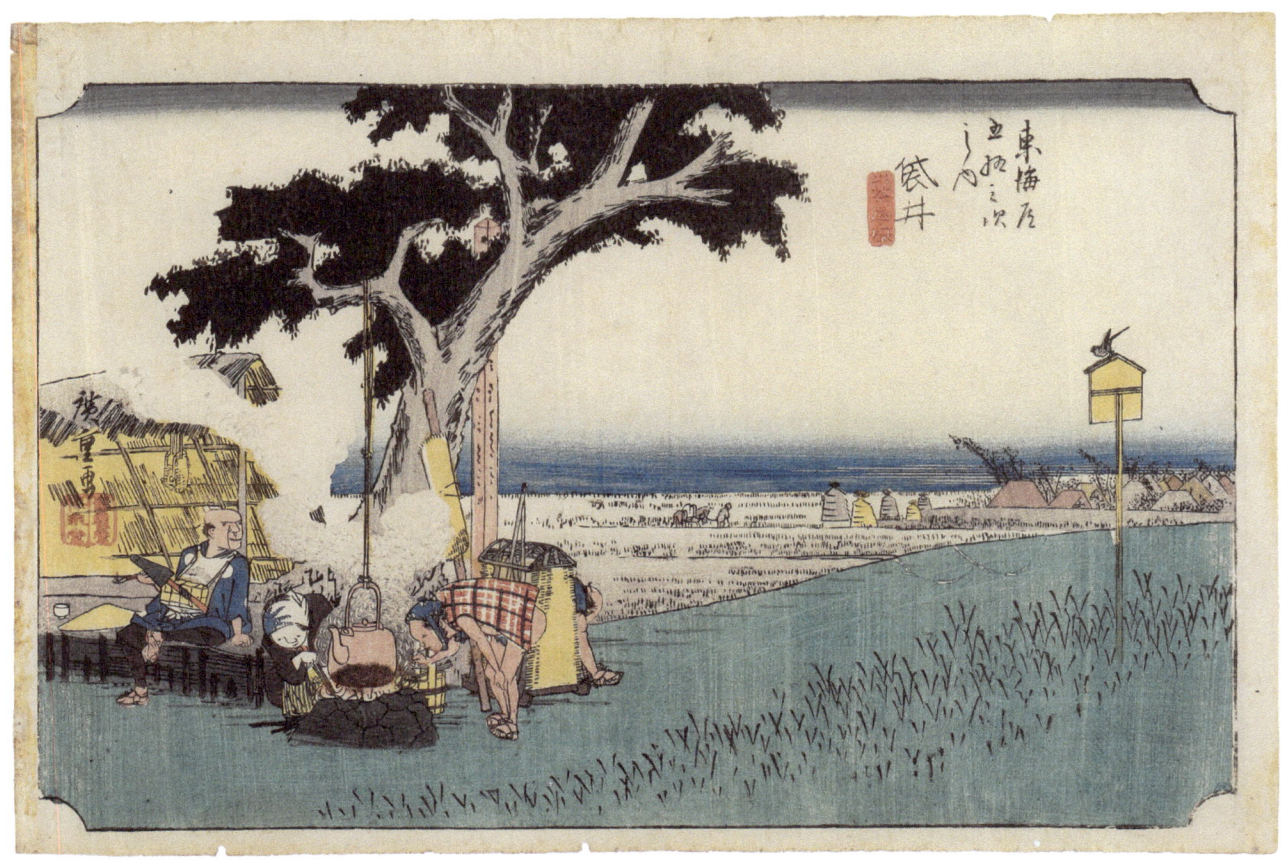

Tōkaidō Gojūsan Tsugi no Uchi, Fukuroi

One of the Fifty-Three Stages of the Tōkaidō Road: Fukuroi

Artist: Utagawa Hiroshige I
Publisher: Takeuchi Magohachi, Tsuru-ya Kiemon
ca. 1833-1835

48

This is another print from the Fifty-Three Stages of the Tōkaidō Road. The landscape is of Fukuroi, just half way between Edo and Kyoto.

A very modest teahouse is seen in the left background. A woman is heating a huge kettle of water for tea over the fire. The three men are the guests. The one sitting is a mailman. The other two are palanquin carriers. They are enjoying a tea and tobacco break. One is bending over to obtain a light for his pipe from the outdoor brick-walled fire of the teahouse. One can clearly see the rising smoke from the fire.

「東海道五拾三次之内　袋井　出茶屋ノ図」
初代広重の著名な東海道シリーズの内、袋井の図。袋井は、日本橋と京を除いた53の宿場の内27番目の宿場で、ちょうど真ん中の宿場である。
道ばたには簡易な茶屋が作られていて、三人の男性客が休憩している。一人は定飛脚で、二人は駕籠かきである。駕籠かきの一人は、茶屋の竈の火から、たばこの火を取ろうとしている。

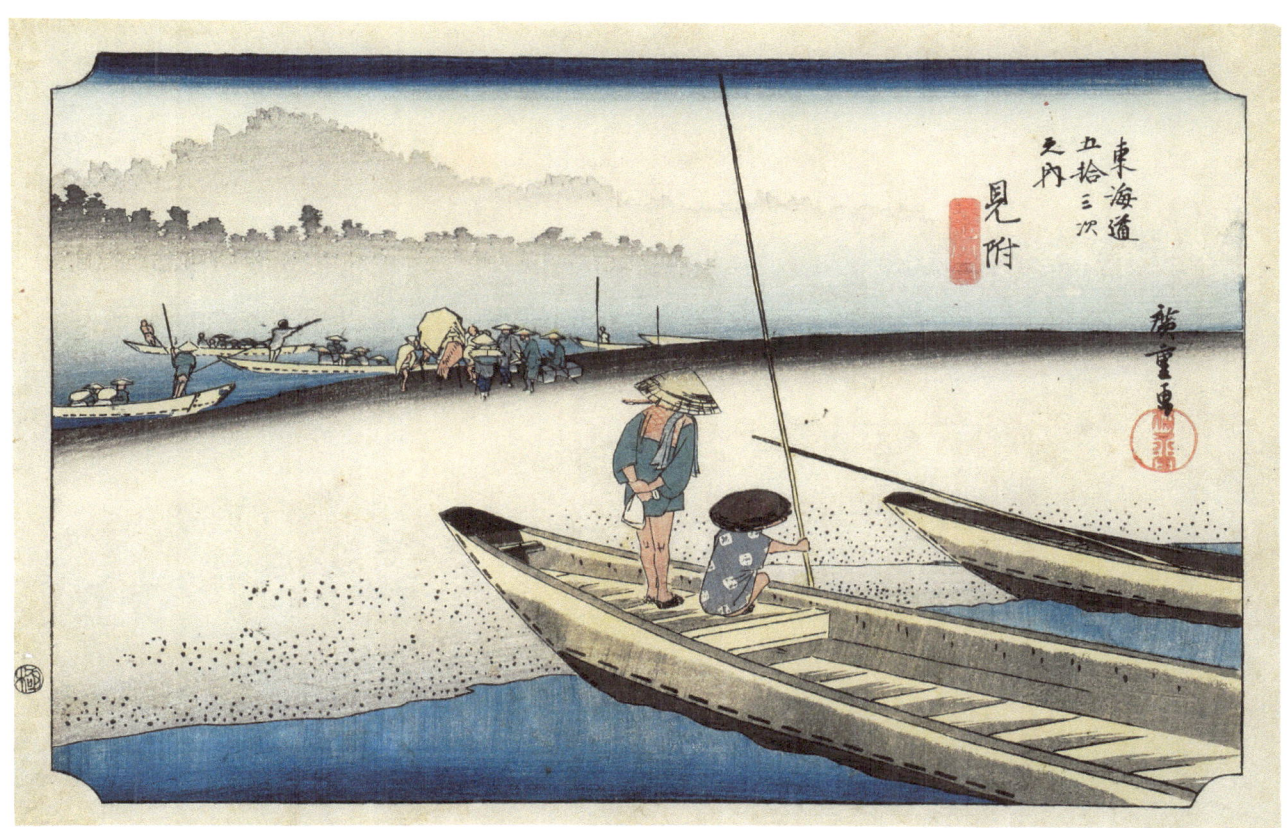

Tōkaidō Gojūsan Tsugi no Uchi, Mitsuke

One of the Fifty-Three Stages of Tōkaidō Road: Mitsuke

Artist: Utagawa Hiroshige I
Publisher: Takeuchi Magohachi
ca. 1833-1835

49

Still another print from the Fifty-Three Stages of the Tōkaidō Road. This landscape is of the Mitsuke Stage by the Tenryū River. During the Edo period, travelers had to charter a ferry to cross this river. Since the river splits into two at this point, the travelers had to change ferries on the sandbank in the river.

In front of the sandbank two ferrymen are waiting for travelers. The one standing is smoking, and the other sitting is holding a pole in the sand as an anchor. The pole is also used to row the boat, as one can see it used in the boats on the other side of the sandbank. A group of travelers on the far edge of the sandbank are waiting to cross to the other side of the river.

「東海道五拾三次之内　見附　天竜川図」
初代広重の著名な東海道シリーズの内、見附の図。見附には、天竜川が流れ、当時、この川を渡るには舟を使用しなければならなかった。ここでは天竜川は二筋に分かれており、人々は中洲で舟を乗り換えていた。
画面手前では、二人の船頭が、一服しながら、あるいは腰掛けながら、客を待っている。

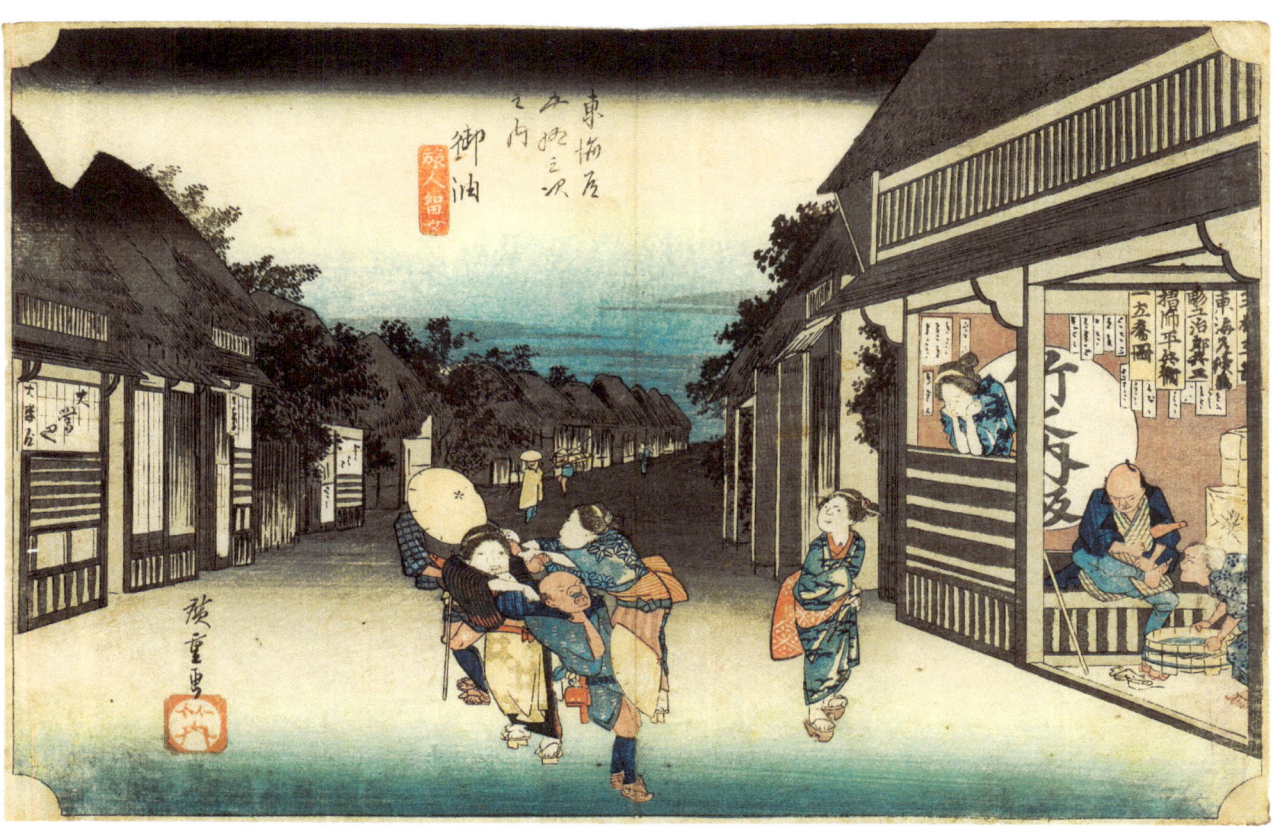

Tōkaidō Gojūsan Tsugi no Uchi, Goyu

One of the Fifty-Three Stages of the Tōkaidō Road: Goyu

Artist: Utagawa Hiroshige I
Publisher: Takeuchi Magohachi
ca. 1833-1835

50

This is still another print showing one of the Fifty-Three Stages of the Tōkaidō Road, the stage of Goyu. Many inns can be seen on both sides of the road. It is dusk. Note the traveler on the far right is about to wash his feet in a tub of water with the help of an old woman. Two of the three women in the center are trying to take the travelers into their inn. The Goyu stage as well as the next Akasaka stage was notorious for such woman hustlers enticing the travelers into their inns.

「東海道五拾三次之内　御油　旅人留女」
初代広重の著名な東海道シリーズの内、御油の図。街道の両側には多くの宿屋が見られるが、二人の女性が強引に客引きをしている。彼女たちは留女と呼ばれ、街道で客引きをし、宿屋で給仕をするかたわら、旅人相手に売色することも多かった。この御油と次の宿場赤坂は、こうした留女が多いことで有名であった。

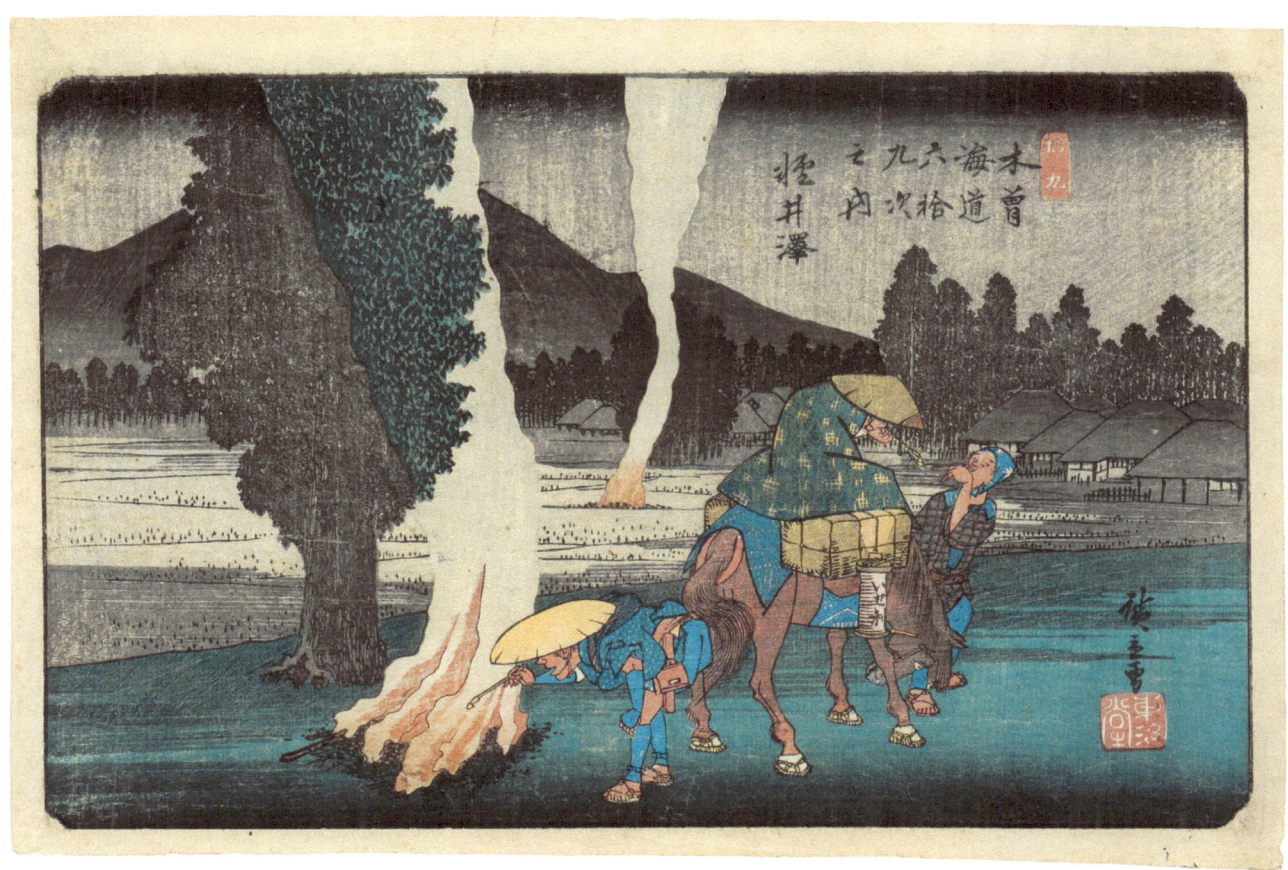

Kisokaidō Rokujūkyū Tsugi no Uchi, Karuizawa

One of the Sixty-Nine Stages of the Kisokaidō Road:
Karuizawa

Artist: Utagawa Hiroshige I
Publisher: Takeuchi Magohachi
ca. 1836-1837

51

This is a print of one of the Sixty-Nine Stages of the Kisokaidō Road. The landscape is of Karuizawa, now famous as a summer resort. It is Autumn. Three men are smoking. One is getting a light from an open air fire. The traveler on a horse is trying to get a light from the horseman's kiseru pipe. Note another fire in the harvested fields. Smoke is rising high from both fires. The tree is partly illuminated by the fire in the foreground. The baggage on the horse is illuminated by a hanging lantern.

「木曽海道六拾九次之内　軽井沢」
初代広重の東海道五十三次シリーズは大変評判が良く、次いで、広重と渓斎英泉との分担制作で、木曽海道六十九次シリーズが出版された。
軽井沢は、現在では避暑地としてたいへん有名であるが、この絵は、その軽井沢の晩秋を描いているように見える。三人の男性が描かれていて、三人ともたばこを吸っている。一人は焚き火から火を取っており、馬上の旅人は馬方からもらい火をしている。

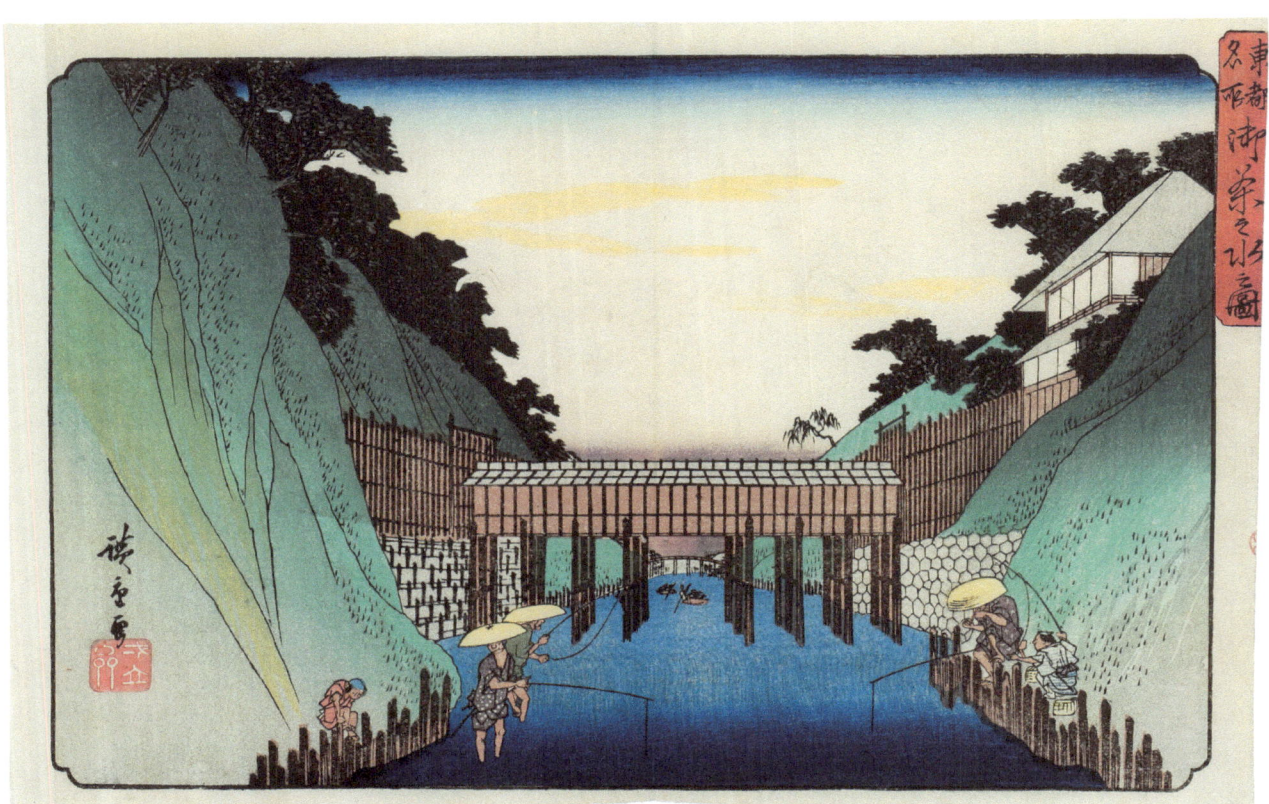

Tōto Meisho, Ochanomizu no Zu

Beautiful Scenery of Edo: Ochanomizu

Artist: Utagawa Hiroshige I
Publisher: Sano-ya Kihē
ca. 1830-1844

52

This is a view of the Ochanomizu area. The river shown is Kandagawa. In the Edo period, there were many samurai residences on both sides of the Kandagawa. A huge wooden water pipe, which looks like a bridge, can be seen in the center. The Edojō Castle is farther away behind the tree-covered riverbank on the left. The water pipe went all the way to the Castle.

Three men and a boy are fishing on the riverbank. The man on the right bank is trying to smoke while holding his fishing rod between his legs. On the left are two fishermen standing in the river casting their lines.

「東都名所　御茶之水之図」
お茶の水の図。画中の川は神田川である。当時は、川の両側には、数多くの武家屋敷があった。川の上部に描かれているのは上水樋である。近隣の水道橋の地名は、この橋のように見える上水道に由来する。画面左の奥には江戸城があり、この上水は江戸城にも引き入れられていた。
川では、三人の男性と一人の少年が釣りをしている。一人の男性は、釣り竿を足で支えながら、たばこを吸おうとしている。

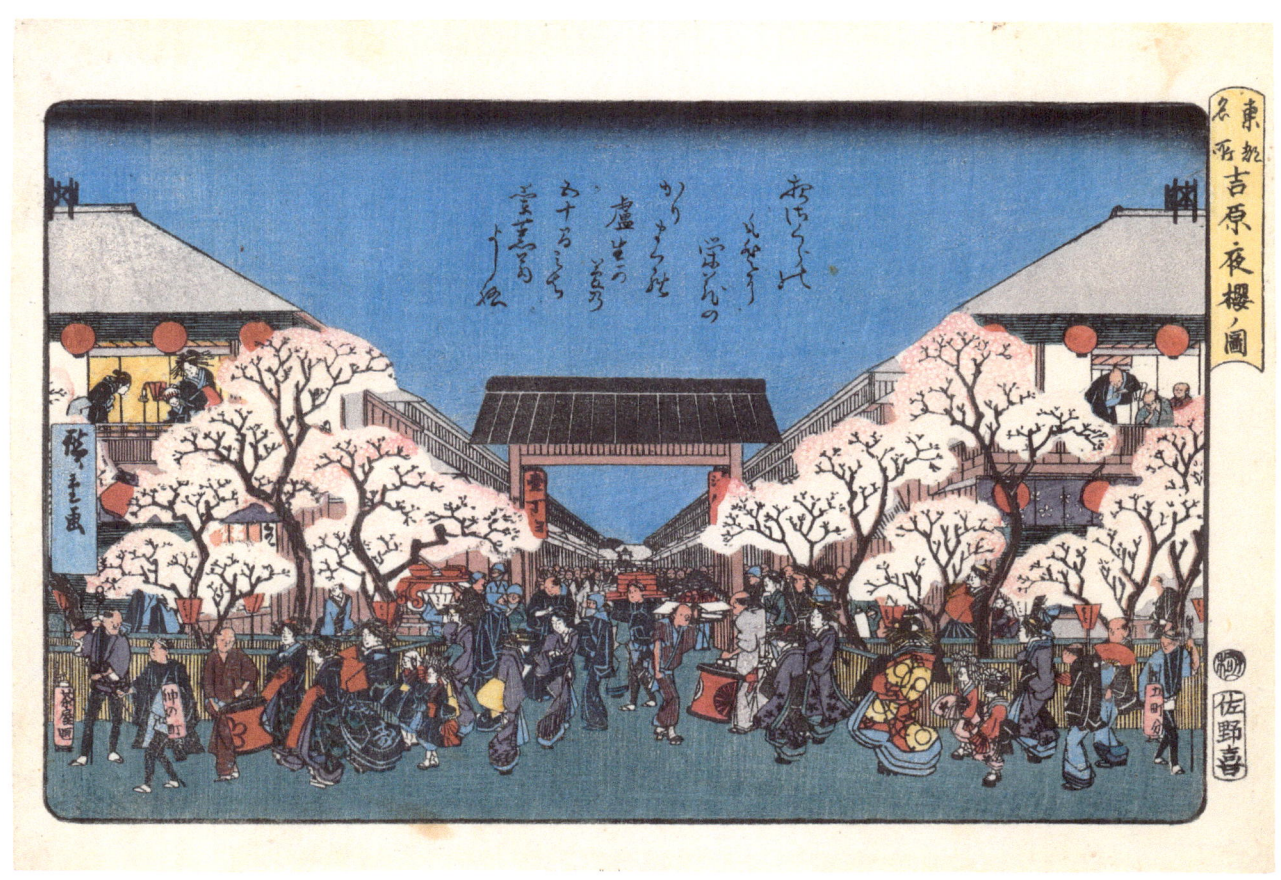

Tōto Meisho, Yoshiwara Yozakura no Zu

Beautiful Scenery of Edo: Yoshiwara and
Cherry Blossoms at Night

Artist: Utagawa Hiroshige I
Publisher: Sano-ya Kihē
ca. 1830-1844

53

Cherry trees were planted temporarily on the main street of Yoshiwara for the cherry blossom season. When the cherry blossom viewing season was over, the trees were removed. In this print, many people are enjoying strolling under the trees in the evening. Some are viewing the flowers from the balconies of the houses on both sides of the street. The gate depicted in the center is the entrance to the Edochō 1-chome area, where many of the pleasure quarters of Yoshiwara were located.

「東都名所吉原夜桜ノ図」
当時吉原では、桜の花盛りの時期だけ、桜の樹を植えていた。花が終わると抜いてしまい、それを毎年繰り返していた。この絵では、多くの人々が夜桜を楽しんでいる。客に呼ばれ、禿を従えて進む花魁の姿も見え、遊女屋の桃燈を持つ若い衆は、たばこ入れを腰から提げているのがわかる。
画面中央に描かれている門は江戸町一丁目の入口である。この入口の両側の手前の方に見えているのは茶屋で、後には遊女屋が軒を連ねている。

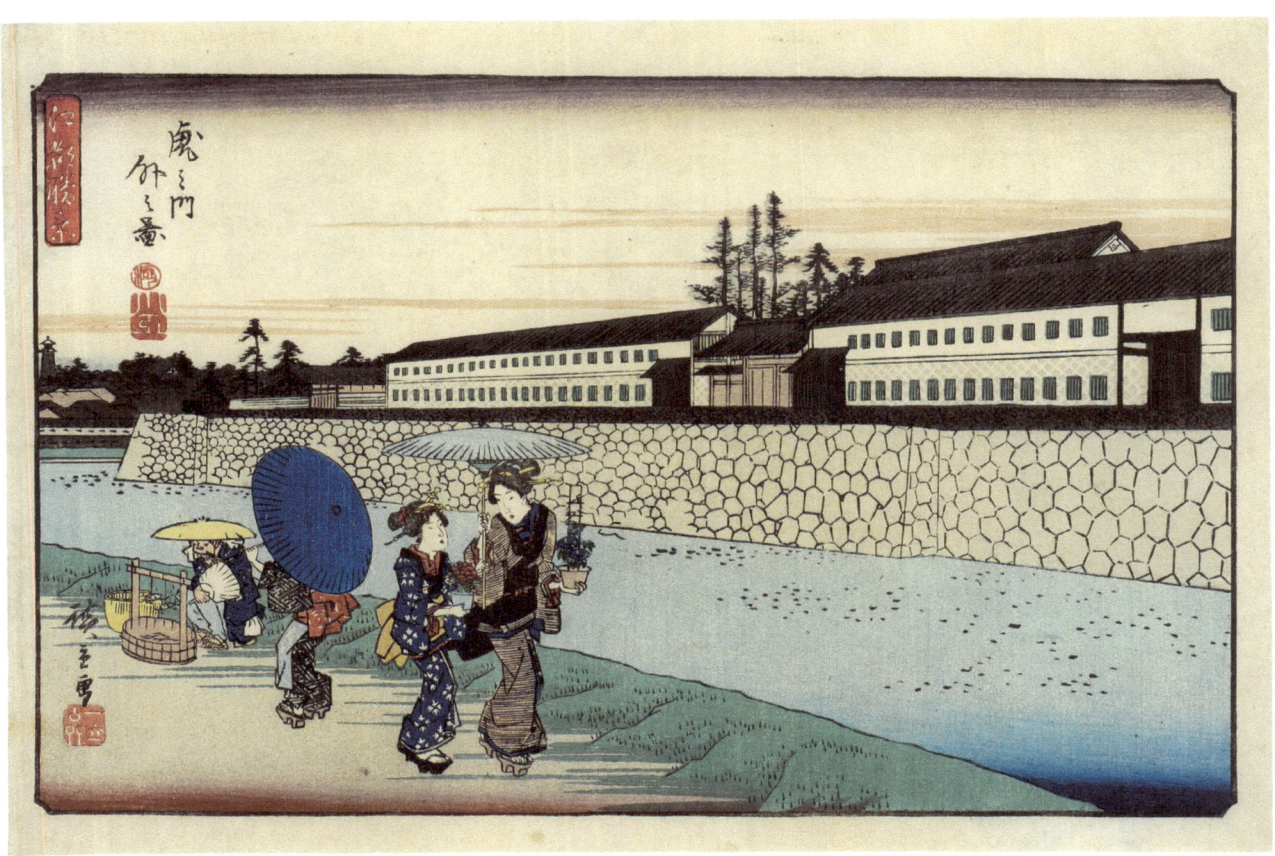

Edo Shōkei, Toranomon-gai no Zu

One of Various Landscapes of Edo:
Near the Toranomon Gate

Artist: Utagawa Hiroshige I
Publisher: Kawaguchi-ya Shōzō
ca. 1830-1844

54

This is a scene near the Toranomon Gate by the outer moat of the Edojō Castle. The water is a section of the outer moat. Across the moat are samurai residences. A massive stone embankment is present.

In the foreground, a mother and a daughter are carrying potted plants.The mother's plant is a morning glory. A man is selling tortoises while smoking. Tortoises were used for a religious ceremony called Hōjō-e held on August 15th. On this day, people set living creatures free.

「江都勝景　虎之門外之図」
虎ノ門近辺を描いている。虎ノ門は江戸城の外濠に設けられた城門であった。濠の向こうに石垣や武家屋敷が見えるが、この屋敷は、位置的に延岡藩内藤家のものと思われる。
母娘と見られる二人連れが、日傘に身を寄せ合い鉢植えを持っている。母の持つ鉢は朝顔である。男性がたばこを吸いながら亀を売っているが、この亀は、8月15日の放生会に放す亀であろう。

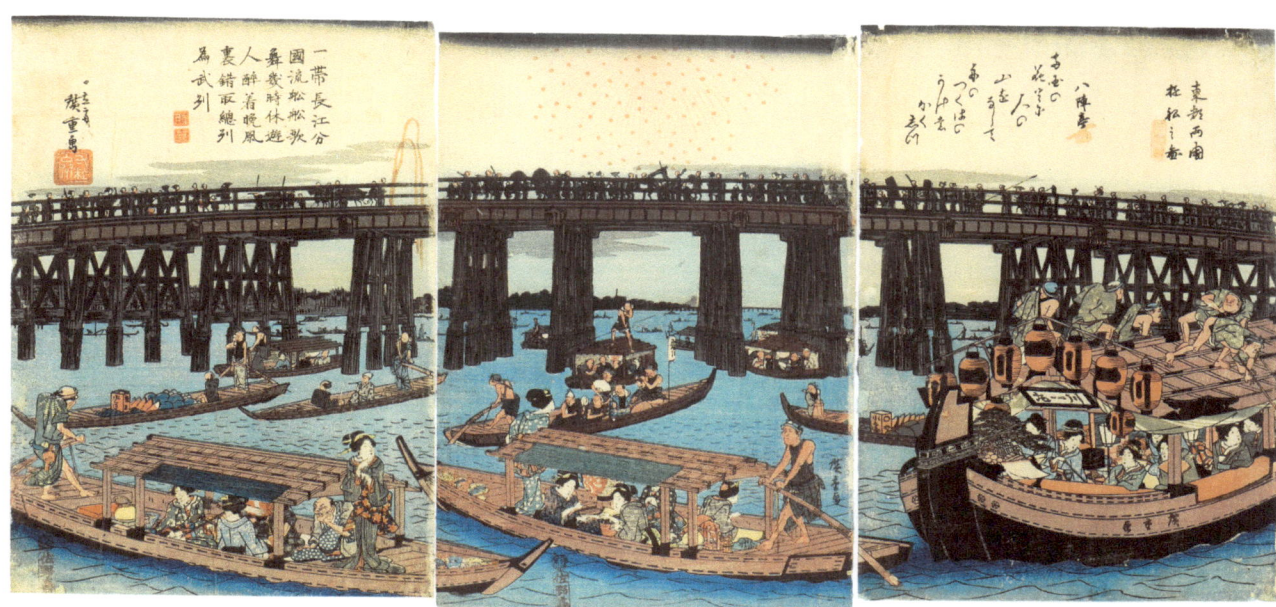

Tōto Ryōgoku Yūsen no Zu

Ryōgoku in Edo, Viewing Fireworks from Boats

Artist: Utagawa Hiroshige I
Publisher: Sano-ya Kihē
ca. 1830-1844

55

The Ryōgoku Bridge over the Sumida River in Edo is depicted. Different fireworks are seen above in the left and center of the print. Watching fireworks in Ryōgoku was a much anticipated pastime that gave picturesque charm to the early Summer in Edo. Some of the people on the bridge are watching the fireworks. Others have chartered pleasure boats. Those who are on the boat are enjoying eating, drinking, and playing finger games. Some vendor boats selling fruits or boats with musicians are also present. All these have added to the merry-making of the event.

「東都両国遊船之図」
隅田川にかかる両国橋を描いている。当時、両国の花火は、江戸の夏の風物詩であった。人々は、橋の上や大小の遊船から花火を眺めているが、船中の人々は、飲み、食べ、あるいは拳（数拳という指で行うゲーム）を打ち、くつろぎながら花火を楽しんでいる。遊船にまじり、水菓子（くだもの）売りの船や、音曲を演奏する一団を乗せた船も見られる。

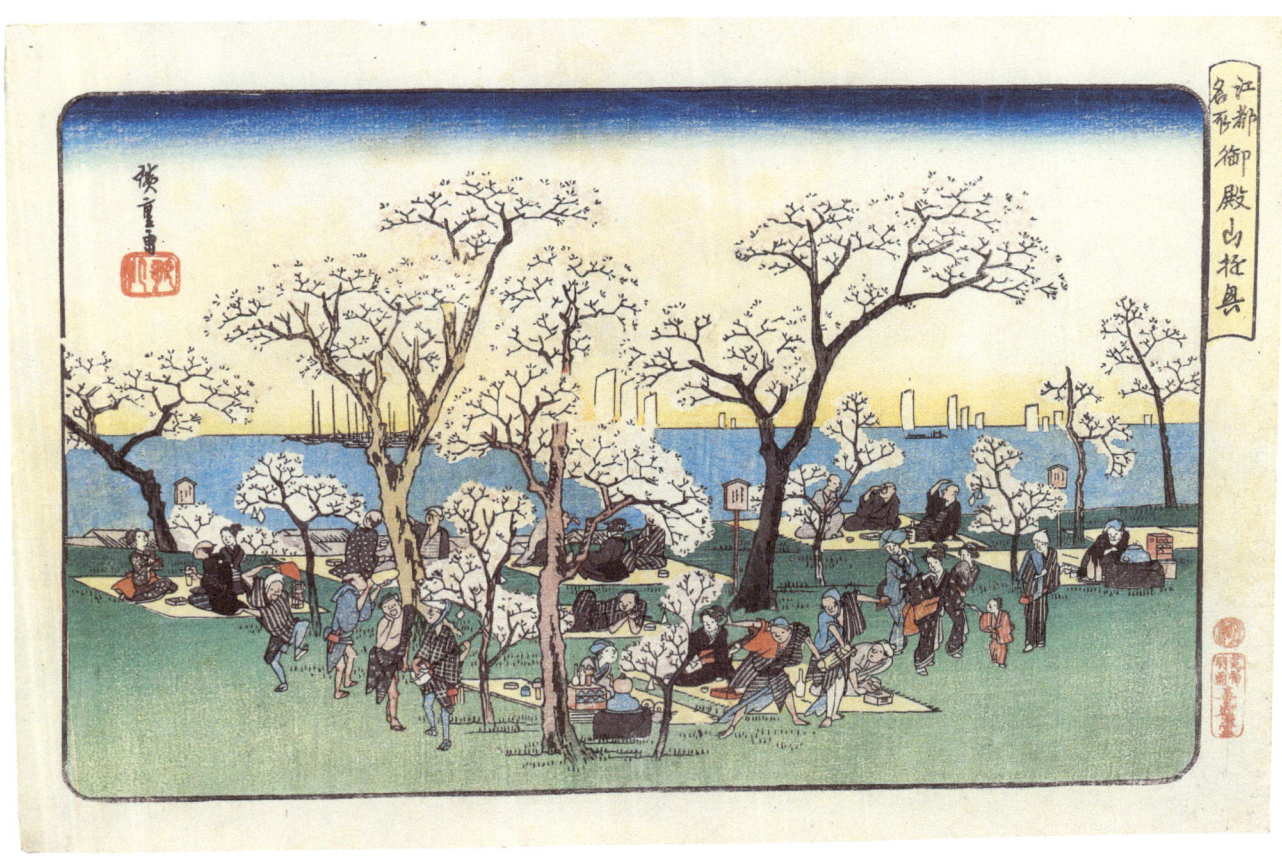

Edo Meisho Gotenyama Yūkyō

Famous Landscapes of Edo: Enjoying Cherry Blossoms
at the Gotenyama Mountain

Artist: Utagawa Hiroshige I
Publisher: Sano-ya Kihē
ca. 1830-1844

56

In this scene people are enjoying the Gotenyama mountain area,
which was very famous for its cherry blossoms. They are eating,
drinking, singing, and dancing. It is a very happy occasion and a
pleasurable experience for everyone.

They loved this area very much because it had a view of the
ocean with gently sailing boats. Unfortunately towards the end of
the Edo period, the soil from Gotenyama mountain was used to
build pedestals for cannons for marine defense.

「江都名所　御殿山遊興」
人々が、桜の下に敷物を敷き、飲み、食べ、
歌い、踊っている。寝そべってたばこを吸
い、くつろぐ男性もいる。ここに描かれて
いるのは御殿山で、御殿山は、海を背景に
して開放感を味わいながら桜を楽しめる名
所として、人々に人気があった。しかし残
念なことに、幕末、海防として品川沖に台
場を設けるため、御殿山の土は使われてし
まった。

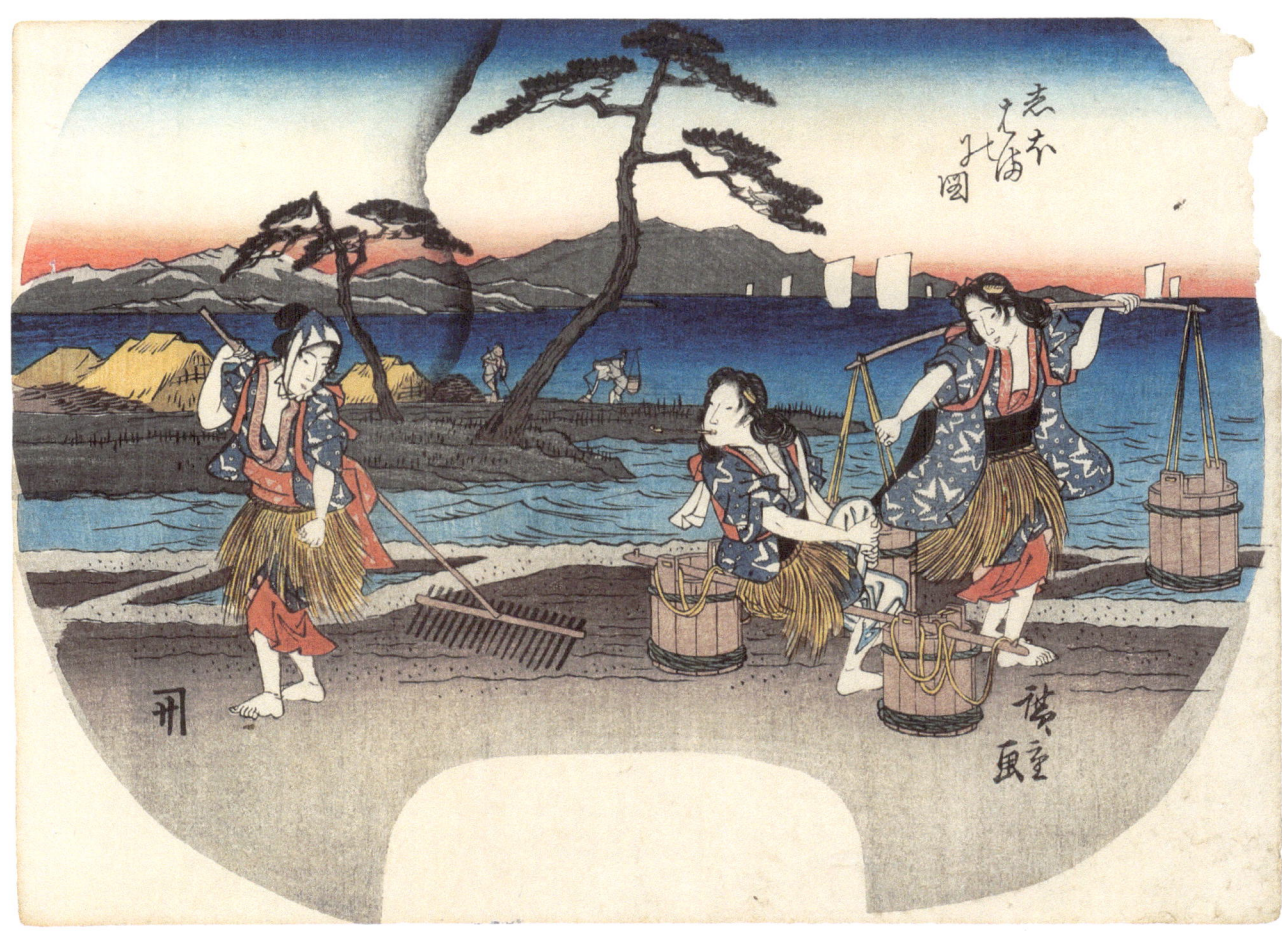

Shiohama no Zu

A Salt Terrace

Artist: Utagawa Hiroshige I
Publisher: Suruga-ya Sakujirō
ca. 1844-1848

57

This print was used to decorate a Japanese fan. People loved to have prints like this on their fans.

This is a scene from a salt terrace. Since no salt mines nor salt lakes exist in Japan, the Japanese made salt from sea water and still do for food use. In the Edo period many salt terraces were prepared near the sea to concentrate seawater by evaporation.

Three women are working on a salt terrace. Two of them are carrying heavy buckets of sea water. One of the two is having a tobacco break. The third woman on the left is spreading the sea water on the terrace. Contrary to this scene, most of the work was carried out by men because of the hard labor. A little jet of smoke in the left background is rising from a fire used to evaporate sea water in containers.

「しほはまの図」
この絵は団扇絵で、当時人々は、このような絵を団扇に貼り、楽しんでいた。
ここに描かれているのは塩浜である。日本には岩塩や塩湖といった塩資源がないため、当時は塩浜を使って塩を作っていた。人々は、海に近い場所に広い塩浜を作り、海水を濃縮し、その濃縮した海水を煮詰めて塩を得ていた。この絵では、手前で三人の美女が塩浜で働いているが、二人は汐汲みに従事し、もう一人は、浜をならす仕事をしている。汐汲みの女性一人は、たばこを吸って休んでいる。ここでは、女性を配し、美しい情景が描かれているが、実は、塩作りはたいへんな重労働で、男性が中心となって行う労働であった。

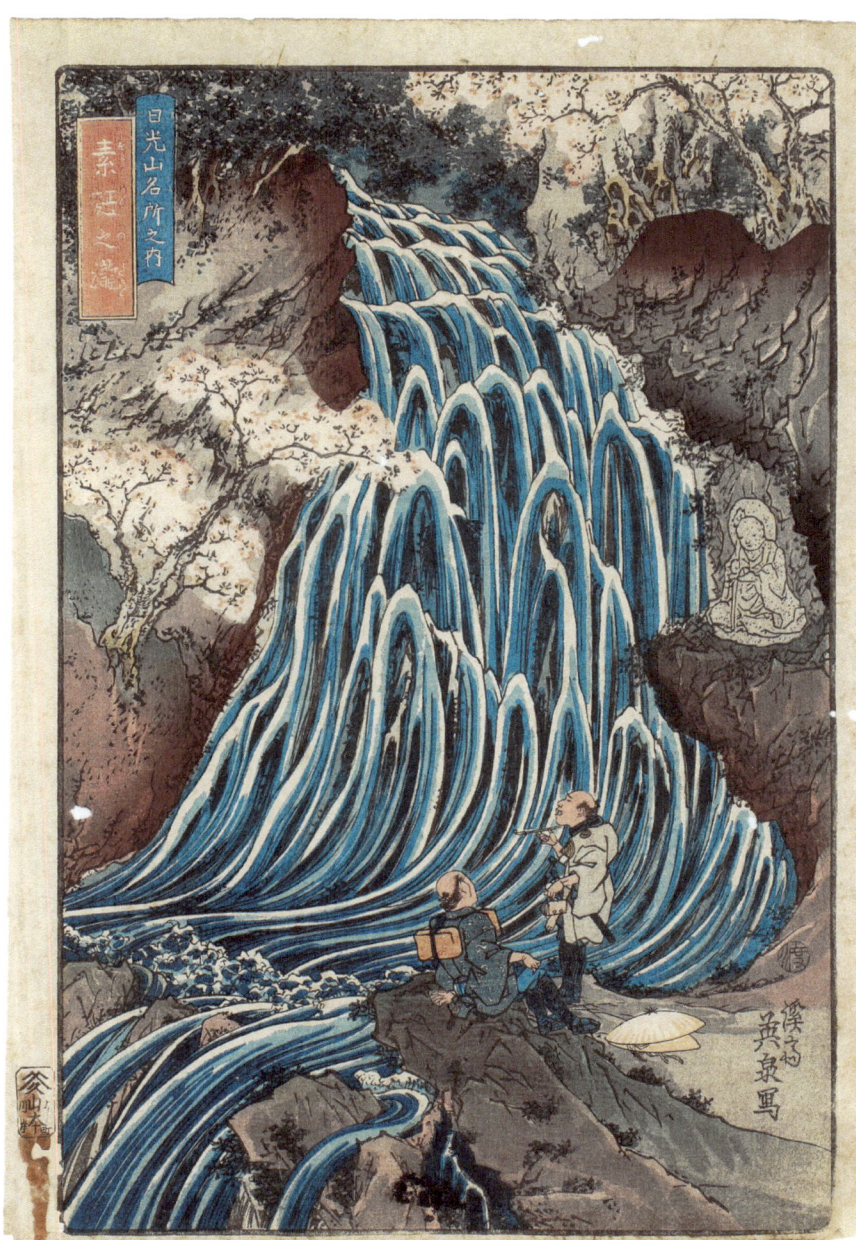

Nikkō San Meisho no Uchi,
Sōmen no Taki

One of the Scenic Spots of Nikkō:
The Sōmen Waterfall

Artist: Keisai Eisen
Publisher: Yamamoto
ca. 1844-1848

58

This print is one of the series which depicted the scenic scenes of Nikkō. This waterfall is presumed to be the Dragon Head Falls. Its nickname is Sōmen. Sōmen is a Japanese vermicelli eaten mostly in Summer. On both sides of the waterfall are cherry trees in blossom, indicating it is Spring.

Two male tourists are watching the beauty of the waterfall and cherry blossoms while enjoying a smoke. Their hats are on the ground. On the right hand side in the middle there is an image of Buddha in the stone.

「日光山名所之内　素麺之瀧」
日光の名所を取り上げたシリーズの1枚。素麺の瀧と題されているが、これは龍頭の瀧のことと考えられている。瀧の傍らには桜が描かれ、春であることを示している。二人の旅人が休憩を取り、たばこと美しいながめを楽しんでいる。

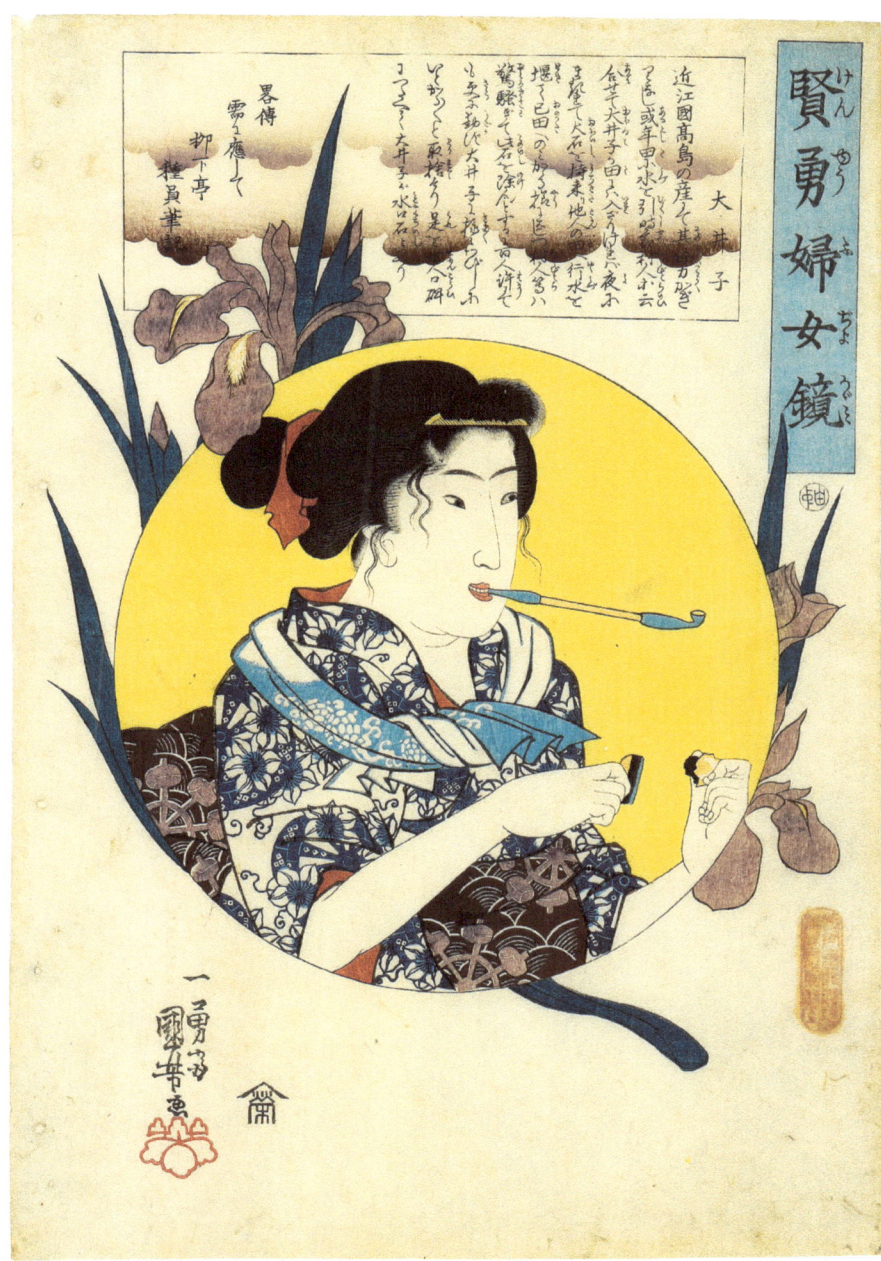

Ken'yū Fujo Kagami Oine

A Model of Heroic Women: Oine

Artist: Utagawa Kuniyoshi
Publisher: Unknown
ca. 1844-1848

59

This is a portrait of a rice field worker named Oine. She was known as a woman of great physical strength. She has a very simple dress style and holds a kiseru pipe in her mouth. A flint stone and a little piece of grass charcoal are in her left hand, and a piece of metal in her right. Sparks were created when these were struck together to light tobacco. The fire for the light thus made was kept burning with a special grass charcoal.

「賢勇婦女鏡　大井子」
百人力で知られる近江国おいねが描かれている。おいねは、百人かかっても動かすことのできない石を軽々と動かすことができたという。この絵でおいねが手にしているのは、火打金と火打石、火口である。当時の人々は、火打金と火打石を打ち付けて火花を起こし、その火花を火口に取って、火種とした。

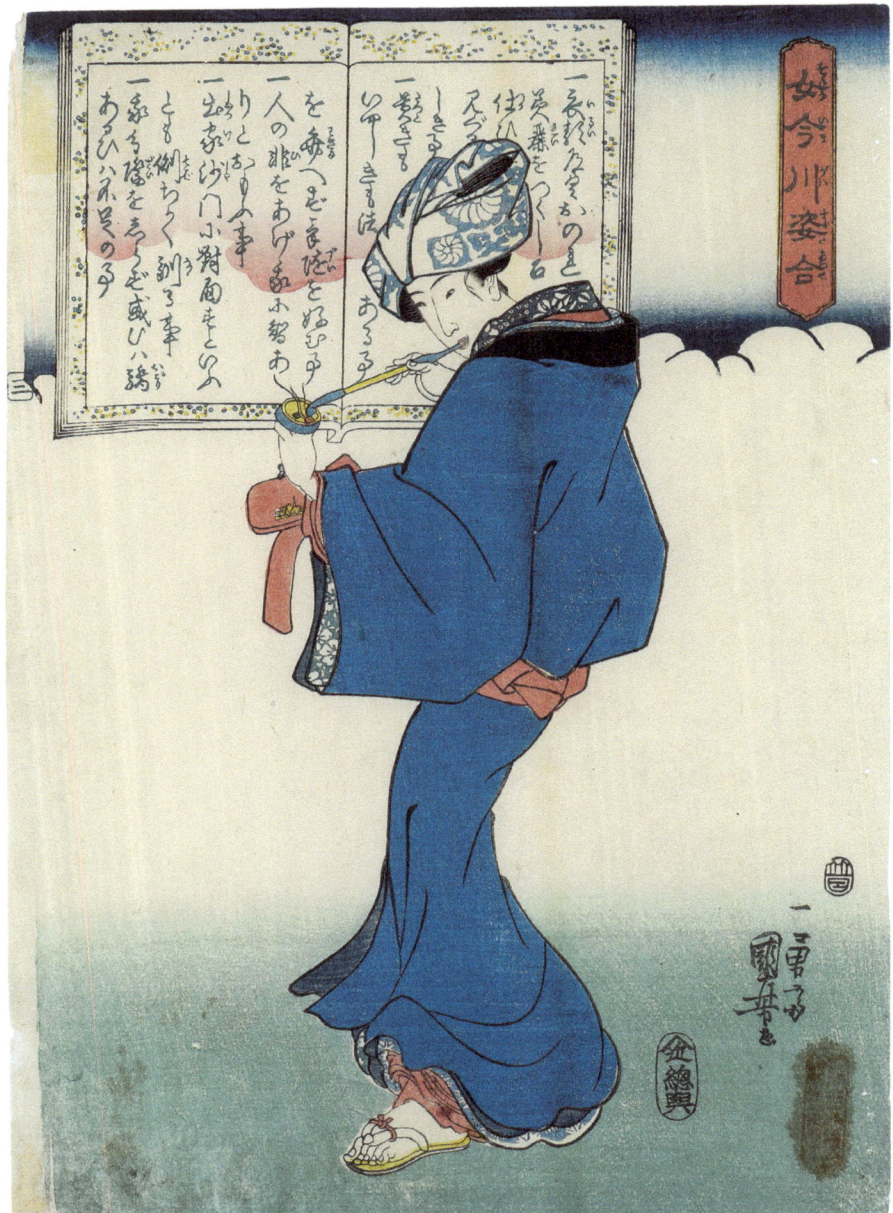

On'na Imagawa Sugata Awase

A Series of Smart Women

Artist: Utagawa Kuniyoshi
Publisher: Sōshū-ya Yohē
ca. 1844-1848

60

This print depicts a woman of high morals and integrity. Since this is one of the Ukiyo-e series intended to teach women, she is wearing a plain solid color kimono. She neither needs to wear a colorful kimono nor to use many ornamental hairpins.

She uses her simply shaped functional netsuke to collect ashes from her kiseru pipe. Netsuke is a fastener to secure a hanging pouch from a kimono sash. The pouch held personal belongings such as tobacco. Originally netsukes were made for a practical use but they developed into highly refined art objects during the Edo period. Today many netsukes are admired for their artistic qualities.

「女今川姿合」
地味な着物を着た女性がたばこを吸っており、彼女は、たばこ入れの根付を灰皿のように使用している。根付は本来は、帯からたばこ入れや印籠を提げるための実用品であり、飾りのあるものや何かを象った根付も多いが、このようにただ丸く、灰を落とすため（火はたき）に使用できるような実用を追求したものも多かった。この絵は、女性の教育を目的としたシリーズの中の1点であるため、身につける着物や使用するたばこ入れが地味に描かれている。

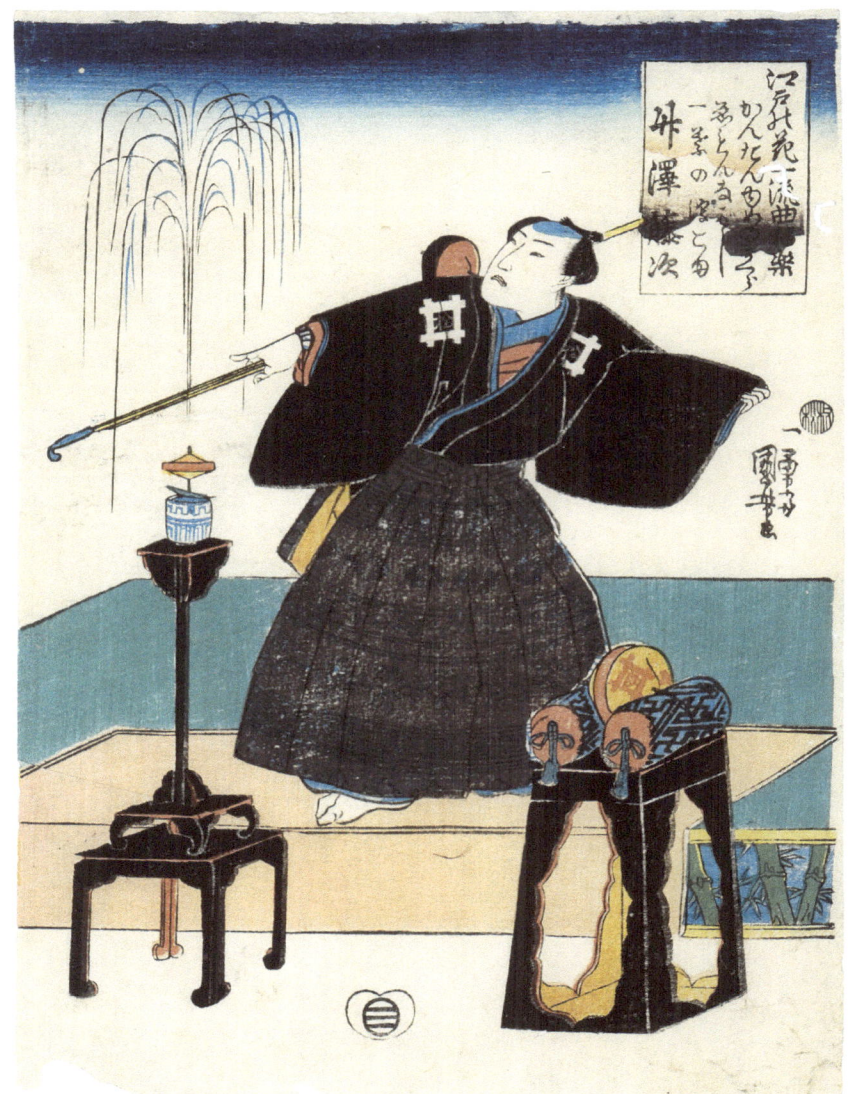

Edo no Hana Ichiryū Kyoku Goma,
Takezawa Tōji

Takezawa Tōji's Spinning Top Magic

Artist: Utagawa Kuniyoshi
Publisher: Iba-ya Senzaburō
ca.1844-1848

61

The Japanese entertainer in this print is Takezawa Tōji.
He was very famous for his skills of spinning a top. There
are many woodblock prints depicting his performances. In
some he used a very long kiseru pipe as shown in this print.
Sometimes Tōji spun his top on the bowl of his long kiseru
pipe.

Note the small spinning top is on an interesting stand on top
of another small stand. It is spraying water like a fountain. In
the right forefront is another stand which holds two pillows
and a much bigger top. These will be used for his next act.
Tōji has a commanding pose indicating he is in complete
control. In the upper right, the Japanese words name the
three segments of his show.

「江戸の花一流曲独楽　竹沢藤次」
江戸のスター芸人、曲独楽の竹沢藤次を描い
ている。当時、見世物芸人として大人気であっ
た竹沢藤次は、数多くの浮世絵に描かれてい
る。そのうちいくつかの絵には、藤次が長い
きせるを使い、独楽を操っていた様子が描か
れている。

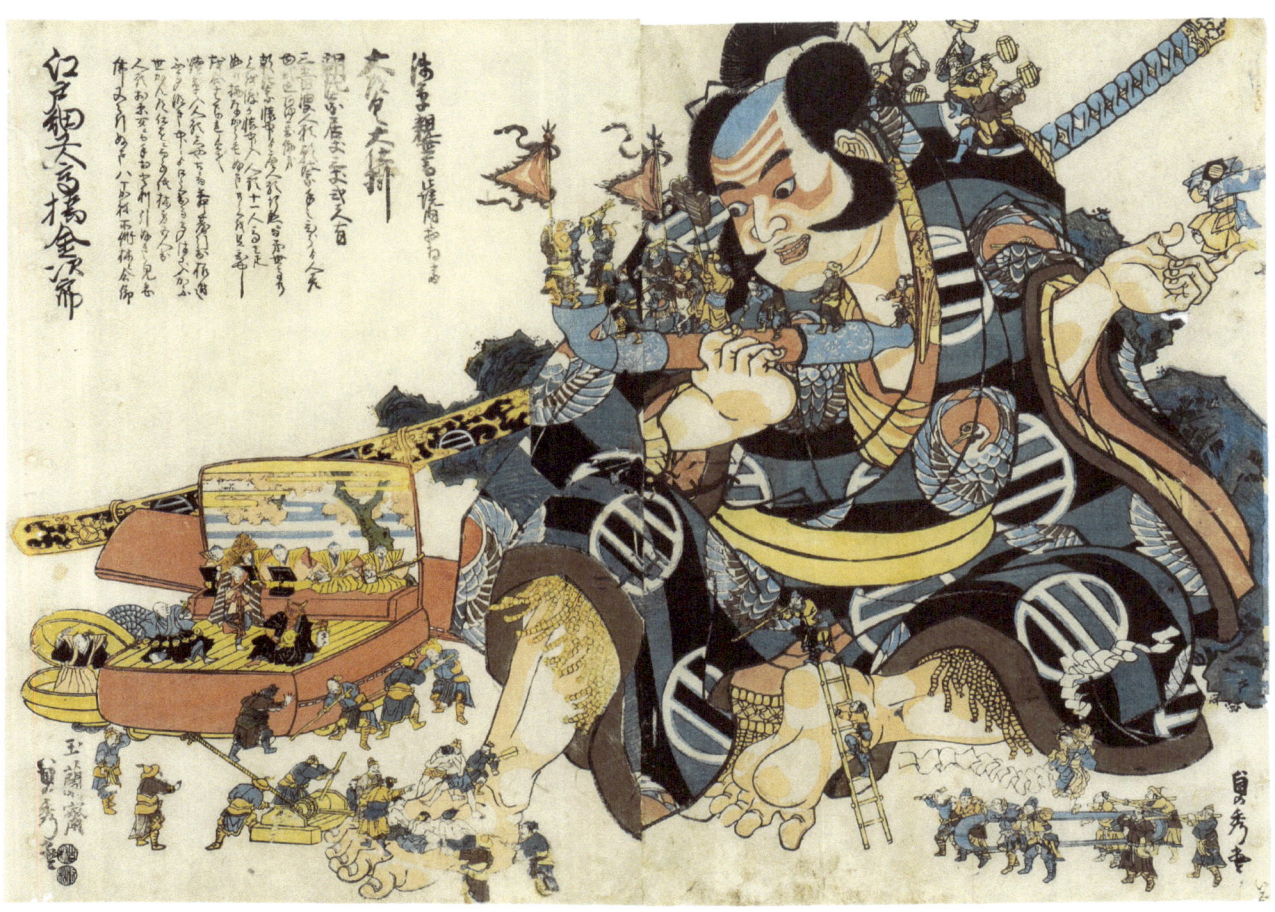

Asaina Ōningyō no Misemono

A Huge Asaina Mechanical Model Show

Artist: Utagawa Sadahide
Publisher: Unknown
1847

62

An enormous mythical giant called Asaina Saburō Yoshihide is depicted. Asaina first lived as a samurai in the 13th century. In the Edo period, there were interesting myths of the giant Asaina traveling to many strange worlds. The stories may be compared to those of the Gulliver's Travels.

Small Chinese men have come out of Asaina's clothes. On the left is a little kabuki stage with actors that appears when he opens his tobacco pouch. Note the elaborate details. Asaina holds a large kiseru pipe in his right hand with Chinese men on it. A Japanese entertainer called Sanbasō is dancing on his left forefinger. The Japanese text in the upper left states the size of Asaina and the details of the show.

This print was prepared as an advertisement for a giant Asaina mechanical show planned in 1847. The show, however, was prohibited because of the gigantic size of the Asaina model.

「朝比奈大人形の見世物」

鎌倉時代に実在していた武将朝比奈三郎義秀は、合戦に敗れた後の後半生が未詳で、不思議な国々を巡ったと考えられていた。弘化4年（1847）、この朝比奈の大人形を制作し、見世物興行を行う企画が持ち上がった。朝比奈の袂から、唐人の人形が踊りながら現れ、開いたたばこ入れの中から芝居のワンシーンがせり上がるというものだが、あまりにも大きすぎたため、事前に禁止されたという。興行は実現しなかったが、この絵は、見世物の予告として制作された。

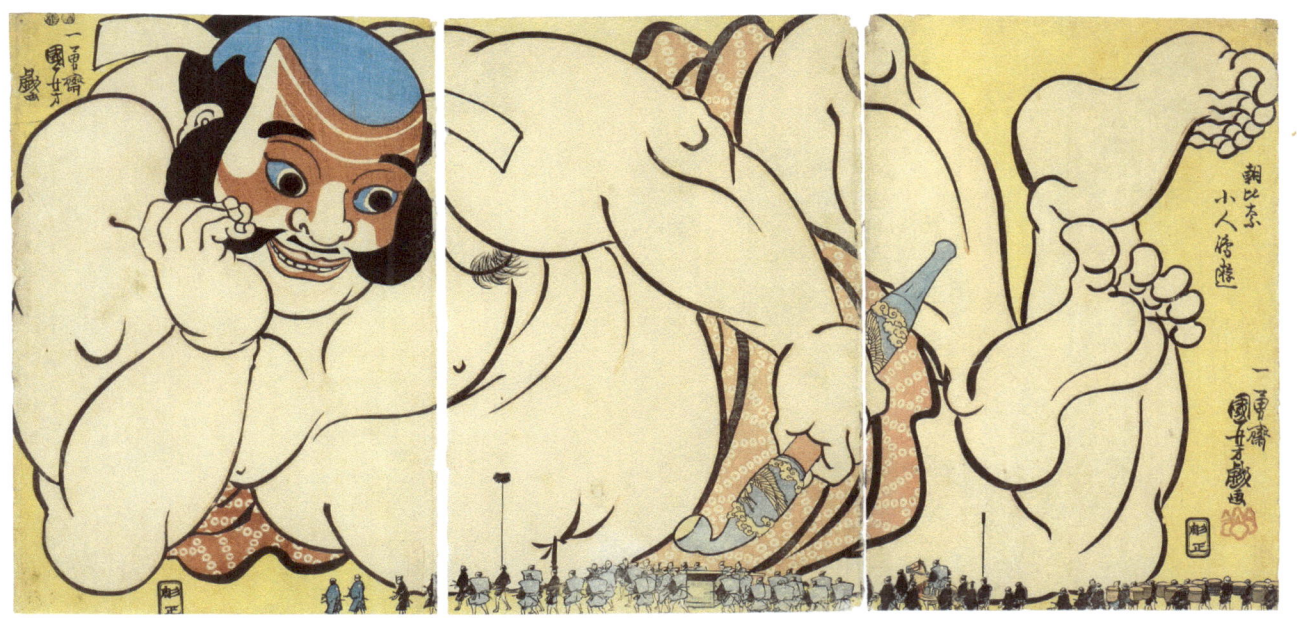

Asaina Kobito-Jima Asobi

Asaina's Delight in the Land of Little Humans

Artist: Utagawa Kuniyoshi
Publisher: Hori Masa
1847

63

Another version of the mythical giant Asaina. Again Asaina is in the land of little humans. He is gazing down on a parade of a Japanese feudal lord and his vassals. Asaina has a very large kiseru pipe in his left hand. He used the symbol of a crane as his crest. Note that only one half of the crane pattern, showing head and one wing, can be seen on his kiseru pipe. A much larger crane pattern appears above his belt on the kimono he wears in print #62.

This print was made in 1847, the same year as for print #62. The canceled event of the huge Asaina mechanical show might have prompted the artist to make this print.

「朝比奈小人島遊」
この図も朝比奈三郎義秀を描いている。朝比奈は、不思議な国々を巡る島巡りの説話で、江戸時代、たいへん人気があった。ここに描かれた朝比奈は小人島で遊んでおり、寝そべって大名行列を見下ろしている。本図も、前図同様に弘化４年（1847）の出版で、この年に企画が持ち上がり、結局実現せずに終わった朝比奈の大人形の見世物と関係があると思われる。なお、この絵で朝比奈が手にしているきせるには、朝比奈が用いていた鶴の紋様が見える。

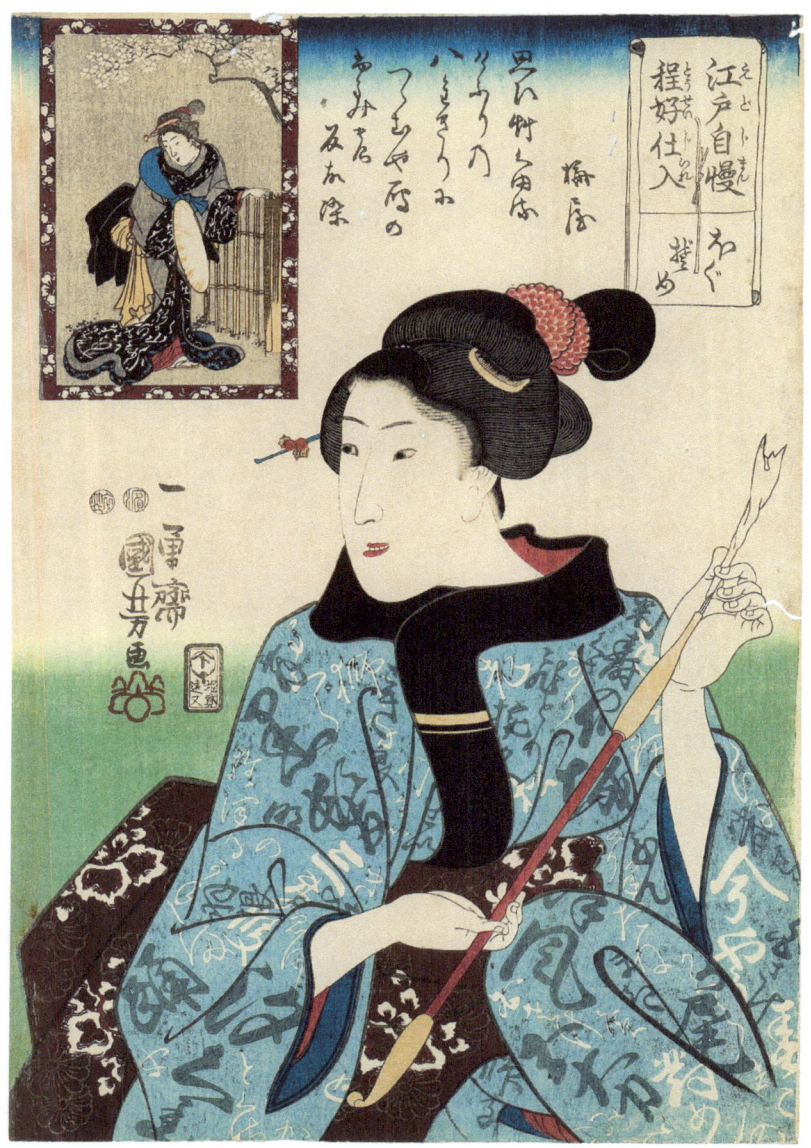

Edo Jiman Tōsei Jiire, Hoguzome

The Latest Kimono Design,
Hoguzome

Artist: Utagawa Kuniyoshi
Publisher: Enshū-ya Matabē
1848

64

This print is one of a series featuring the latest fashions. The kimono the woman is wearing represents a new fashion trend. In those years common people with little money often wore clothes made of used paper. It created a new fashion in Kimono design called Hoguzome, which means a wastepaper design. It has many Japanese letters dyed as a design on cloth as seen on the woman's kimono in this print. The woman is not poor, but she is wearing a trendy wastepaper design kimono.

In the framed picture of the upper left, a woman named Yaegiri in kabuki dramas is depicted. She is a poor woman, and the name Yaegiri was always associated with poverty in those days. Note Yaegiri's kimono made of wastepaper with many letters.

The woman is cleaning her kiseru pipe. It was necessary to clean such pipes often so that smoke could go through easily. The tobacco tar was removed with a twisted, stiff paper string as shown also in print #40.

「江戸自慢程好仕入ほぐぞめ」
流行のスタイルを取り上げた1枚。この女性が身につけている着物のデザインは、反古染めと呼ばれたもの。貧しい人々は反古紙でできた着物を着ていたが、反古染めは、それをデザイン化したものである。左上部のコマ絵に描かれた女性八重桐は、歌舞伎などに貧しい人物として登場する。ここでは、その八重桐が身につける反古紙の着物と、流行としての反古染めが対比されている。
この女性は、紙縒できせるの手入れをしている。きせるの手入れを怠ると、煙が通りにくくなり、羅宇を替えなければならないこともあった。

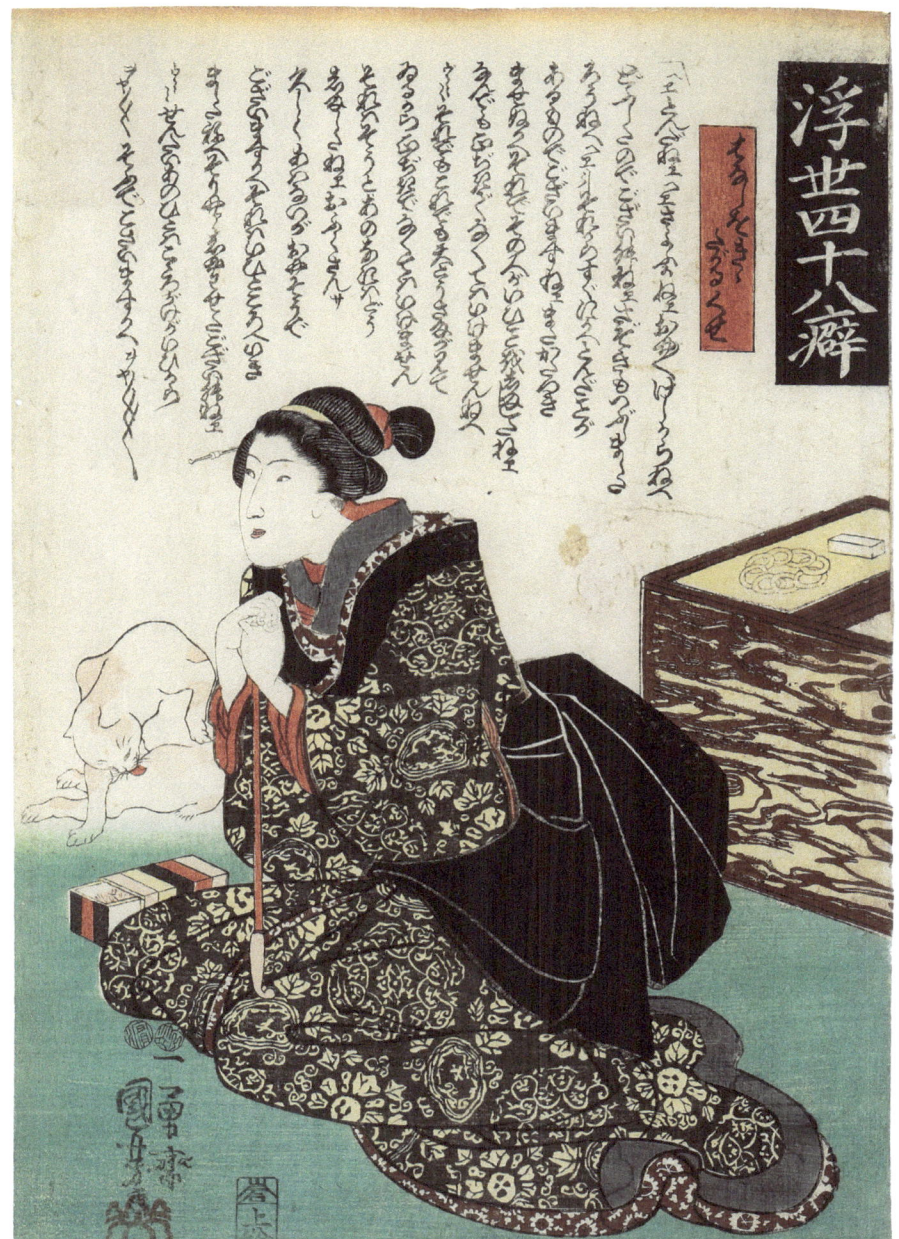

Ukiyo Shijūhachi Kuse, Hanashi
wo Kikitagaru Kuse

Forty-Eight Habits of Ordinary
People: An Eager Gossiper

Artist: Utagawa Kuniyoshi
Publisher: Kazusa-ya Iwakichi
ca.1844-1848

65

This print is one of a series named Forty-Eight Habits of
Ordinary People. This scene depicts a woman fond of
listening to rumors. She is hearing gossip from her friend
who is not shown. Note the white cat licking its hind leg.
Behind the woman is a charcoal brazier enclosed in a
wooden box. On her right there is a small colorful wooden
case. The case is half slid open. Shredded tobacco leaf
is inside. She is holding a kiseru pipe. It seems she is too
intrigued with the gossip that she forgets to smoke. The
writing above indicates she is asking for more details of
the story.

「浮世四十八癖　はなしをききたがるくせ」
ちまたの人々の癖を描いたシリーズで、この
作品では、噂を聞きたがる婦人の姿が描かれ
ている。この婦人の傍らには彩りの美しい木
箱があり、箱が開いているので、中には刻み
たばこが入っているのがわかる。この婦人は、
きせるを抱えており、箱から刻みを取り出そ
うとしたのだろうが、噂話に夢中で、たばこ
のことを忘れているようだ。

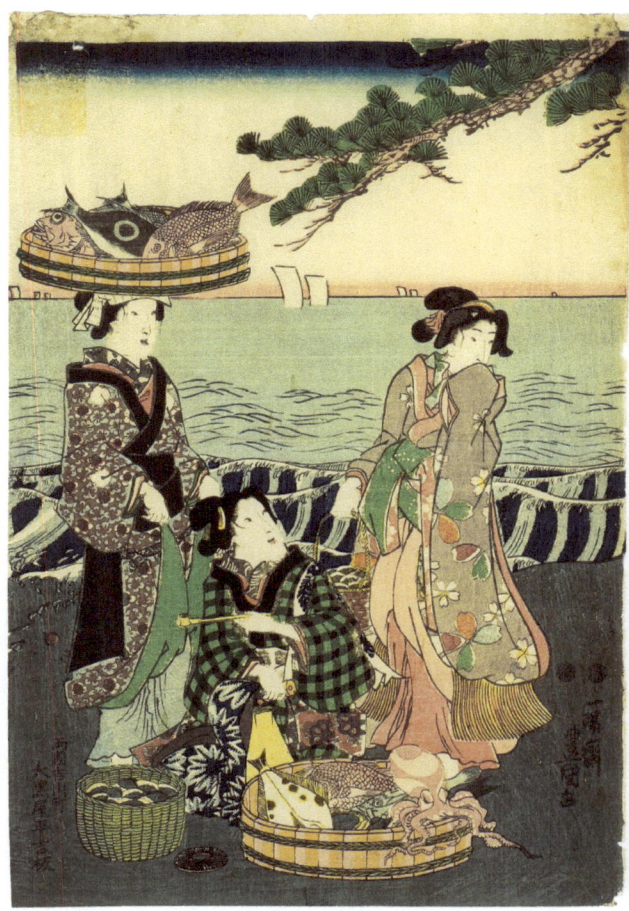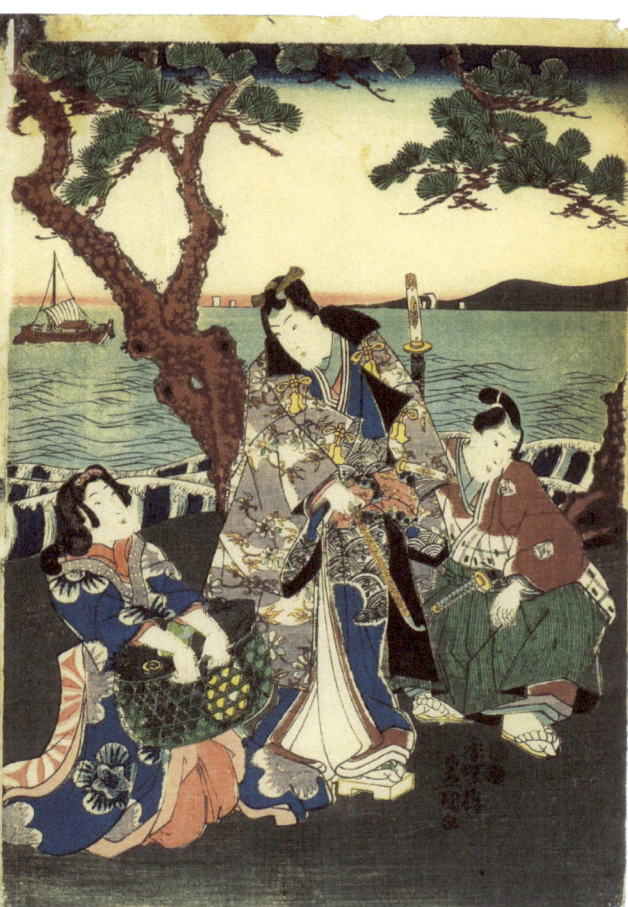

Akashi-no-Ura Kei

The Beautiful Landscape of Akashi-no-Ura Seashore

Artist: Utagawa Toyokuni III
Publisher: Daikoku-ya Heikichi
ca.1848-1854

66

In the latter half of the Edo period the novel named Nise Murasaki Inaka Genji was very popular. People loved its principal character Mitsuuji. In this novel, Mitsuuji enjoys his extravagant life. Because of his less praiseworthy character, the sale of the book was banned during the Tenpō Reforms. Many prints depicting him were continued to be made, however. This is one of such prints.

The right panel shows Mitsuuji standing at the Akashi-no-Ura seashore. In this area there were many professional women divers. In the left panel some women are carrying fish and shells. In the left panel, the woman sitting has a special bamboo pipe called Takappo Kiseru. The sea with a few boats in the water is seen in the background of both panels. A very pleasant view of the seashore.

「明石の浦景」
『偐紫田舎源氏』は、江戸後期に人気を博した大衆向けの小説である。天保の改革で発禁処分となったが、その後も、この小説の主人公を描いた絵が数多く制作されていった。この絵も『偐紫田舎源氏』に取材しており、主人公の光氏が明石の浦に滞在し、海女たちと交流するシーンを描いている。海女の一人はタカッポきせるという竹のきせるを手にしている。

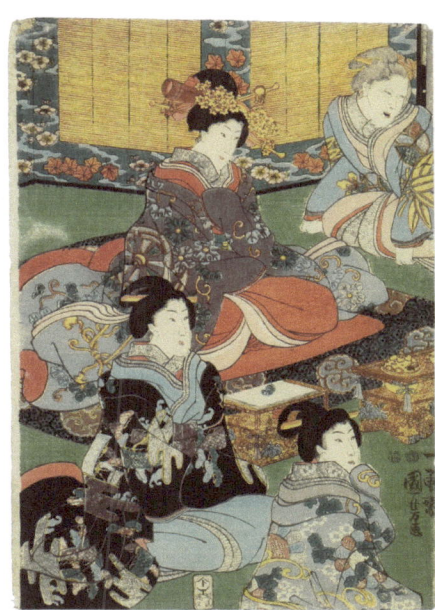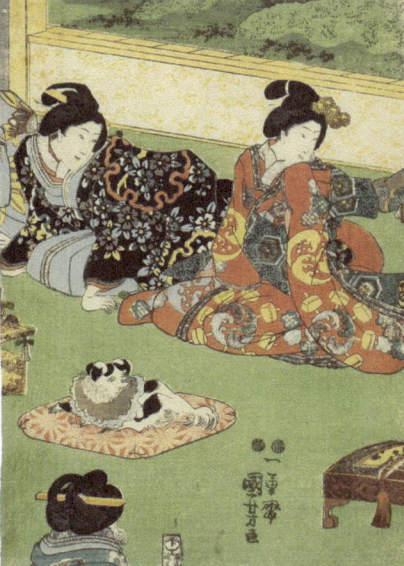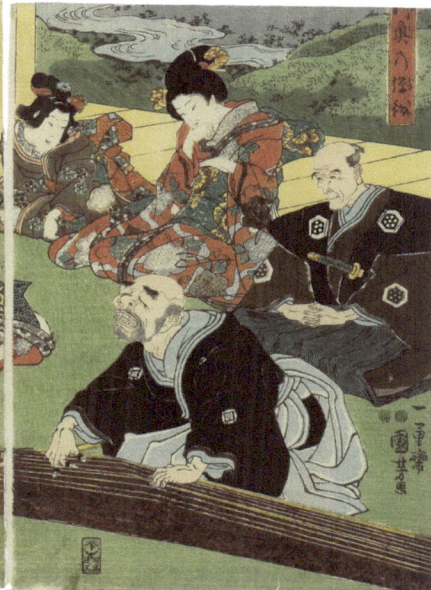

On-oku no Hikizome

New Year's Koto Play
in the Room of a Nobleman's Daughter

Artist: Utagawa Kuniyoshi
Publisher: Enshū-ya Matabē
ca.1848-1854

67

There are three panels to this elaborate print which depicts a nobleman's daughter and her young and old valets. They are in the daughter's room, listening to the koto music and a storytelling performed by a blind man. Between the middle and the left panel is a gorgeous tobacco tray and a fancy box in front of the daughter. A Japanese spaniel dog is sitting on a cushion in the center. In the Edo period, many noble families had such dogs which were treated as precious pets.

「御奥の弾初」
高貴な家の娘とその侍女たちが、座頭の琴の演奏と語りを聞いている。娘の傍らには、豪華な火入れと鼻紙台が置かれているが、この火入れはたばこ盆としても用いることができる。
絵の中央には、座布団の上に座っている狆が描かれているが、江戸時代、狆はたいへん珍重され、富裕層の家庭で大切に飼われていた。

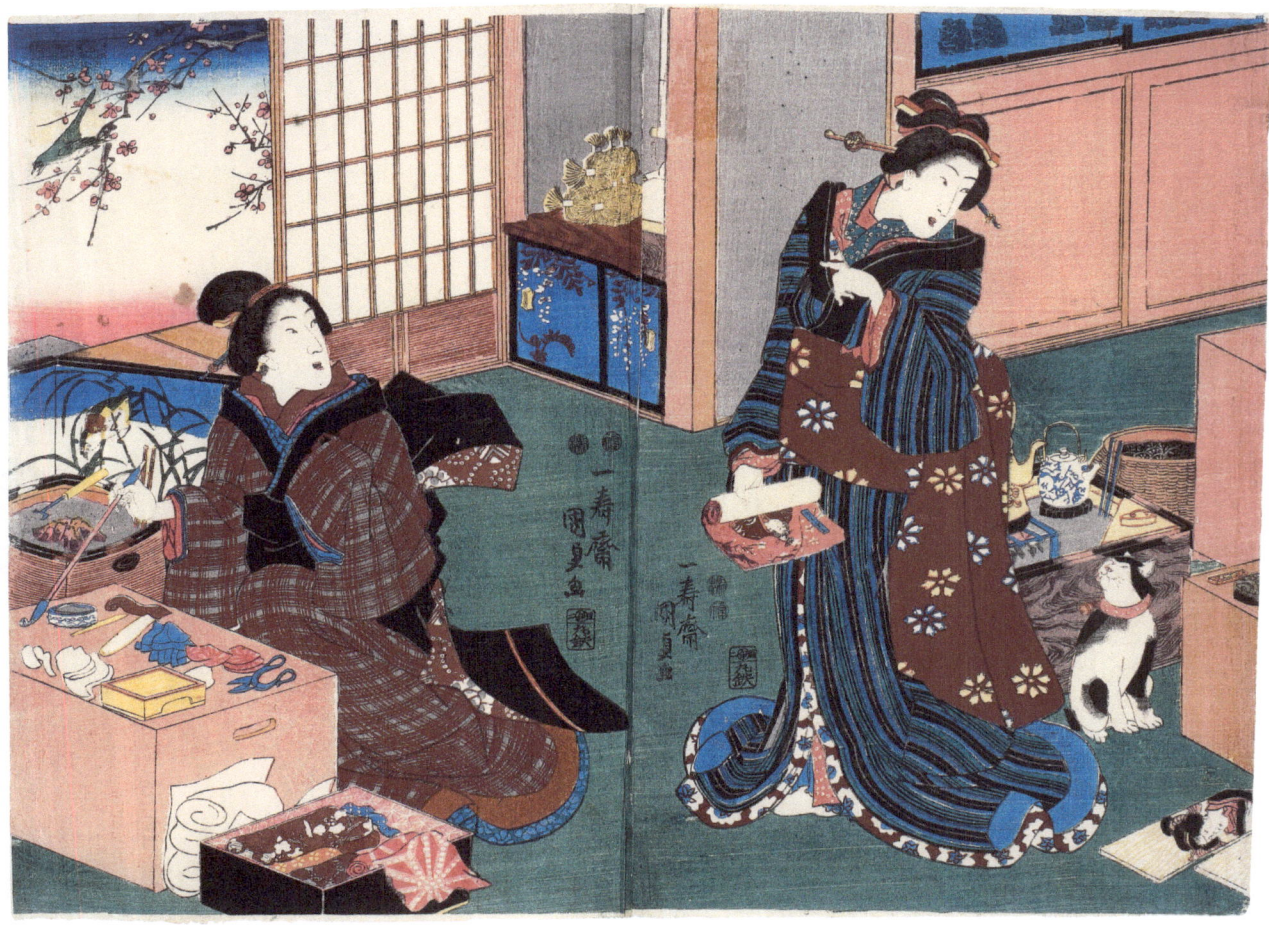

Oshie Zukuri

Making the Oshie Hand Work

Artist: Utagawa Kunisada II
Publisher: Kobayashi Tetsujirō
ca. 1848-1854

68

There are two women in this print. The woman standing has a partially unrolled woodblock print in her right hand. There are some painted battledore paddles on the floor at the right hand corner. The game of battledore and shuttlecock is an early Japanese version of badminton.

The lady sitting is smoking. In front of her on the table are many cloth patches and a pair of scissors. There are some wads of cotton and a large box on the floor with some more patches of cloth. It shows that the woman is making Oshie handwork to decorate the Japanese paddle on the floor. Note the beautiful items in the background.

The original print had three panels, but the far right one was lost.

「押絵作り」
二人の女性が描かれているが、立っている女性は浮世絵を手にしており、その傍らには人物の絵が描かれた羽子板がおかれている。座っている女性はたばこを吸って休憩しているが、彼女の前に置かれたテーブルには、小さく切られた布や小箱、ハサミがあり、床にも布地の入った大きな箱や綿が置かれている。羽子板を布のお細工物で飾る、押絵を作る様子が描かれている。この作品は、本来3枚続きで、右側の1枚が欠けている。

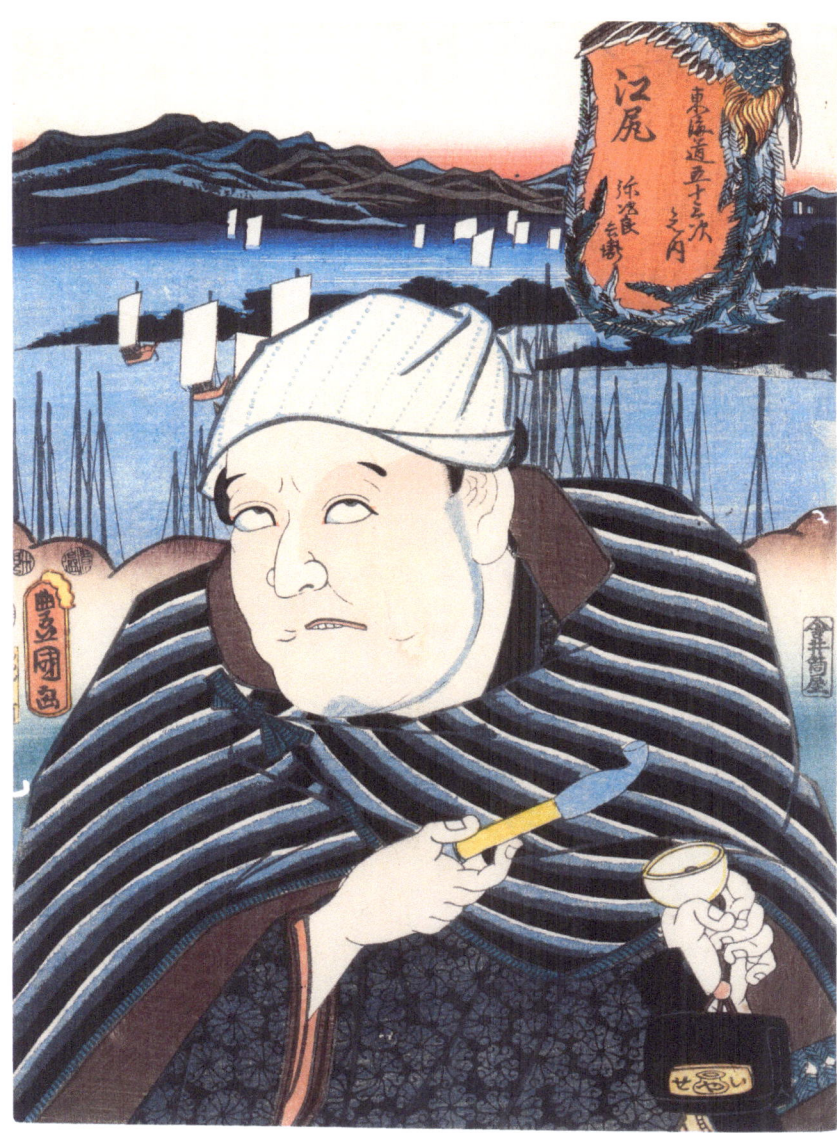

Tōkaidō Gojūsan Tsugi no Uchi,
Ejiri, Yajirōbē

Tōkaidō Fifty-Three Stages and
Kabuki Actors

Artist: Utagawa Toyokuni III
Publisher: Izutsu-ya
1852

69

The kabuki actor Nakayama Bungorō is depicted against the landscape of Ejiri, one of The Fifty-Three Stages of the Tōkaidō Road. This series is commonly known as the Actors' Tōkaidō. It is a separate series from the well-known Hiroshige's Tōkaidō Road series.

Here the actor has a kiseru pipe in his right hand and the rope handle of a tobacco pouch in his left hand. On the front of the tobacco pouch there is a label showing the Japanese letters *i*, *se*, and *ya*. This indicates that it is a paper tobacco pouch of the Ise Tsubo-ya brand. It was a very popular souvenir of the Ise district.

In this print Nakayama Bungorō is depicted as Yajirōbē, the main character of the popular novel Tōkaidōchū Hizakurige by Jippensha Ikku. This novel deals with a humorous trip in the Edo period. Nakayama Bungorō as Yajirōbē is wearing a cape for this trip. Apparently he went to the Ise shrine to pray and then bought a paper tobacco pouch. In the background a lovely sea with many sailing ships is seen.

「東海道五十三次之内　江尻　弥次良兵衛」
　　　　　　　　　（通称役者東海道）
歌舞伎役者の背景に東海道五十三次各地の光景を描いた、役者東海道と呼ばれるシリーズ。『東海道中膝栗毛』の登場人物、弥次郎兵衛に扮する中山文五郎が左手に持つたばこ入れは、前金具の「いせ」の文字と、「や」と記された壺形のマークから、当時伊勢土産として有名であった壺屋製の紙たばこ入れであることがわかる。中山文五郎の弥次郎兵衛は道中合羽をまとった旅姿でもあり、お伊勢参りに行き、土産にこの紙たばこ入れを買ったのであろう。

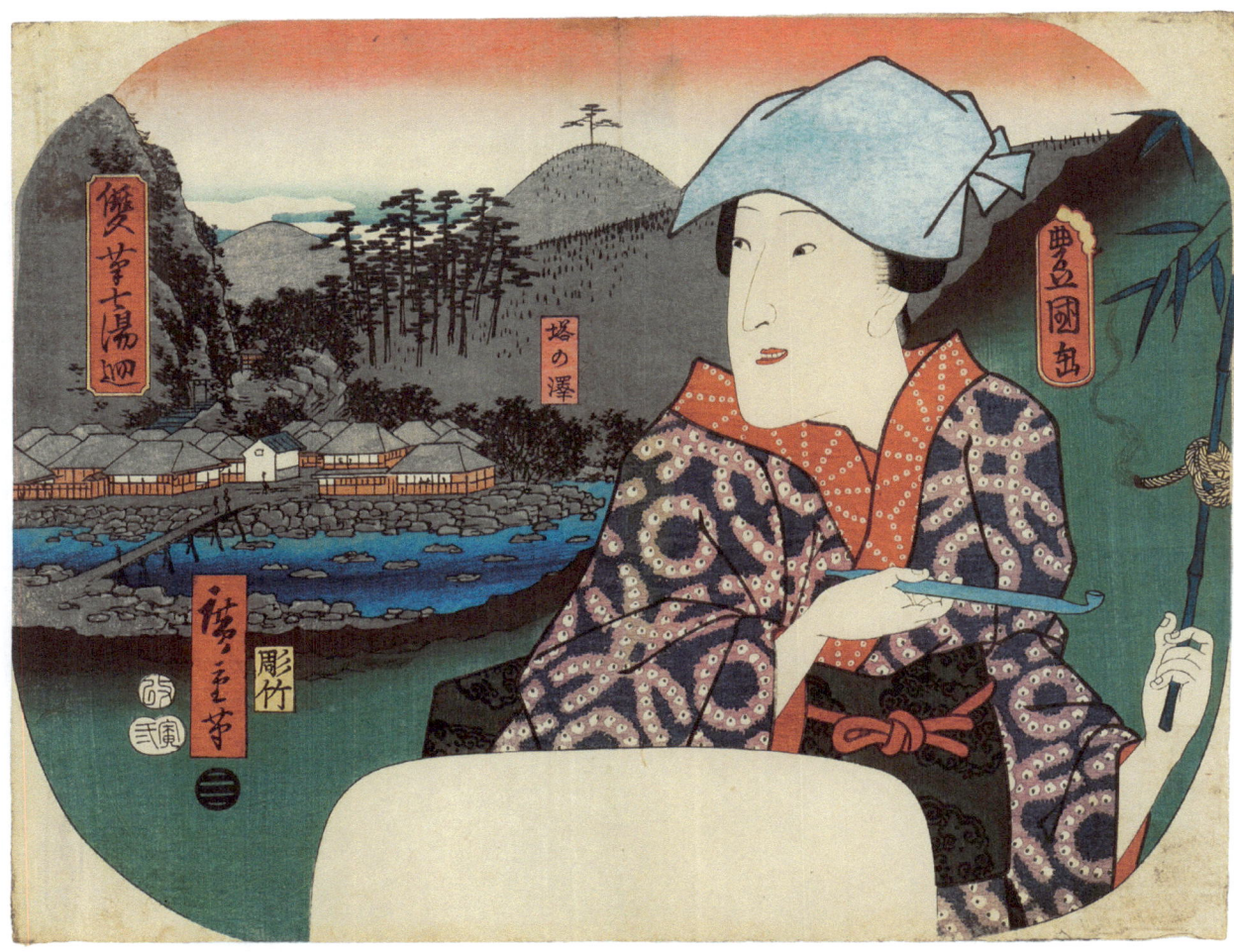

Sōhitsu Shichiyu Meguri

The Series of Seven Famous Spas of Hakone

Artists: Utagawa Toyokuni III
　　　　Utagawa Hiroshige I
Publisher: Iba-ya Senzaburō
1854

70

This print was used for a Japanese fan. It involved the unique collaboration of two famous artists. Utagawa Toyokuni III drew the woman and Utagawa Hiroshige I drew the background landscape of a famous spa in Hakone called Tōnosawa Onsen.

The woman is a visitor to this spa. She has a kiseru pipe in her right hand and a short bamboo branch in her left. The bamboo branch is partially hidden. In the middle of the branch is a slowly burning rope called a Hinawa. It is hardly visible. In those days, Japanese travelers carried such a burning rope to light their tobacco. Also they could tell from the remainder of the burning rope how much time had past.

The woman is glancing at the splendid scene of the winding little stream, a bridge, spa, trees, and the far away hill with a single tree on top.

「双筆七湯廻」
この団扇絵のシリーズは、三代目の歌川豊国と歌川広重の合作で、前面の女性を豊国が、背景の塔ノ沢温泉の風景を広重が描いている。　女性は旅姿で、右手にきせる、左手に笹を持っている。笹に火のついた火縄がまかれているが、当時、旅人はこのようにして火縄を携帯していた。火縄の火から、たばこの火を得るとともに、火縄の燃えた長さから、時刻の経過を知った。

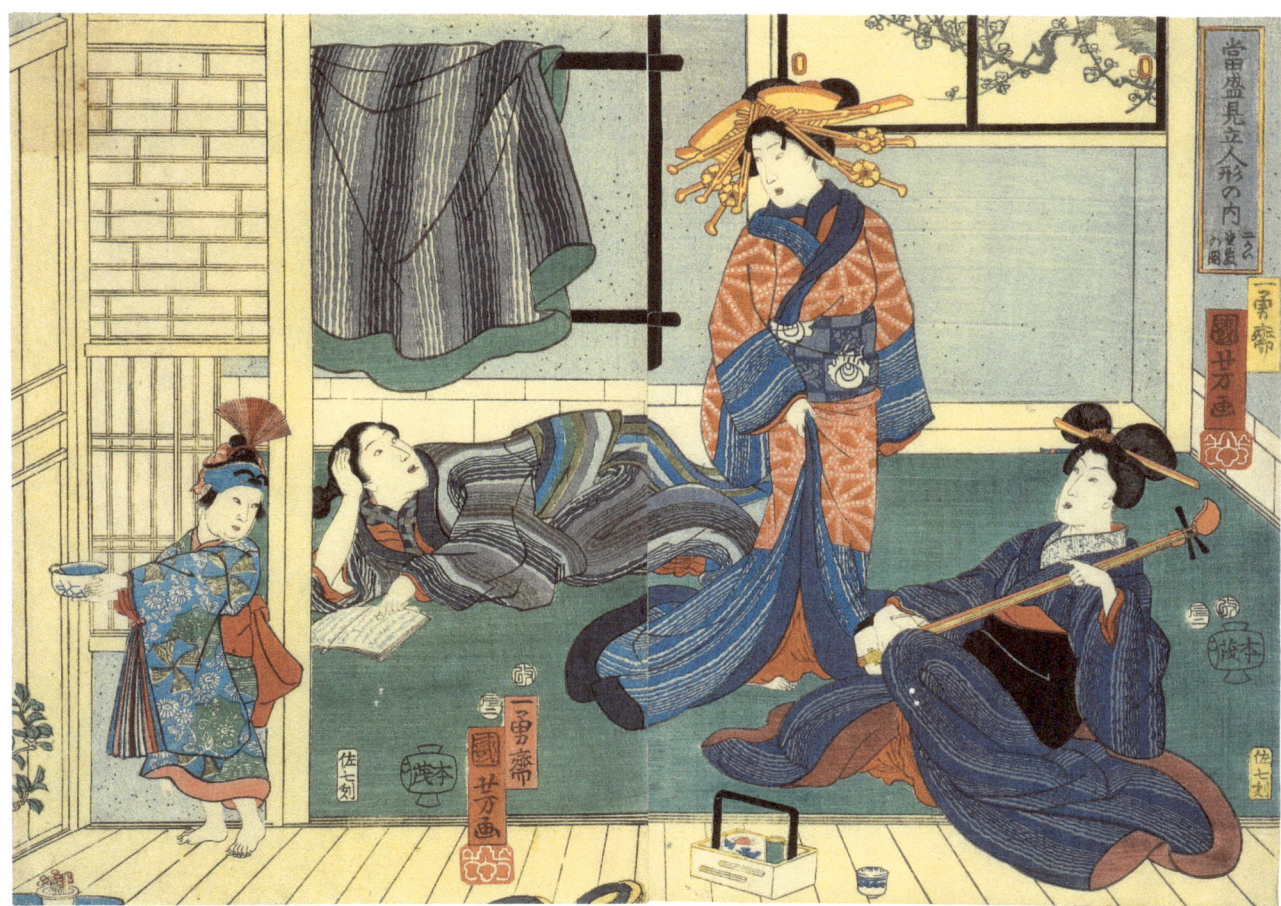

Tōsei Mitate Ningyō no Uchi, Nikai Zashiki no Zu

A Scene of a Courtesan's Private Room from a Life-Size Doll Show

Artist: Utagawa Kuniyoshi
Publisher: Hon Shige
1856

71

This is a very interesting print of life-size dolls (mannequins) of courtesans and their young female attendant on the left. In the middle of the 19th century shows using such mannequins were very popular. They were made to look like real people. These shows often dealt with scenes from an imaginary world or the world that can only be fancied.

In this print the scene is a private quarter of courtesans, which ordinary people were not permitted to see. The woman standing has her undergarments on. Next to her is a relaxed woman lying on her side. The woman in the right front is playing a musical instrument called shamisen. For the background sets, real furniture was used in the show.

「当盛見立人形の内　二かい座敷の図」
この絵は、当時流行していた生人形の見世物を描いている。生人形興行では、架空の世界や遊女のプライベートな時間など、普段見ることの出来ない世界が人形と精巧なセットで表現されていた。吉原遊廓は、前年10月の地震で焼失しており、当時は、別の場所（仮宅という）で営業していたが、この絵も、吉原ではなく仮宅の遊女を描いている。立っている遊女は下着姿で描かれていて、くつろいでいる様子が再現されていることがわかる。

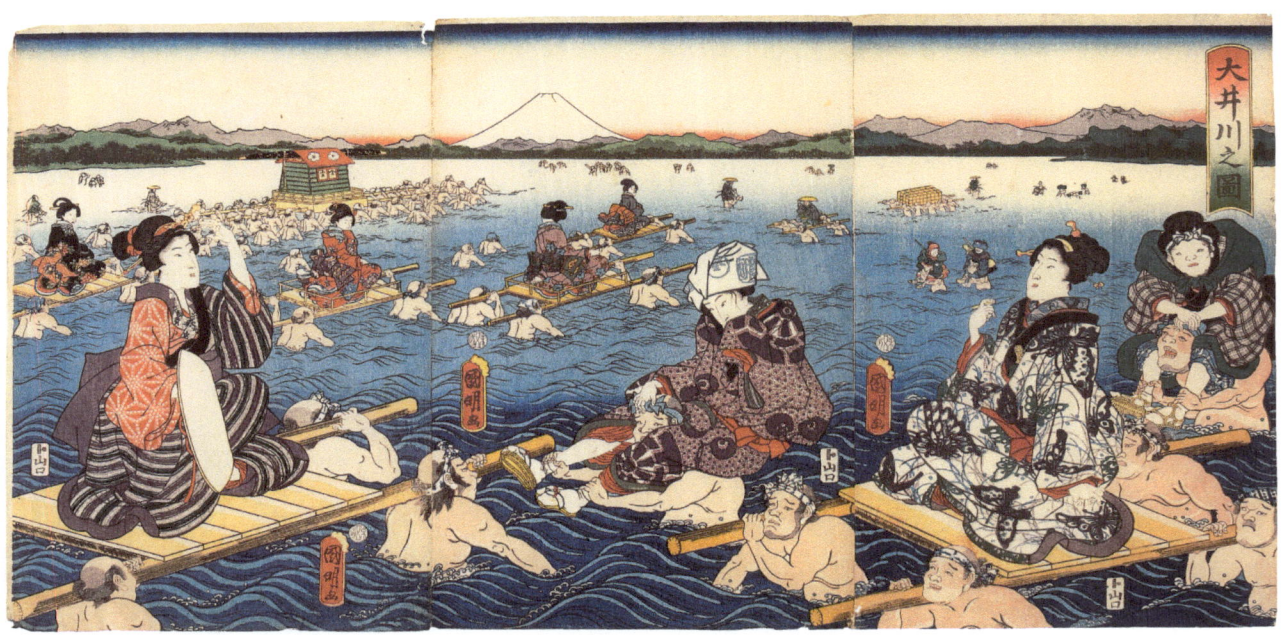

Ōigawa no Zu

Crossing Ōigawa River

Artist: Utagawa Kuniaki
Publisher: Yamaguchi-ya Tōbē
1859

72

The wide river in the background is the Ōigawa River in Shizuoka Prefecture. In the Edo period, the government did not allow building of bridges over this river to safeguard Edo from attack. Furthermore, boats were also not permitted.

This print shows different modes of crossing the river. Some rent a special raft to be carried by four bearers. Another sits on the bearer's shoulders as seen in the right center. The print shows that those who cross the river on rafts were able to relax and even enjoy smoking while viewing Mt. Fuji in the distance.

「大井川之図」
よく知られているように、江戸時代、大井川は、架橋も渡船も禁じられていた。人々が川を渡る場合は、川渡しの人足や輦台を雇ったり、あるいは人足の肩車などで渡らなければならなかった。

この絵を見ると、人々が様々な方法で川を渡っていることがわかるが、輦台を使用すれば、ゆったりと川を渡ることができ、富士山を眺めながらたばこを吸うことさえできたということがわかる。

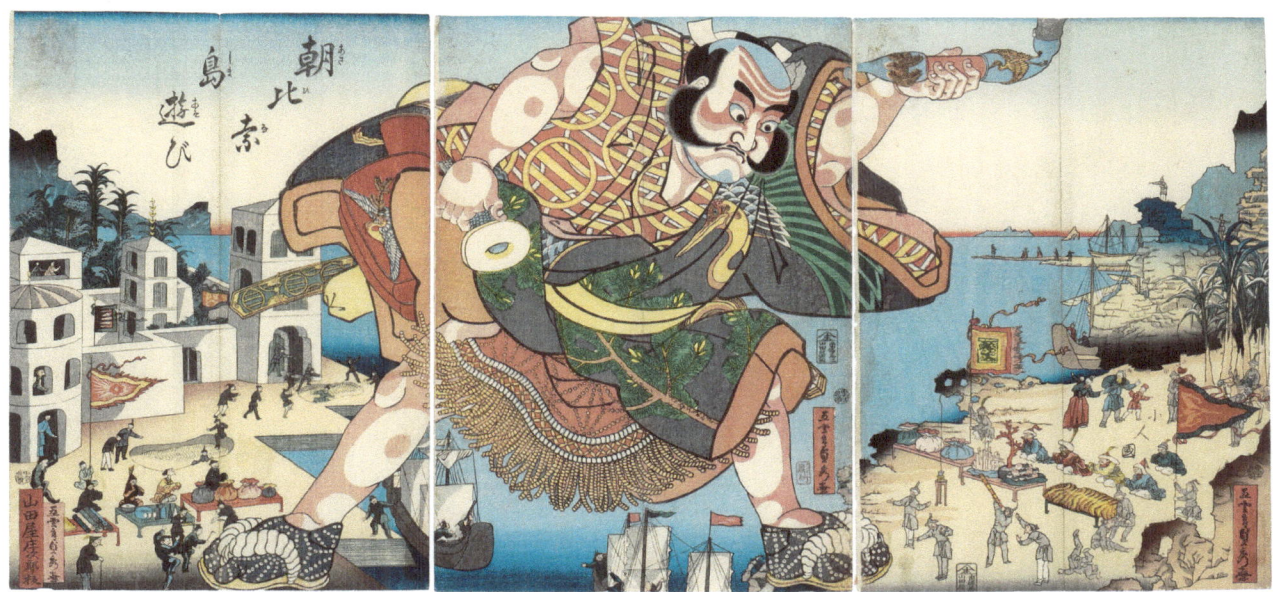

Asaina Shima Asobi

Asaina's Adventure in a Wonder Land

Artist: Utagawa Sadahide
Publisher: Yamada-ya Shōjirō
1860

73

This is another remarkable print of the mythical giant Asaina Saburō Yoshihide. As described previously in print # 62, Asaina made his name as a brave samurai in the 13th century.

As the mythical giant he traveled to many strange lands. In this print, Asaina again enjoys visiting the land of little humans. He has a large kiseru pipe in his left hand and a tobacco pouch in his right. He is standing astride over an inlet of an ocean. It is clear that this story is taken from one of the Seven Wonders of the World, the Colossus of the Island of Rhodes in the Aegean Sea.

「朝比奈島遊び」
鎌倉時代の武将、朝比奈三郎義秀を描いたもの。朝比奈は、江戸時代たいへん人気があり、勇猛な武将として知られ、数々の不思議な国を旅する物語も作られていた。この絵で朝比奈は左手できせるを高く掲げており、右手にはたばこ入れを持っている。朝比奈は海をまたいでいるが、海をまたぎ左手でトーチを掲げるのは、世界七不思議の一つ、ロードス島の巨人像の絵の構図であり、この絵はその構図をまねていることがわかる。

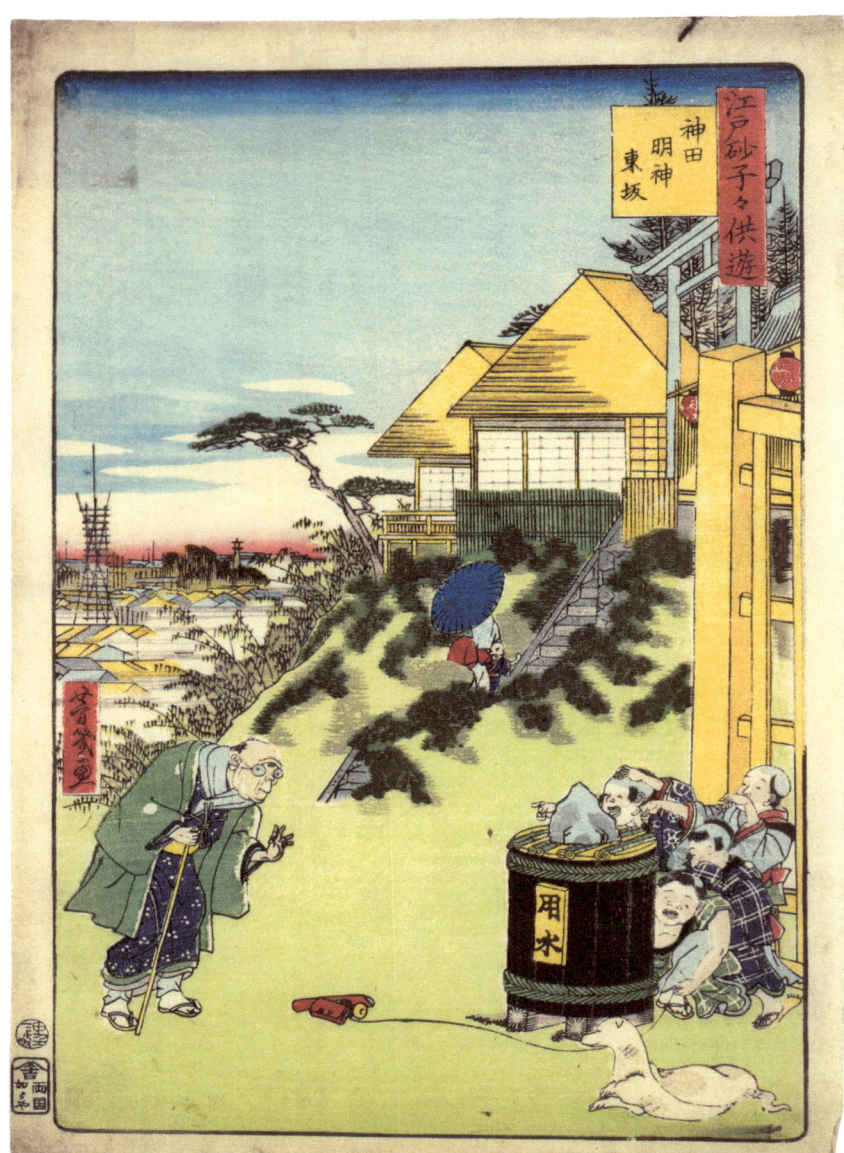

Edo Sunago Kodomo Asobi,
Kandamyōjin Kurumazaka

Children Playing at Kurumazaka Hill,
Near the Kandamyōjin Shrine, Edo

Artist: Utagawa Yoshiiku
Publisher: Kaga-ya Kichibē
1860

74

This scene is near the Kandamyōjin Shrine. It is one of a series of prints by the artist Utagawa Yoshiiku who depicted children at play. Note that the children are hiding behind a big water tub. In those days, such water tubs were placed on a street for extinguishing fires. The children are playing a trick on an old man. They are slowly pulling a red tobacco pouch with an attached string from behind the water tub. The old man has very poor eyesight. He is trying to pick the pouch up as it slowly moves away from him.

「江戸砂子々供遊　神田明神車坂」
神田明神の近くで、子どもたちが、用水桶の後に隠れている。当時通りには、防火用にこのような用水桶が備えられていた。子どもたちは、赤いたばこ入れに紐をつけて引っ張り、老人にいたずらをしている。この老人は、目が悪いらしく、たばこ入れを拾おうと追いかけている。
この絵では、いたずらをしているが、絵師の芳幾は、このシリーズで、子どもたちのかわいらしい姿を描いている。

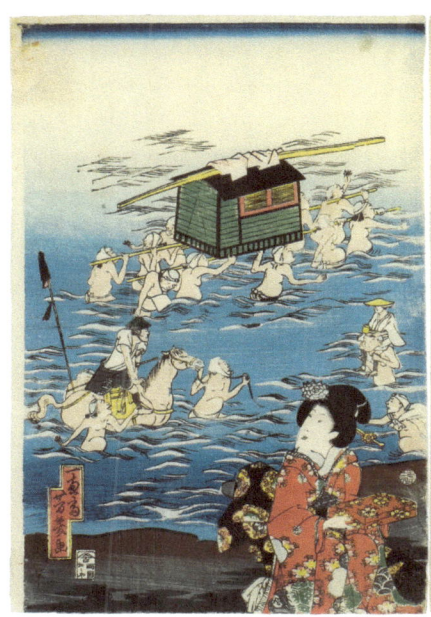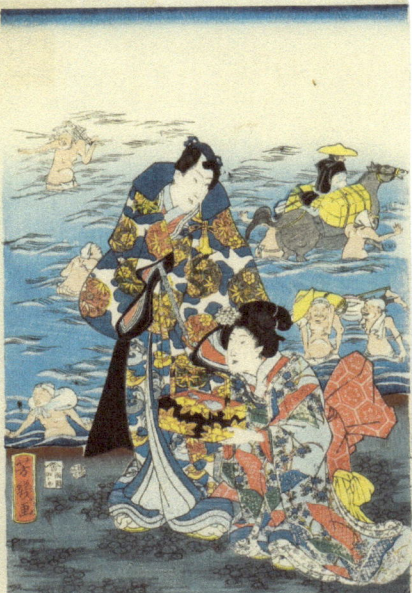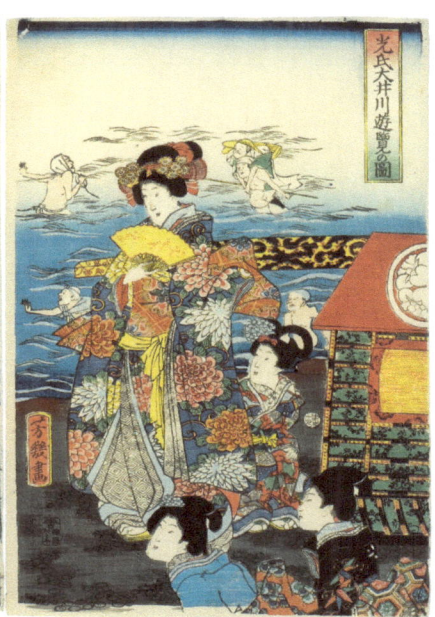

Mitsuuji Ōigawa Yūran no Zu

Mitsuuji's Pastime by the Ōigawa River

Artist: Utagawa Yoshiiku
Publisher: Kaga-ya Kichibē
1860

75

During the Edo period, there was a novel by the name of Nise Murasaki Inaka Genji. It was very popular among ordinary people. Although the novel was banned by the Tenpō Reforms, many prints depicting Mitsuuji, the main character of the novel, have been made since then. This is one of such prints.

Mitsuuji is in the center panel. He is standing at the shore of the Ōigawa while smoking a fine kiseru pipe. As mentioned in print #72 there were no bridges across the Ōigawa river. He is watching the many different ways of crossing the river. This is a very busy scene with Mitsuuji surrounded by a number of elegant women.

「光氏大井川遊覧の図」
『偐紫田舎源氏』は、江戸後期に人気を博した大衆向けの小説である。天保の改革で発禁処分となったが、その後、この小説の主人公光氏を描いた絵が数多く制作されていった。この絵では、光氏は大井川を眺めている。当時、大井川には橋がなく、川を渡るには、人足を雇い、輦台を借りる必要があった。この絵では、そのような人々の川渡りの様子を、光氏は着飾り優雅にたばこを吸いながら、ながめている。

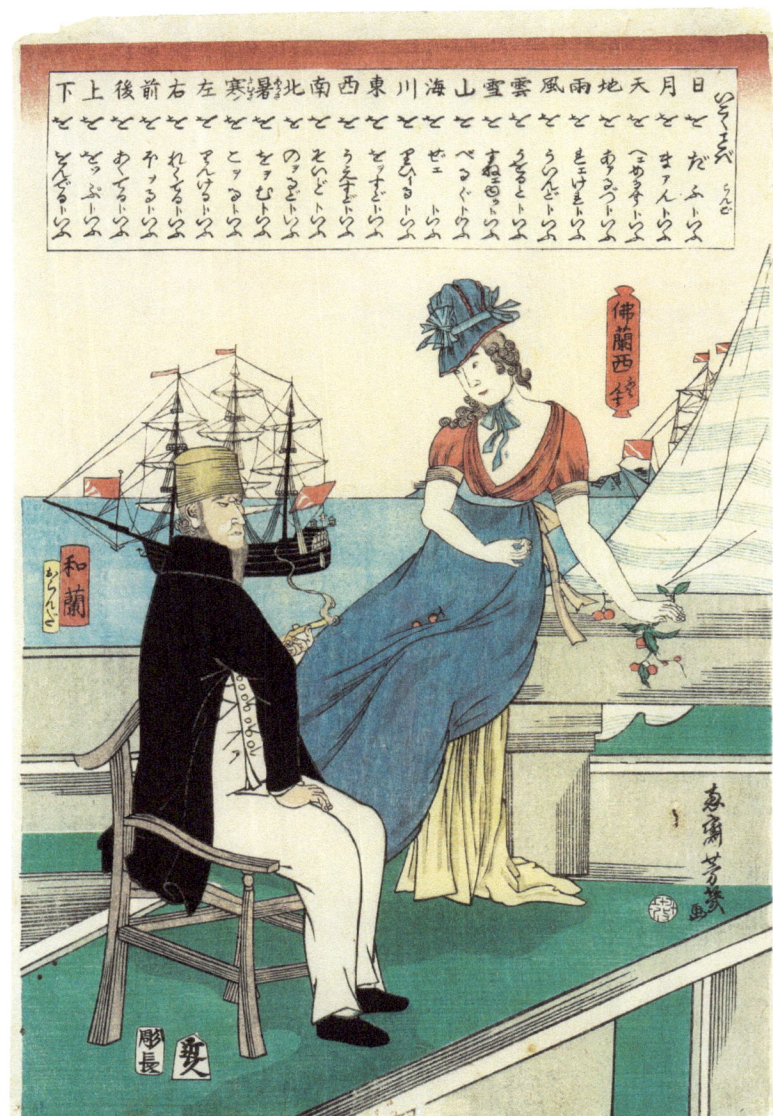

Ikoku Kotoba Rango

The Foreign Language, Dutch

Artist: Utagawa Yoshiiku
Publisher: Ōmi-ya Kyūjirō
1860

76

As it is well known, during the Edo period, no Europeans except the Dutch were admitted into Japan. At the end of the Edo period, the Americans forced Japan to open its ports for trade. As a result Japan concluded a commercial treaty with America, and later with other European countries. The port of Yokohama was opened as a trading port and a colony for foreigners was established there. The Japanese were very interested in the unusual clothes and manners of the foreigners. Since the beginning of the 1860's, many woodblock prints were published depicting foreigners. Such prints were called Yokohama-e.

In this print, foreign ships can be seen in the background. A French woman and a Dutch man smoking a cigar are shown. The French lady is leaning on her left hand on a railing with a branch of flowers. She is dressed in French clothes of the time. Shown at the top of the print are some Japanese words with corresponding Dutch words written in Hiragana.

「いこくことバ　らんご」
江戸時代、日本と諸外国との交流は限られており、ヨーロッパ諸国の中では、オランダだけが正式に通商関係を持っていた。しかし、江戸時代末期、アメリカによって開国が迫られると、日本も数カ国と通商関係を締結していき、横浜港などが開港されていった。横浜には、外国人のための居留地も築かれたが、日本人にとって、横浜に滞在する外国人はたいへん珍しく、万延元年（1860）頃から、外国人を描いた絵が、多数出版されていった。これらの絵は横浜絵と呼ばれている。
この絵では、フランスの婦人と葉巻を吸うオランダの男性が描かれ、背景には外国船も見える。絵の上部には、オランダ語の単語の意味も記されている。

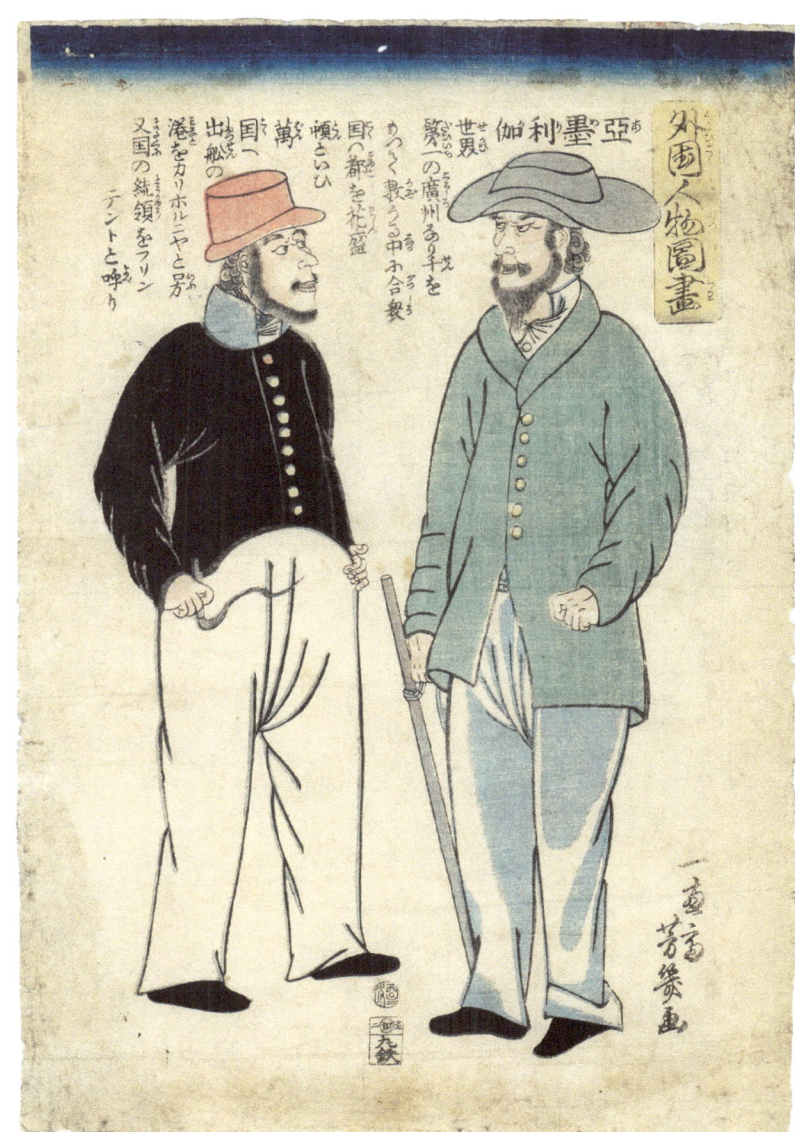

Gaikoku Jinbutsu Zuga, Amerika

Sketches of Foreigners: Americans

Artist: Utagawa Yoshiiku
Publisher: Maru-ya Tetsujirō
1861

77

Like print # 76 this is also a Yokohama-e, published in
1861. The artist depicted two American men. The one on
the left is smoking a cigar. The Japanese writing at the top
of the print is an explanation of America. It says: "America
is the largest country in the world. There are many States.
The capital of America is Washington. The large port from
which ships sail to the world is called California. The head
of the country is called *Furintento*. The word President
must have sounded like *Furintento* to Japanese ears. Note
the interesting 19th century clothing which, in contrast to
their own, the Japanese of Edo believed Americans would
wear.

「外国人物図画　亜墨利伽」
この絵も横浜絵で、文久元年（1861）に出
版されている。絵師は二人のアメリカ人を描
いているが、一人は葉巻か紙巻たばこを吸っ
ている。
絵の上部には、アメリカについての解説があ
る。それによれば、アメリカは世界で一番大
きな国で、1000 を超える州がある。首都は
ワシントンで、外国との往来のある大きな港
はカリフォルニアである。統領のことを「フ
リンテント」という、となっている。

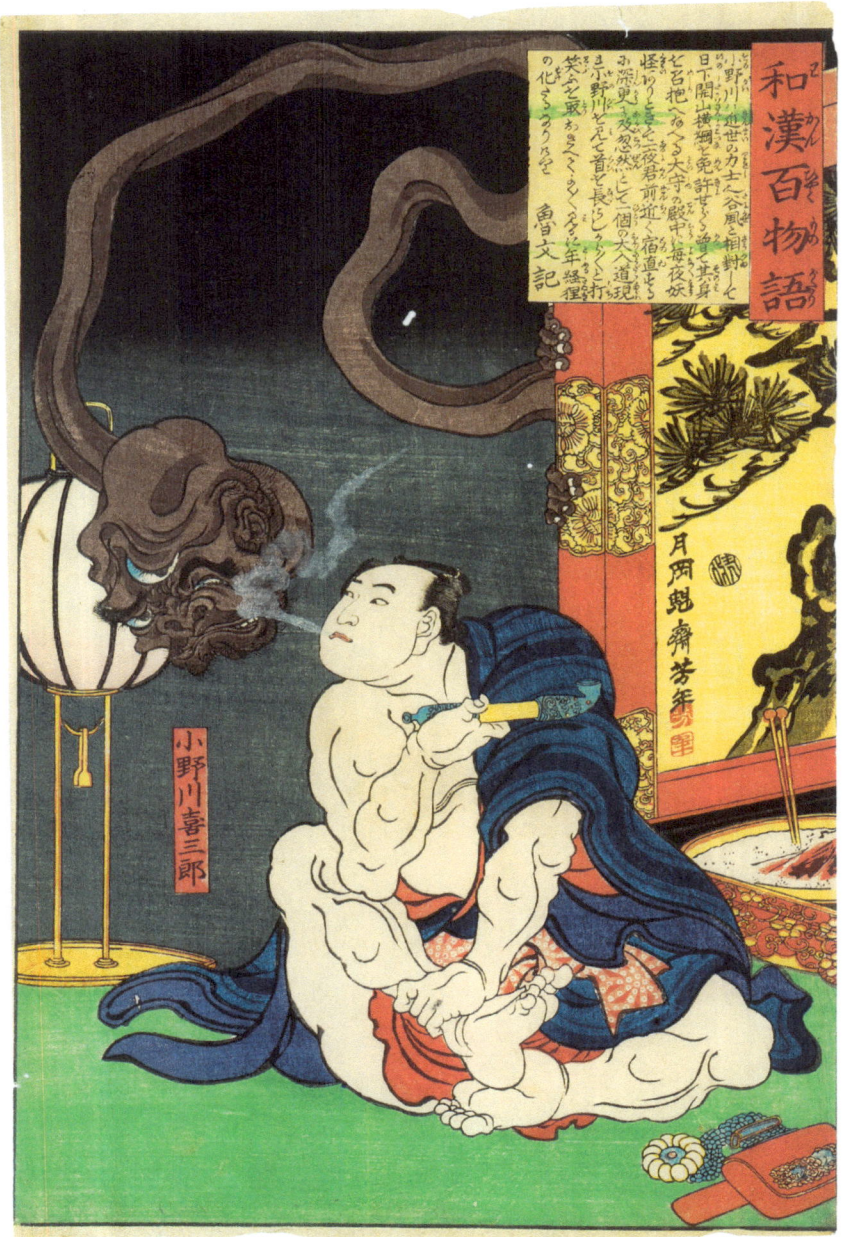

Wakan Hyaku Monogatari

One Hundred Short Horror Stories of Japan and China

Artist: Tsukioka Yoshitoshi
Publisher: Unknown
1865

78

In Japan, Sumō wrestlers have always been very popular. In this print, the Sumō wrestler Onogawa Kisaburō is shown. Onogawa and Tanikaze Kajinosuke were the first Yokozuna, or champions.

Onogawa was a vassal to the Kurume Clan. The feudal lord of the Kurume Clan was said to be haunted by a monster every night.

In this print Onogawa is defying the hobgoblin by blowing smoke into its face. It is pictured with a very long neck and three eyes. It is frowning because of the smoke. One can tell from Onogawa's facial expression that he was confident of his great strength. Note the bulging muscles of this very strong Sumō wrestler.

The captured hobgoblin turned out to be an old raccoon dog.

「和漢百物語」

ここに描かれているのは小野川喜三郎である。小野川は、谷風梶之助とともに、横綱として免許された最初の相撲取りであった。当時の多くの相撲取りがそうであったように、彼も武家に召し抱えられていて、彼の主君は久留米藩の有馬氏であった。その有馬氏は、ある時夜毎妖怪にとりつかれるようになっていた。そのため小野川が主君の側に控えて妖怪を捉えてみたところ、妖怪の正体は古狸であったという（有馬氏は化け猫騒動で有名であるが、ここでは有馬氏を悩ますのは、猫ではなく古狸になっている）。

この絵では、首の長い妖怪が、小野川の吹くたばこの煙に、煙たそうにしている。

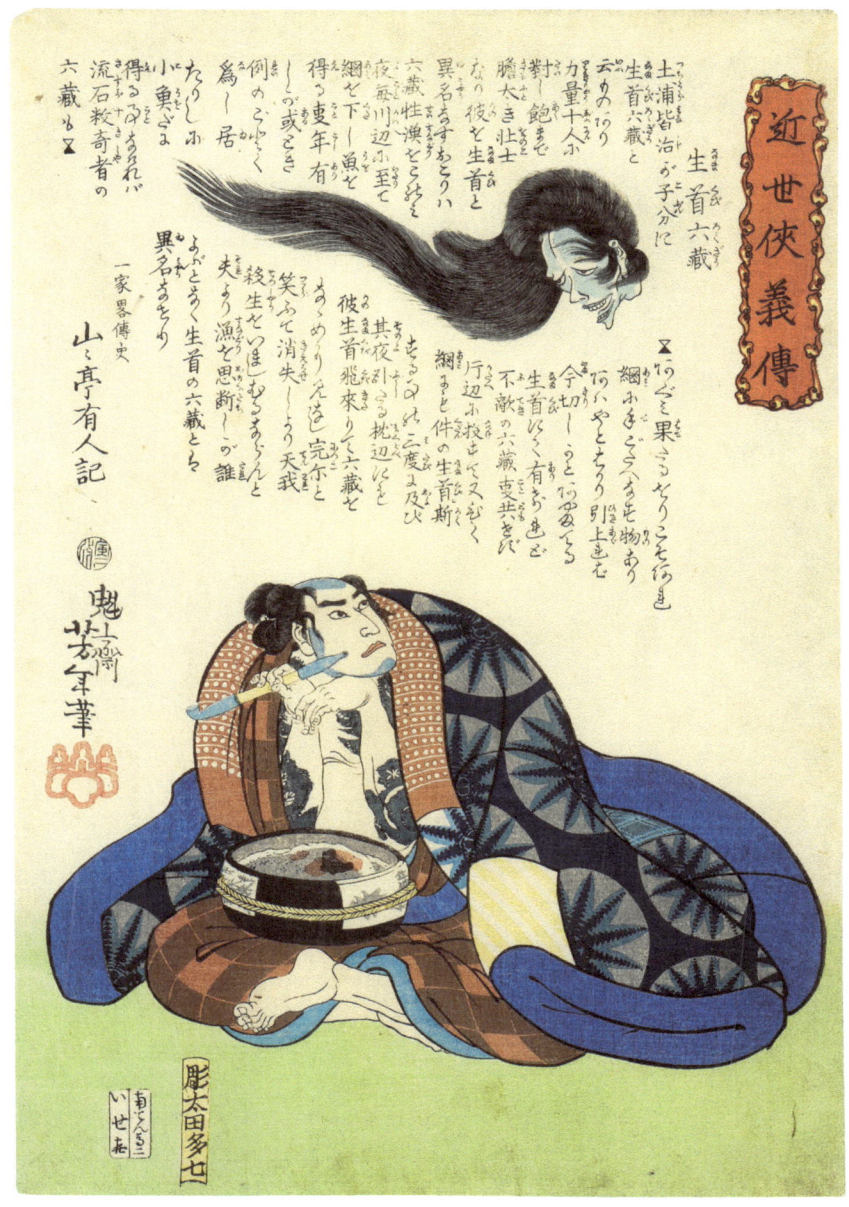

Kinsei Kyōgiden Namakubi Rokuzō

Strong and Courageous Men
Stories: Namakubi Rokuzō

Artist: Tsukioka Yoshitoshi
Publisher: Ise-ya Kisaburō
1866

79

A strong and courageous man named Namakubi Rokuzō is depicted. Rokuzō is looking at the severed head above him while sitting with his legs crossed on a padded futon and smoking. The floating head is looking forlornly at him.

The Japanese writing above describes the story of the man. According to the description, Rokuzō loved fishing with a net. One day he could not catch any fish even though he cast his net repeatedly. Finally he felt a pull, but what he found in his net was a severed head. Rokuzō was not frightened. He threw the head back into the river and cast the net in another spot. But again, the severed head was caught in his net. That night as he went to bed, the head appeared at his bedside with an eerie smile and then disappeared. Rokuzō took these events to be a Buddhist precept against killing and stopped fishing. People began to call him Namakubi Rokuzō. Namakubi means a severed head in Japanese.

「近世侠義伝　生首六蔵」
剛気の者の生首六蔵の話が記されている。それによれば、六蔵はもともと網で漁をするのを好んでいたが、ある日、いくら網を投げても少しも魚がかからなかった。やっと手応えを感じ網を引き揚げると、そこには生首がかかっていた。六蔵は怖じ気づくこともなく生首をその辺りに放り、また網を投げたが、その後は、先ほどの生首ばかりが網にかかった。その夜、六蔵が寝ようとすると、生首が枕元に現れ気味悪く笑い、消えていった。六蔵はこの出来事を殺生の戒めと考え、漁をすることをやめた。この後、六蔵は生首六蔵と呼ばれるようになった。

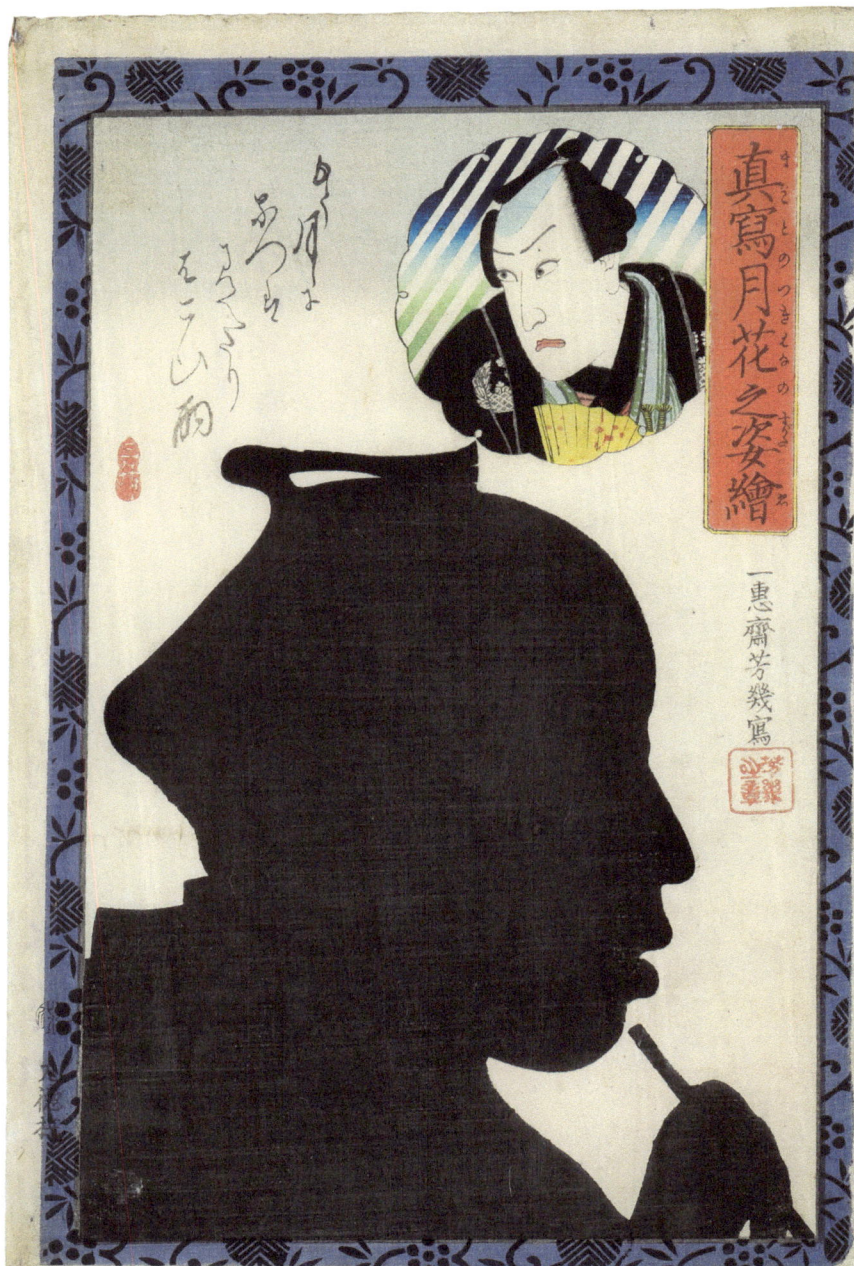

Makoto no Tsuki Hana no Sugata-e

A Series of the Heads of Kabuki Actors

Artist: Utagawa Yoshiiku
Publisher: Maru-ya Tokuzō
1867

80

Each print in this series shows a famous kabuki actor's silhouette profile of his head. The big profile is the main subject. The smaller frontal view is added to show who the actor is.

The series consists of an index, a foreword and 36 prints. In the foreword, the artist illustrated how he made the profiles. It shows that he sat in the dark room next to where the subject was. He traced with the aid of a candlelight the silhouette that appeared on the shōji paper door on to a paper.

This print shows the silhouette of kabuki actor, Kawarazaki Gonjūrō, with his kiseru pipe. Later he became the famous actor Ichikawa Danjūrō IX.

「真写月花之姿絵」
このシリーズでは、役者の横顔の影絵が全面に描かれ、影に対する役者の似顔が、各絵の上部に配されている。このシリーズは、36枚の本編に合わせ、目録、口上で揃いとなる。口上では、絵師がどのように影絵を描いたか図示されているが、それによれば、絵師は隣の部屋にいて、蝋燭の明かりによって障子に映し出された被写体の影を紙に写し取ったということがわかる。
この絵には、河原崎権十郎が描かれている。影絵の権十郎はきせるを手にしており、今まさにたばこを吸おうとしている。この権十郎は、後に、有名な九代目の市川団十郎となる。

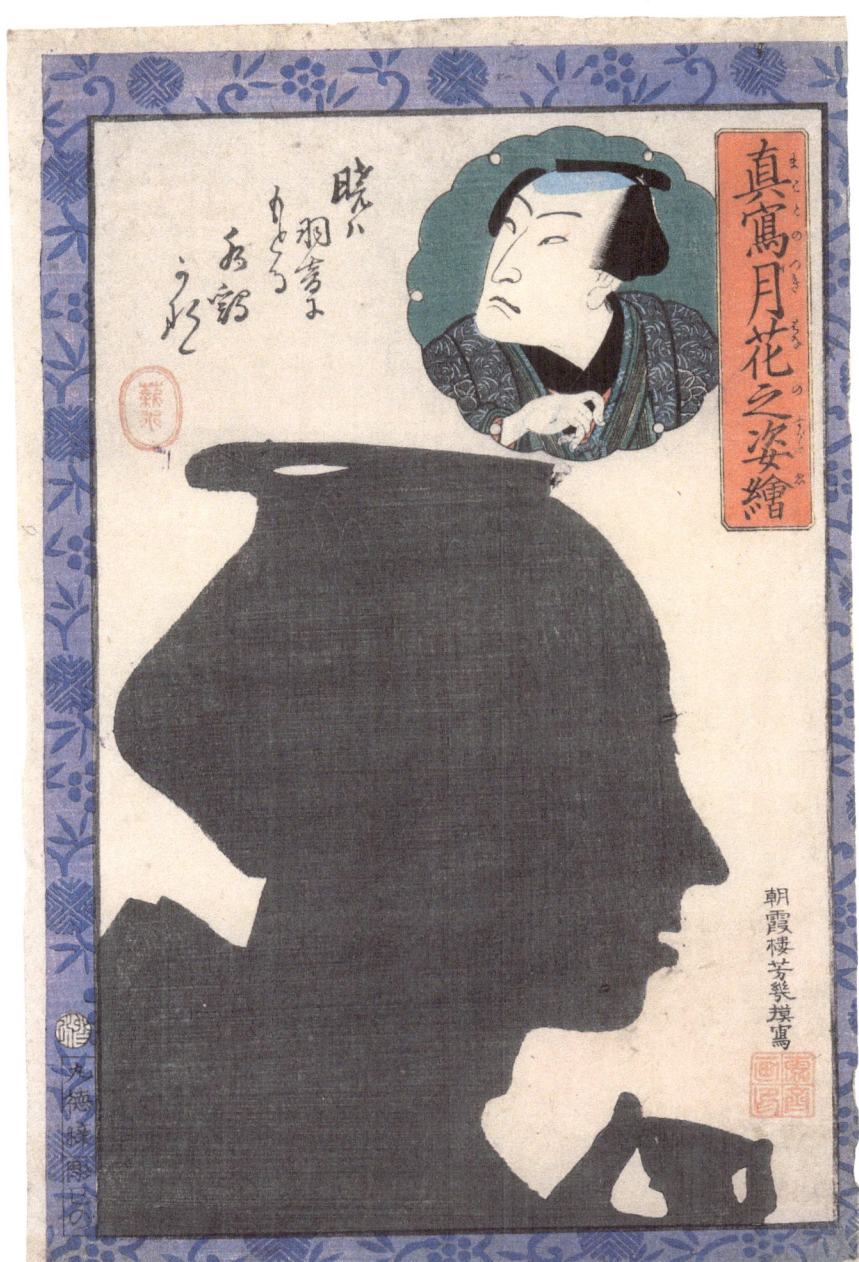

Makoto no Tsuki Hana no Sugata-e

A Series of the Heads of Kabuki Actors

Artist: Utagawa Yoshiiku
Publisher: Maru-ya Tokuzō
1867

81

This is another print from the series of silhouettes of kabuki actors. In many silhouettes, the actors are relaxing while smoking, drinking or reading letters. In this scene, the actor Bandō Hikosaburō V is depicted drinking sake. Note his slim face and his very distinct features.

To represent one's face with his silhouette profile was a very original idea in those days. Ukiyo-e artists always tried to find some original unique designs.

「真写月花之姿絵」
この絵も、前図同様、影絵のシリーズの1枚である。絵師芳幾は、役者の髪型、鼻の高さ、唇の厚さなどを影絵によく描き出している。役者絵としては、たいへん独創的なシリーズである。影絵では、役者達は、たばこを吸い、盃を傾け、手紙を読み、くつろいだ様子で描かれている。この絵には、五代目の坂東彦三郎が描かれているが、影絵の彦三郎を見ても、彼が細面であったことがわかる。

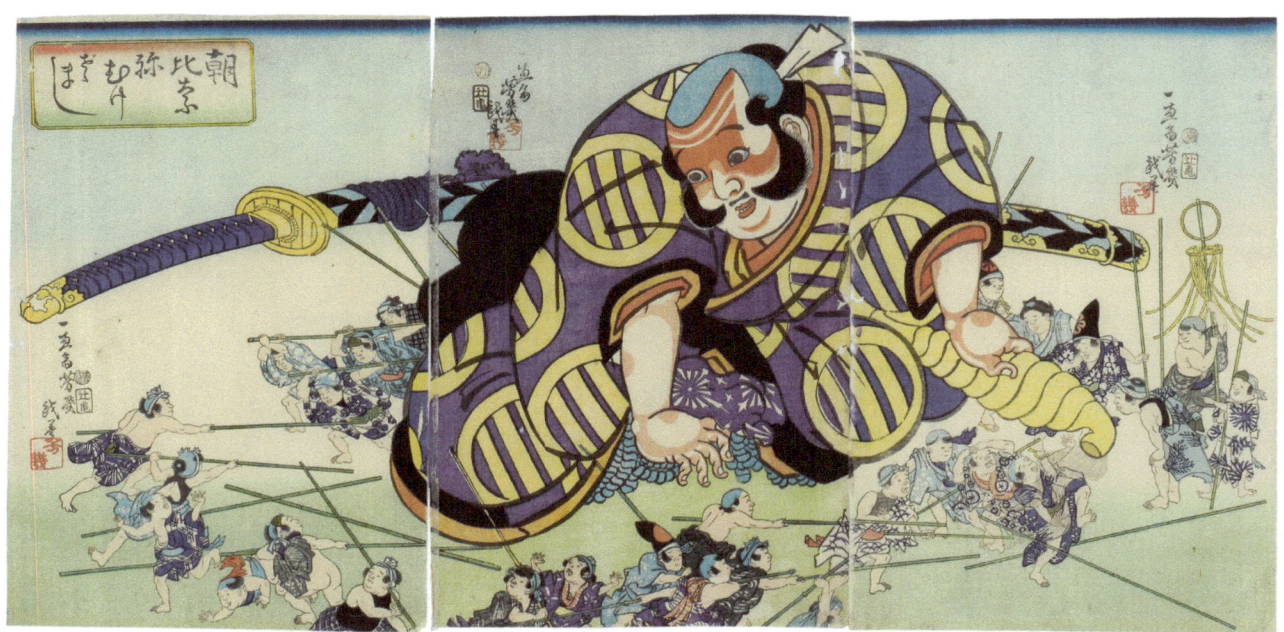

Asaina Nemukezamashi

Awakening Big Asaina

Artist: Utagawa Yoshiiku
Publisher: Tsujioka-ya Kamekichi
1868

82

Here is still another print of Asaina Saburō Yoshihide. In his mythical form of a giant, Asaina is again visiting the land of little humans. He has a puzzled look on his face as he watches the little people fighting a battle. This print, published in May 1868, has a hidden meaning. In that year there was some fighting in Edo and elsewhere between the samurais of the clans supporting the Emperor and of the clans loyal to the weakened Shogunate. Perhaps Asaina represents the Shogunate at the Edojō Castle. The children around him engaging in fights are the two opposing groups of samurai.

「朝比奈ねむけざまし」
朝比奈三郎義秀は、13世紀に実在した侍で、江戸時代の人々にとても愛されていた。勇敢で、ガリバーのように不思議な異国廻りをすると考えられていた。
この絵では、小人島にいる朝比奈が描かれている。きせるを片手に持った朝比奈の周りで、子どもたちが騒しく戦ごっこをしている。この絵は慶応4年（1868）5月に出版されていて、ちょうどこの頃、武士たちは、旧幕府側と新政府側に分かれ激しく覇権を争っていた。そのため、この絵は風刺画として描かれたと考えられる。朝比奈は江戸城で、彼の周りで騒ぐ子どもたちは、二つの勢力に分かれ、争う武士たちと見ることができる。

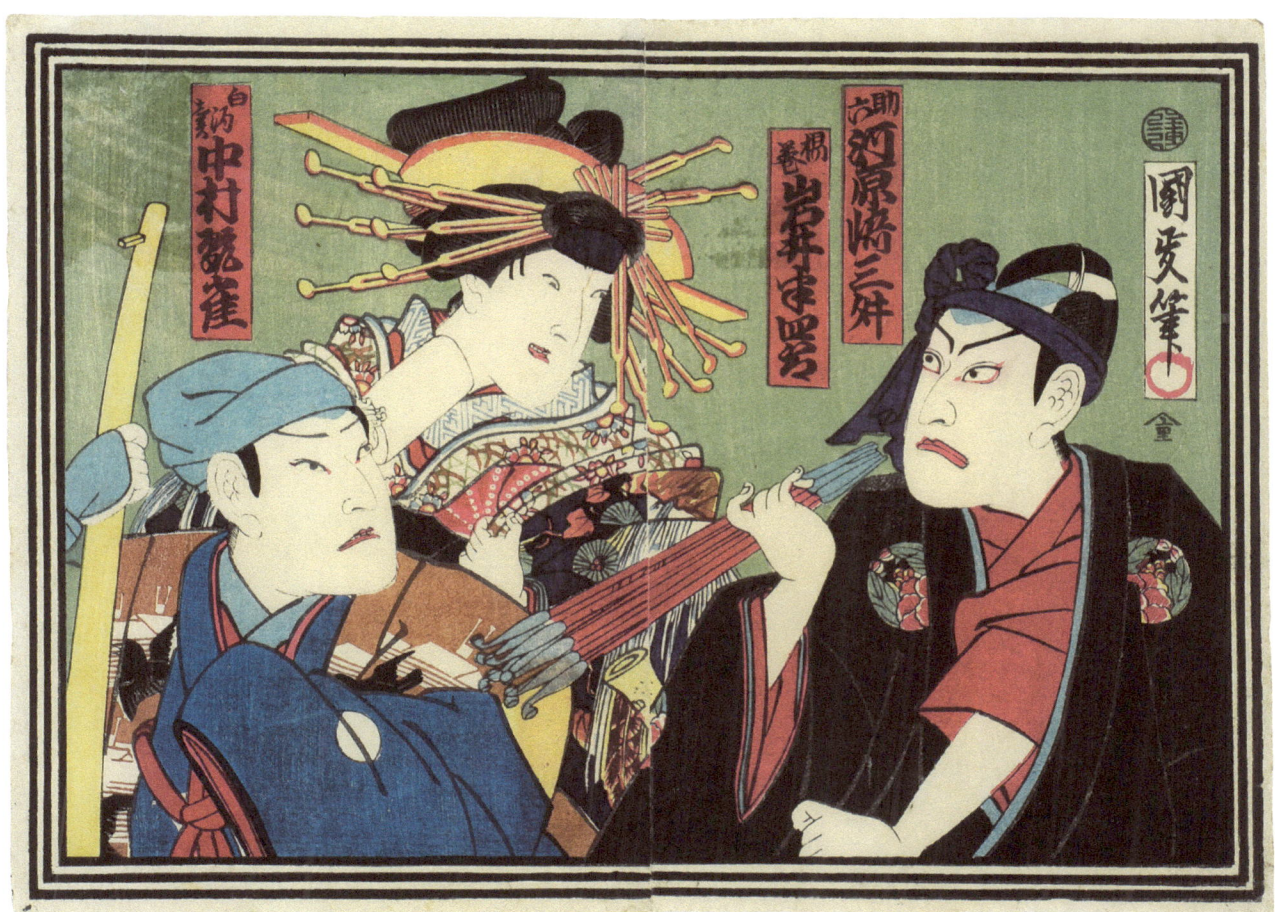

Sukeroku

Sukeroku

Artist: Utagawa Kunimasa IV
Publisher: Jōshū-ya Jūshichi
1872

83

A scene from a famous kabuki drama called Sukeroku named after its principal character. The handsome man with a cool look is holding many kiseru pipes. He is Sukeroku. Many young women were very attracted to him and gave him their used kiseru pipes to demonstrate their affection.

The man at the left is his brother Shinbē, a vendor of white sake called shirozake that is sweet and thick in texture. He is holding a long wooden pole with a peg near the top. It is used to carry sake on his shoulders, hanging a bucket at each end of the pole. The peg prevents the bucket from slipping off the pole.

The woman in the middle is Agemaki, Sukeroku's lover. She has many elegant ornamantal hairpins. Her gorgeous dress indicates her high status.

「助六」
助六は、大変人気のある歌舞伎狂言の主人公である。助六は吉原の遊女たちに気に入られ、彼女たちの吸い付けきせるを渡されるため、この絵でも数多くのきせるを手にしている。この絵に描かれているもう一人の男性は、助六の兄である白酒売新兵衛。助六の馴染みの遊女揚巻も描かれている。

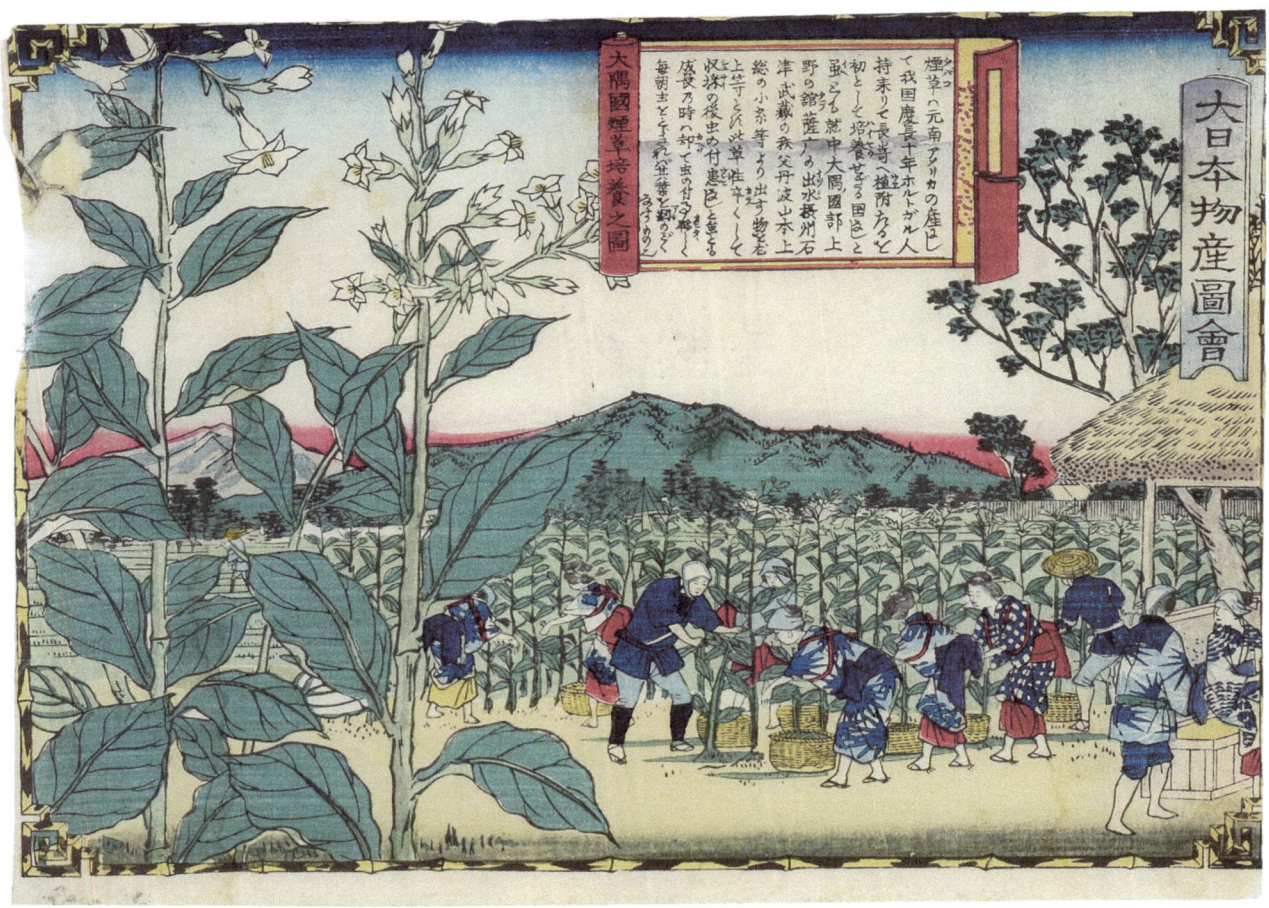

Dainippon Bussan Zue

A Series of Prints on Japanese Products and Industries

Artist: Utagawa Hiroshige III
Publisher: Yorozu-ya Magobē
1877

84

This print is one of a series by Utagawa Hiroshige III called Dainippon Bussan Zue. It was published in 1877 for display at the First Domestic Exhibition of the Products and Industries of Japan.

In this print a famous tobacco field of Ōsumi in Kagoshima, the southernmost part of Kyūshū, is depicted. Ōsumi tobacco was called Kokubu tobacco and had the best reputation among Japanese people.

The Japanese writing in the middle explains the history of tobacco in Japan.

「大日本物産図会」

大日本物産図会は、明治10年（1877）に開催された第一回内国勧業博覧会展示用として制作されたシリーズである。日本各地の産業について、三代目の歌川広重が絵を描いている。

この絵では、大隅地方のたばこ畑が描かれているが、江戸時代、この地方で産出されるたばこは、国分たばこと呼ばれ、高級たばことして知られていた。

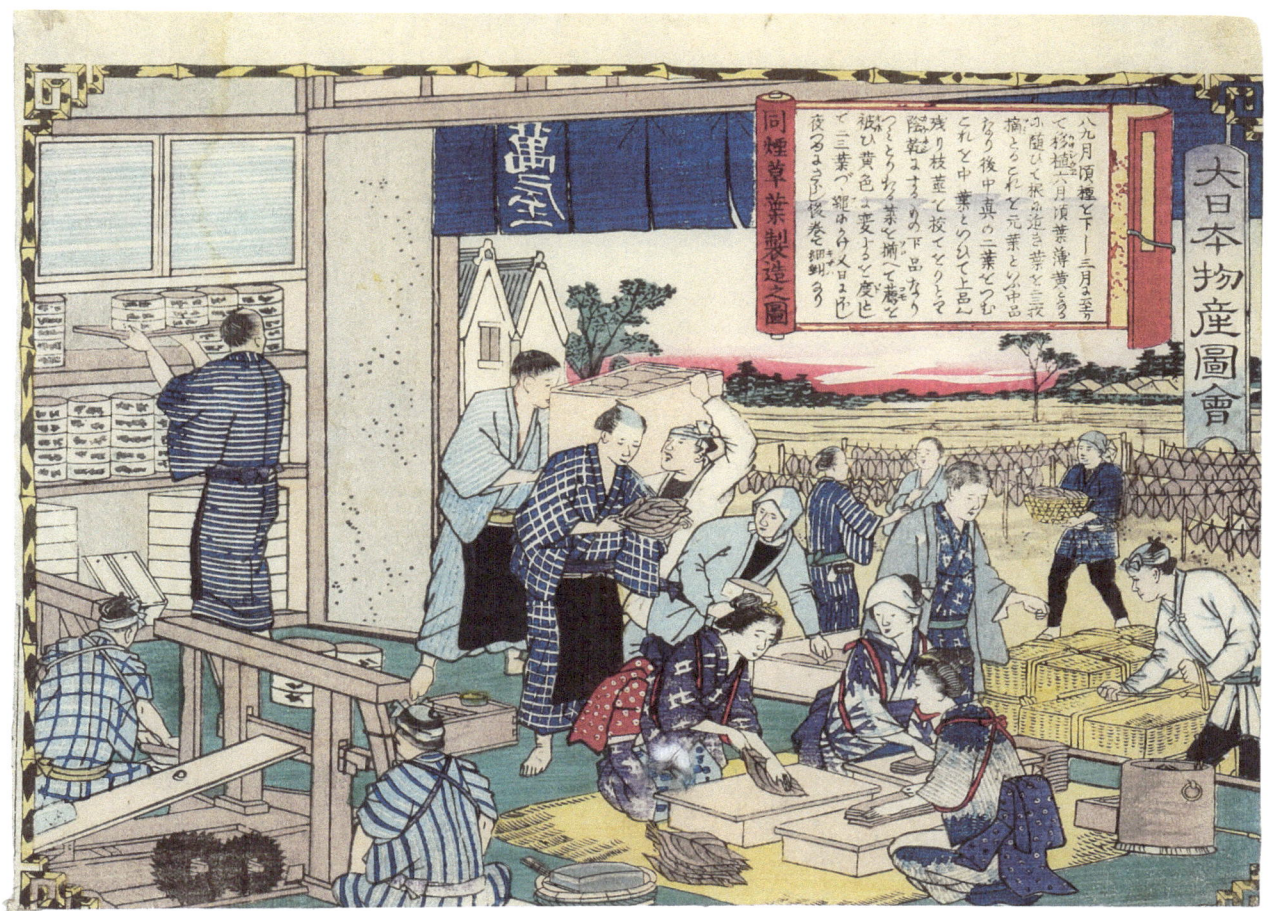

Dainippon Bussan Zue

A Series of Prints on Japanese Products and Industries

Artist: Utagawa Hiroshige III
Publisher: Yorozu-ya Magobē
1877

85

This is another print from the Dainippon Bussan Zue, the Products and Industries of Japan. It shows the inside of a tobacco shredding factory. Tobacco leaves are hung outside for drying. Inside, women are cleaning and binding the tobacco leaves, and men are shredding them. The man above to the left is grading and labeling the packaged products.

The two men below him are operating the shredder machines. This special machine called a cogwheel shredder was invented in the middle of the 19th century for this purpose. This is a very busy scene. The Japanese writing above to the right describes how to grade and shred tobacco leaves.

「大日本物産図会」
この図も大日本物産図会の1図で、前図の対である。
ここでは、刻みたばこの製造所の内部が描かれている。製造所の外では、たばこの葉が干されていて、内部では、女性がたばこの葉を掃き、男性が機械で刻んでいる。この機械は歯車を取り入れた細刻機で、19世紀半ばに開発された。

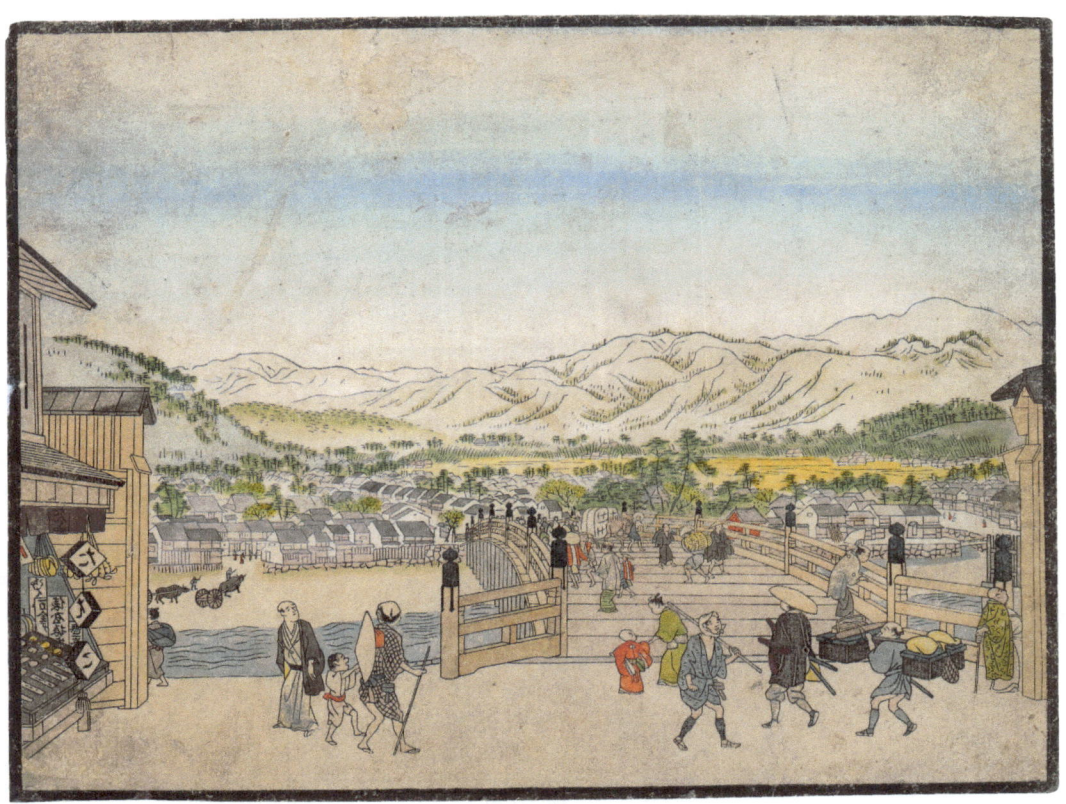

Kyo Sanjō Ōhashi

Sanjō Ōhashi Bridge in Kyoto

Artist: Unknown, possibly Maruyama Ōkyo
Publisher: Unknown
ca. 1751-1764

86

The famous Sanjō Ōhashi Bridge entering Kyoto is depicted. This print is considered to be the work of Maruyama Ōkyo, though his signature is not on it.

The artist made this print in reverse. It was used with a projector which corrected the image to normal. One common way was to view through a hole in a box which had a convex lens within it. Another type used a mirror to reverse the image and a convex lens to enlarge it. You, the reader can see the correct image if you turn this print upside down. Take a hand mirror and hold it 90 degrees perpendicular to the print to visualize the correct image.

The bridge crosses the Kamo River. This bridge was the terminal station for travelers on the Tōkaidō Road from Edo to Kyoto. In the distance one can see the low lying mountains that surround Kyoto. In this former capital of Japan there are many houses, temples and shrines. On the river road, note the ox-pulled carts and the persons by the houses far away. A number of people are crossing the bridge. In the foreground all sorts of interesting travelers are depicted.

Although there are many changes to modern Kyoto since the Edo period, it is worth visiting the back streets of this old Imperial capital to truly appreciate Japan. During the Edo period from 1603-1868, the political power shifted from Kyoto to Edo, today's Tokyo.

「京三条大橋」
この絵には、江戸から京に向かう旅の終着点である京の三条大橋が描かれている。
落款はないが、この絵は円山派の応挙が描いたと言われている。鏡に反射させ、凸レンズを通して見る眼鏡絵と呼ばれるもので、わざと左右逆向きに描かれている。それは、店の中に見える文字が逆向きであることからもわかる。ところでこの店はたばこ店で、江戸時代は、橋のたもとや町はずれなどにたばこ店があることが多かった。三条大橋のたもとにも、応挙が描いたようなたばこ店があったのだろう。

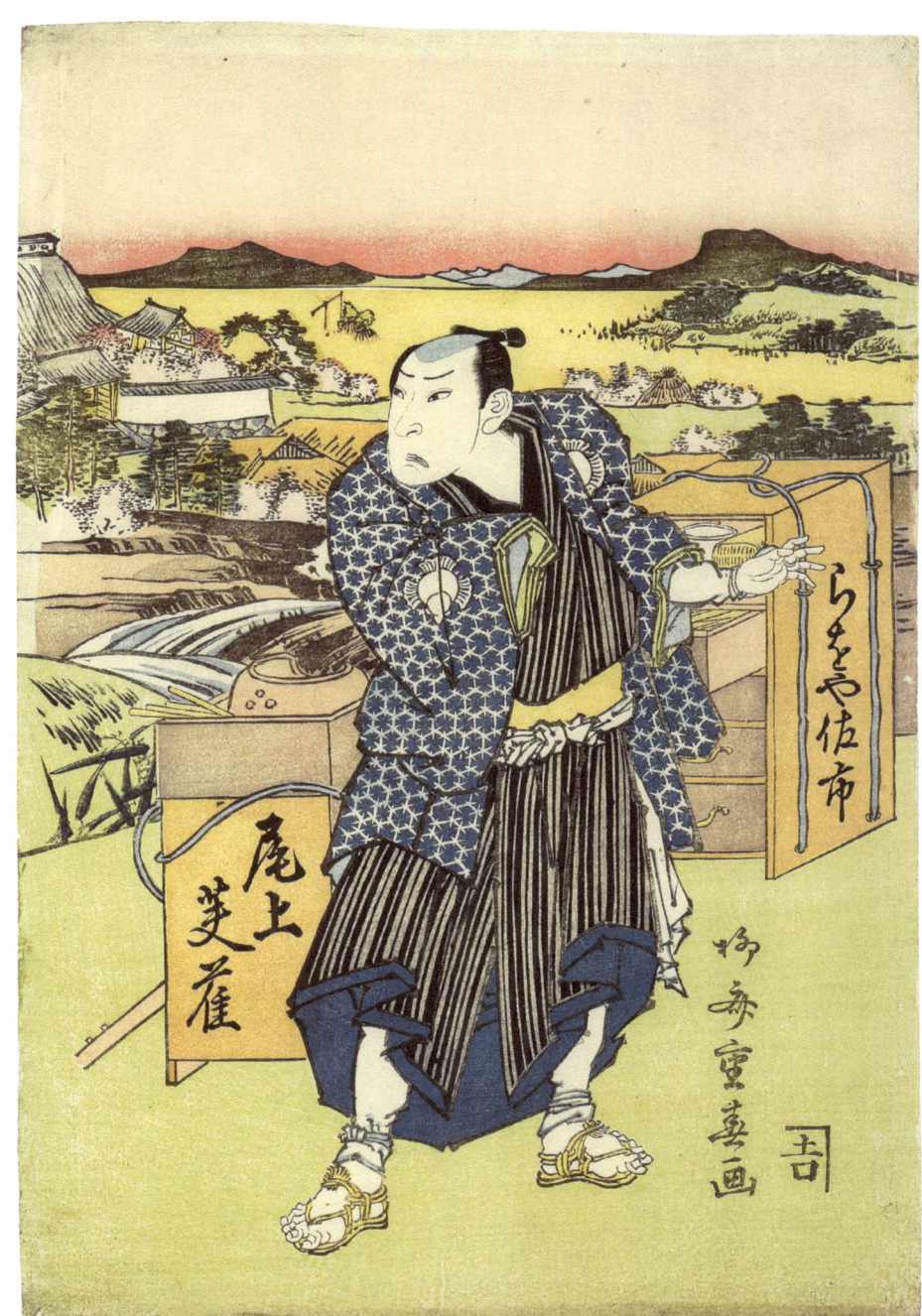

Onoe Fujaku no Raoya Saichi

Onoe Fujaku as a Raoya

Artist: Ryūsai Shigeharu
Publisher: Unknown
1829

87

The kabuki actor Onoe Fujaku is shown. He performed often in the Kyoto-Osaka area known as Kamigata. This print is called a Kamigata-e because it was published in Osaka.

It depicts a scene from a kabuki drama in which Onoe Fujaku plays Raoya Saichi. Saichi is the name and raoya is his trade. Raoyas replace old kiseru pipe stems with new ones. There were many raoyas in the Edo period. Most of them were vendors who carried their tools on their backs. In this print, two very large containers are filled with tools necessary for his trade. Note the splendid background scene behind Saichi. Imagine what he is about to say to his audience in this interesting kabuki play.

「尾上芙雀のらをや佐市」
この絵は上方絵で、ここで描かれているのは上方で活躍していた尾上芙雀という役者である。芙雀は「らをや佐市」に扮している。江戸時代は、きせるの羅宇交換を行う羅宇屋（らお屋とも言った）がいて、道具を担いで町々を廻っていた。この絵にも、羅宇屋の商売道具を入れた荷物が描かれている。

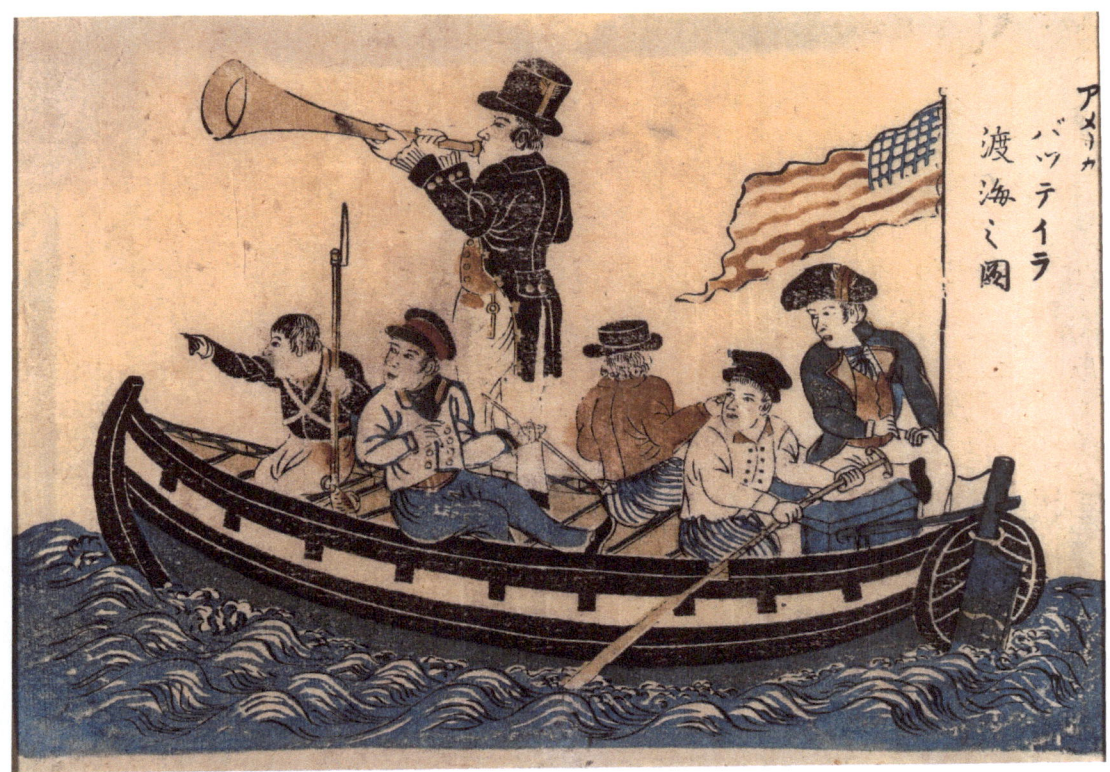

Amerika Batteira Tokai no Zu

American Envoys Sailing
Toward the Shore of Japan

Artist: Unknown
Publisher: Unknown
ca. 1830-1864

88

This print was published in Nagasaki, originally the only place in the Edo period Dutch traders were permitted to enter and stay. In the Edo period, many prints depicting Dutch men were produced as souvenirs in Nagasaki. In the last days of the Edo period, other foreigners were also included. In this print the artist depicted the arrival of American envoys.

The American flag with its Stars and Stripes are shown. The lattice on the flag represents the Stars and the thick waving lines the Stripes. The wind is blowing the American flag toward the shore.

The group of American "envoys" is very revealing. In the bow of the rowboat a soldier with a bayonet is pointing toward the shore of Japan. The gentleman playing the trumpet is dressed in a tuxedo with a top hat and long coattails. There are two oarsmen. Toward the rear one sailor is rowing and in the middle another sailor has his back toward the viewer. Another well dressed gentleman at the stern is sitting with both hands on his lap. The last man has a long stemmed clay pipe in his left hand. It seems that the artist tries to show the diversity of Americans by depicting many differently clothed Americans. The Japanese letters at the far right show the title of this print.

「アメリカバッテイラ渡海之図」
この絵は、長崎で出版されている。江戸時代、長崎は、唯一オランダの商館員や中国の商人たちが滞在することのできる土地であった。 そのため、オランダ人や中国人を描いた絵が、この土地の土産物として出版されていたが、幕末になると、次第に他国の人々も描かれるようになっていった。この絵では、絵師はアメリカの使節を描こうとしている。アメリカの星条旗やアメリカ人の喫煙者を描いているが、喫煙者の持つパイプは、主にイギリスやオランダの人々が用いたクレーパイプである。

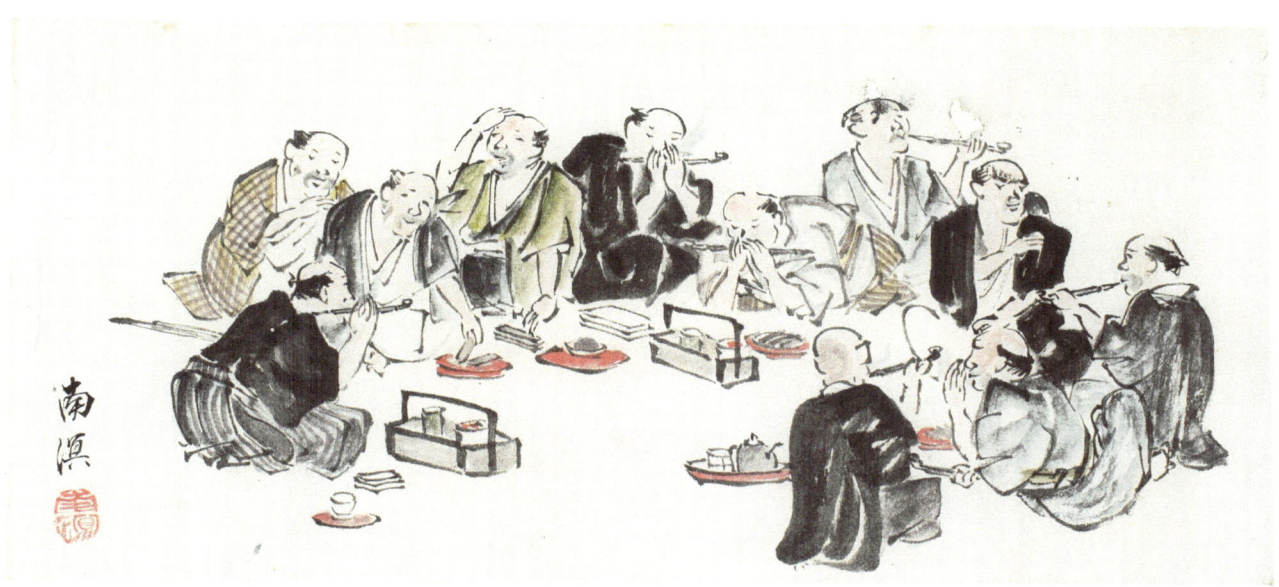

Kokubu Tobacco Shichi-shu no Hyō Narabini San

Evaluations of Seven Kinds of Kokubu Tobacco Brands

Artist: Haruki Nanmei
Original author: Ichiyōdō Kunshi, Nakahara Kan'en
Transcript year: 1832

89

This print depicts a wonderful business scene. It is a part
of a hand painted picture scroll called Evaluations of Seven
Kinds of Kokubu Tobacco Brands.

In the Edo period, the Kokubu tobacco was produced in
Kagoshima, Kyūshū. It was known as the best and the most
expensive grade of tobacco. Kokubu was a general name.
There were several different brands such as Kurumada,
Sunabashiri, Sunagamachi, etc.

In this interesting scroll the several types of Kokubu tobacco
were graded by experts. The tobacco was judged according
to its taste, flavor, sweetness, freshness, quality of ashes,
and easiness for lighting. Each brand was likened to the
temperaments of women such as mild, pleasant, harsh, etc.
In this picture eleven men are evaluating different brands of
tobacco and giving their individual opinions.

「国分煙草七種の評幷讚」
江戸時代、鹿児島産の国分たばこは、最高級
品として珍重されていた。この国分たばこと
いう名は総称で、さらに詳細に、「車田」「砂
走」「砂ヶ町」などの産地名をつけた銘柄に
区別されることもあった。
この絵巻では、国分たばこのうち、七つの品
種が取り上げられている。それぞれについて
の味、風味、甘味、青味、灰の質、火付など
の評が述べられ、さらに女性の気質に譬えら
れている。挿絵では、国分たばこの味競べを
している男性達の様子が描かれている。

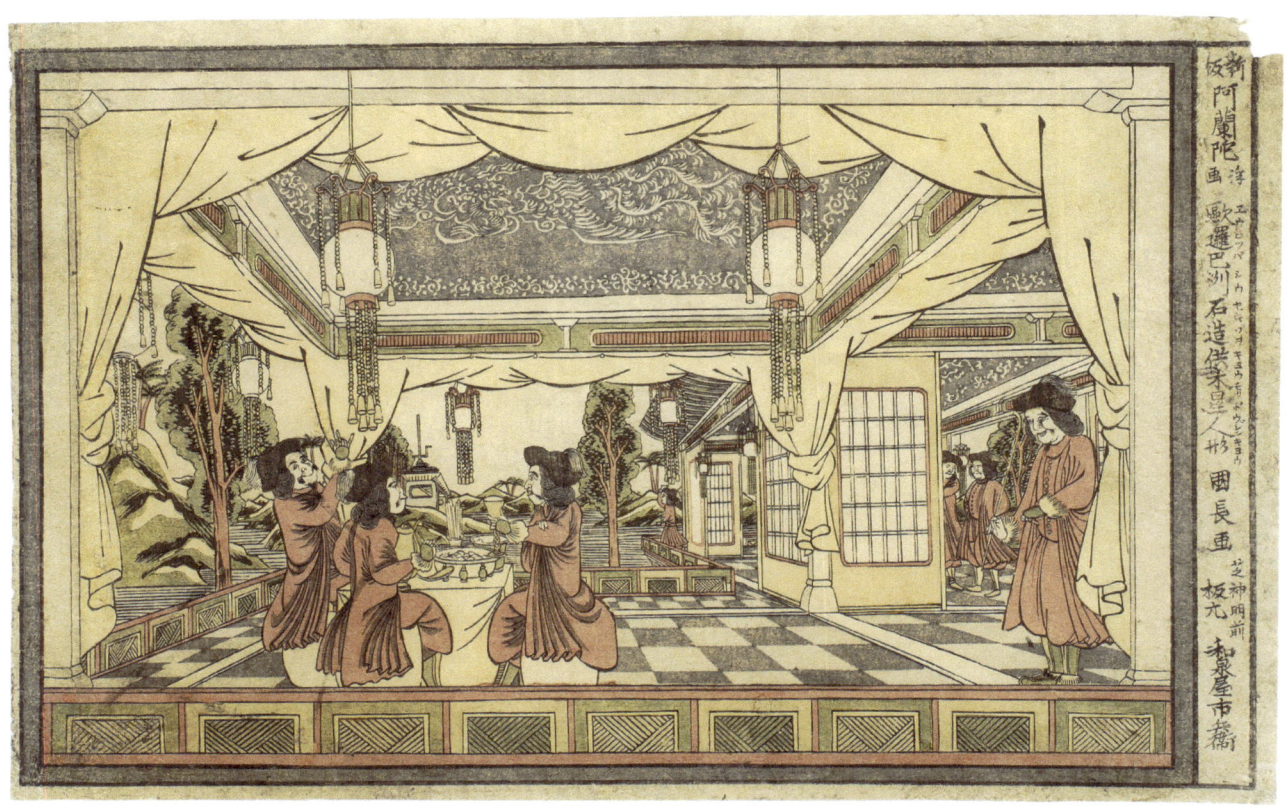

Shinpan Oranda Uki-e Yōroppa-shū Sekizōkyō Mokusei Ningyō

A New Edition of the European Perspective Techniques: The Statue of Zeus

Artist: Utagawa Kuninaga
Publisher: Izumi-ya Ichibē
ca. 1804-1818

90

This print was made using the European perspective technique, which allowed the artist to give the drawing the appearance of three dimensions. This is called uki-e, which was very popular in the Edo period because of its exotic effect.

In this print, various foreigners are eating and drinking. Their attires and behaviors must have been of great interest to the Japanese of those years. This is one of the series dealing with the Seven Wonders of the World. It is generally believed that the artist Kuninaga used the illustrations of the Seven Wonders as a reference for the series.

According to the title of this print, Kuninaga was supposed to depict the Statue of Zeus at Olympia, one of the Seven Wonders. This print, however, bears no likeness to it. Perhaps he did not know the meaning of the Seven Wonders of the World, or he may have been confused by the titles and figures in the reference book he used.

「新板阿蘭陀浮画欧邏巴洲石造供木星人形」
江戸時代、何人かの浮世絵師はヨーロッパ風の遠近画法を習得し、その画法を用いて浮世絵を描こうとしていた。このような絵は浮絵と呼ばれるが、浮絵は、その異国風の雰囲気が人気を集めていた。この絵では、異国の人々が室内で食事をとっており、一層江戸時代の人々の興味をかきたてたことと思われる。
この絵は、世界七不思議を取り上げたシリーズで、絵師の国長は、中国の書物の日本語版に載る挿絵などを参考にこのシリーズを描いたと思われる。ギザの大ピラミッド、マウソロスの霊廟、バビロンの空中庭園、ロードス島の巨人像などを描いたものが現存している。この絵も、タイトルからは、オリンピアのゼウス像を描こうとしたと考えられるが、全く異なるものが描かれている。おそらく絵師の国長は、世界七不思議の意味を理解せずに、参考書のタイトルと他の挿絵を混同したのだろうと思われる。

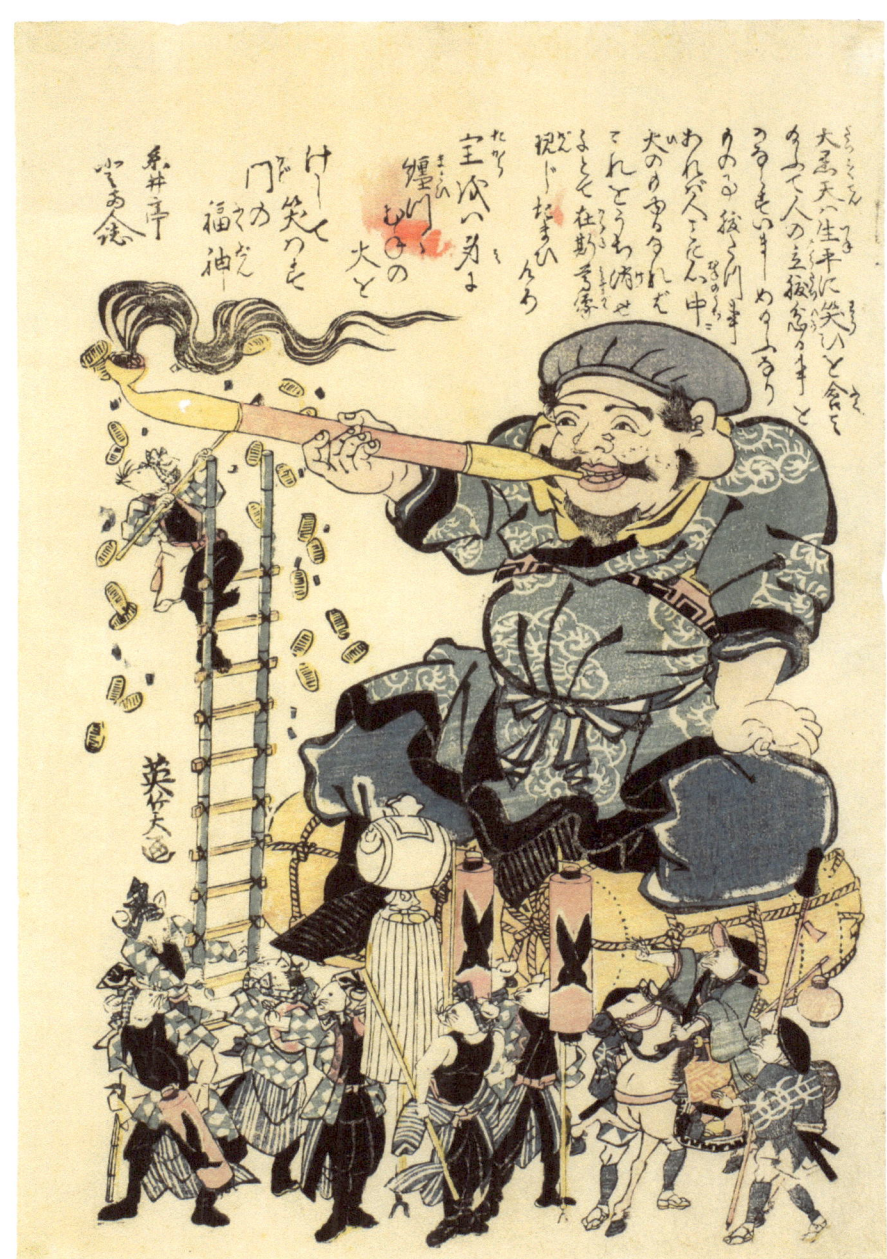

Daikokuten no Kitsuen

Smoking Daikokuten Deity

Artist: Eishō
Pubulisher: Unknown
ca. 1818-1830

91

In Japanese mythology one of the Seven Deities of Good Luck is Daikokuten. He is usually shown wearing a large hood, carrying a large sack of treasure over his shoulder, holding a small mallet in his right hand, and standing or sitting on two straw bales of rice, followed by mice.

In this print, many mice dressed like fire fighters are trying to extinguish the fire in the bowl of Daikokuten's very large kiseru pipe. Along with the smoke, a flood of money falls from the pipe's bowl.

The Japanese writing on top of the print tells the moral of the scene. It says that an angry person is like carrying a burning fire inside him and it must be extinguished. The Daikokuten here is shown burning the anger through kiseru into money. The moral is that if you can suppress your anger, good luck will come to you.

「大黒天の喫煙」

七福神の大黒天が描かれている。大黒天は、頭巾をかぶり、米俵の上に乗り、小槌を持ち、ねずみを従えた姿で知られるが、本図では、ねずみたちは、火消しとして描かれている。画面上部の詞書きを見ると、腹を立てている人は、腹の中で火が燃えているようなものなので、これを消さなければならない、とある。ここでは、大黒天は腹立ちの炎を燃やし、たばこの煙にしてしまっているが、代わりに小判があふれ出ている。絵の意味は、腹立ちを消すことができれば、福が訪れるということであろうか。

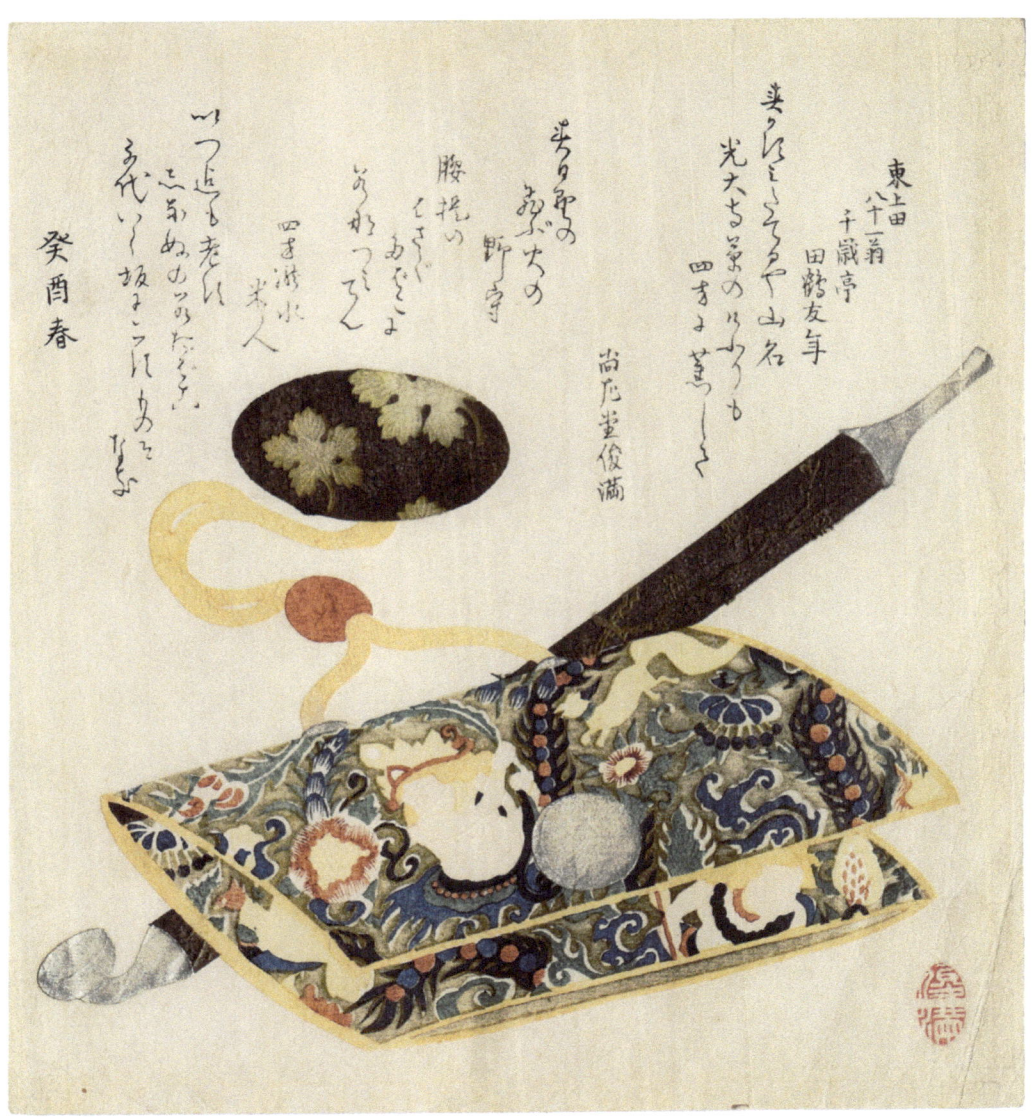

Hitotsu Sage Tabako Ire

A Greeting Card with a Tobacco Pouch Design

Artist: Kubo Shunman
1813

92

This print is in the form of a season's greeting card. In the Edo period, people made such prints and affixed their own short kyōka or haiku poems. This print was designed by the professional woodblock artist, Kubo Shunman.
A kiseru pipe and a tobacco pouch are shown. In the center of the tobacco pouch is a symbol outline of an embossed angel. The exotic design of the pouch was made on Dutch gilded leather imported through Dutch-Japanese trade. Some wealthy Japanese carried gilded leather tobacco pouches. The large, round ornament at the end of the cord is a netsuke, a stopper for hanging a pouch from the sash.

「一つ提げたばこ入れ」
江戸の人々は、摺物を作り、狂歌や俳諧を添えて、互いに交換していた。この摺物には、きせるとたばこ入れが描かれていて、分かりづらいが、たばこ入れには、正面に天使の模様が見える。このエキゾチックな紋様は、日蘭貿易を通して輸入された金唐革の紋様で、実際に、当時の富裕層は、金唐革をたばこ入れや小物などに使用していた。

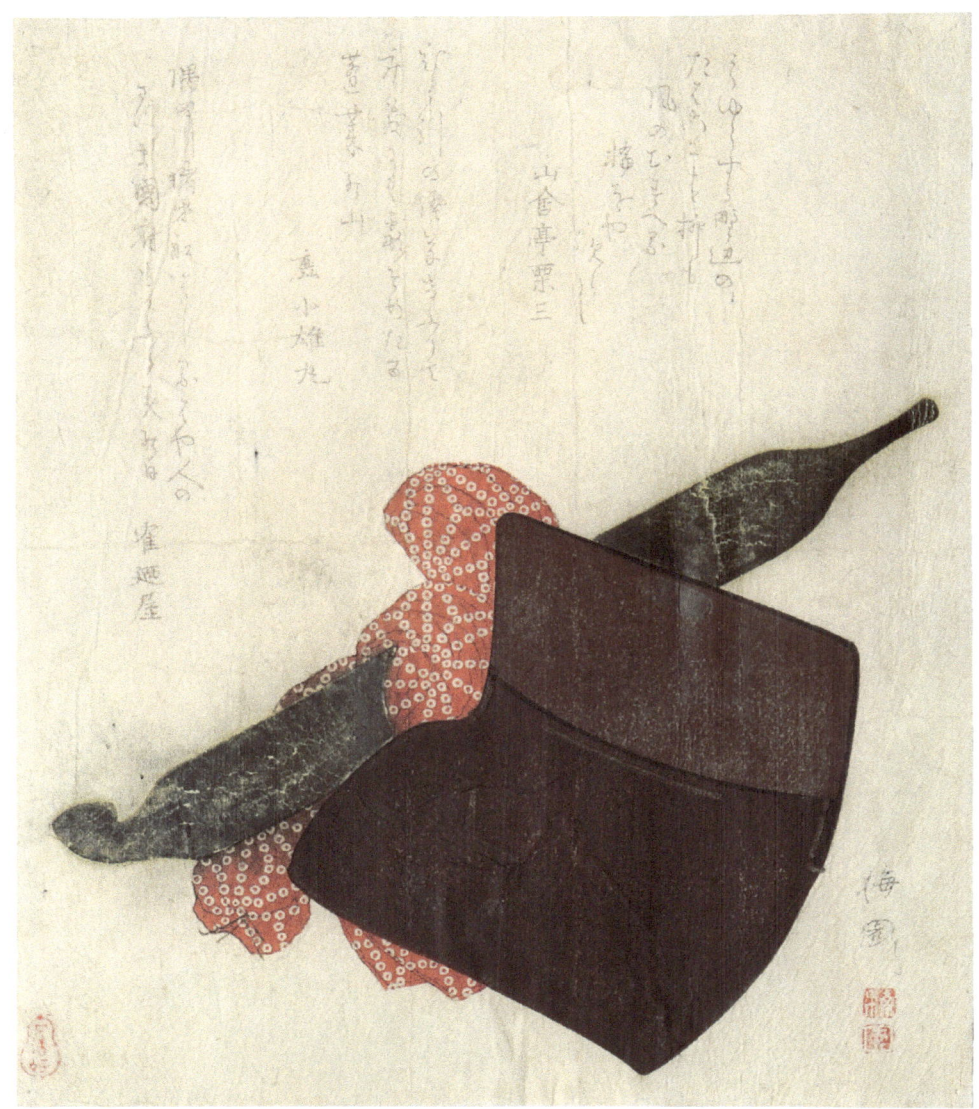

Kaichū Tabako Ire to Natamame Kiseru

A Greeting Card with a Tobacco Pouch Design

Artist: Baien Joshi or Tani Seikō
ca. 1830-1844

93

This print is also a season's greeting card. During the Edo period, many people exchanged such cards. The print was designed by a professional female artist, Baien Joshi or a male artist, Tani Seikō. A tobacco pouch and a thick stemmed kiseru pipe are depicted. The tobacco pouch is most likely made of leather. The kiseru pipe is in the shape of a sword bean. The red colored cloth tied to the kiseru pipe is a case for the pipe.

「懐中たばこ入れと鉈豆きせる」
江戸の人々は、摺物を作り、狂歌や俳諧を添えて、互いに交換していた。この摺物には、女流絵師の梅園と、谷清好の名が見られ、いずれかによって描かれたものと思われる。たばこ入れときせるが描かれていて、たばこ入れは革製らしく、きせるはナタ豆の形をしている。きせるに巻かれている赤い袋は、きせる入れである。

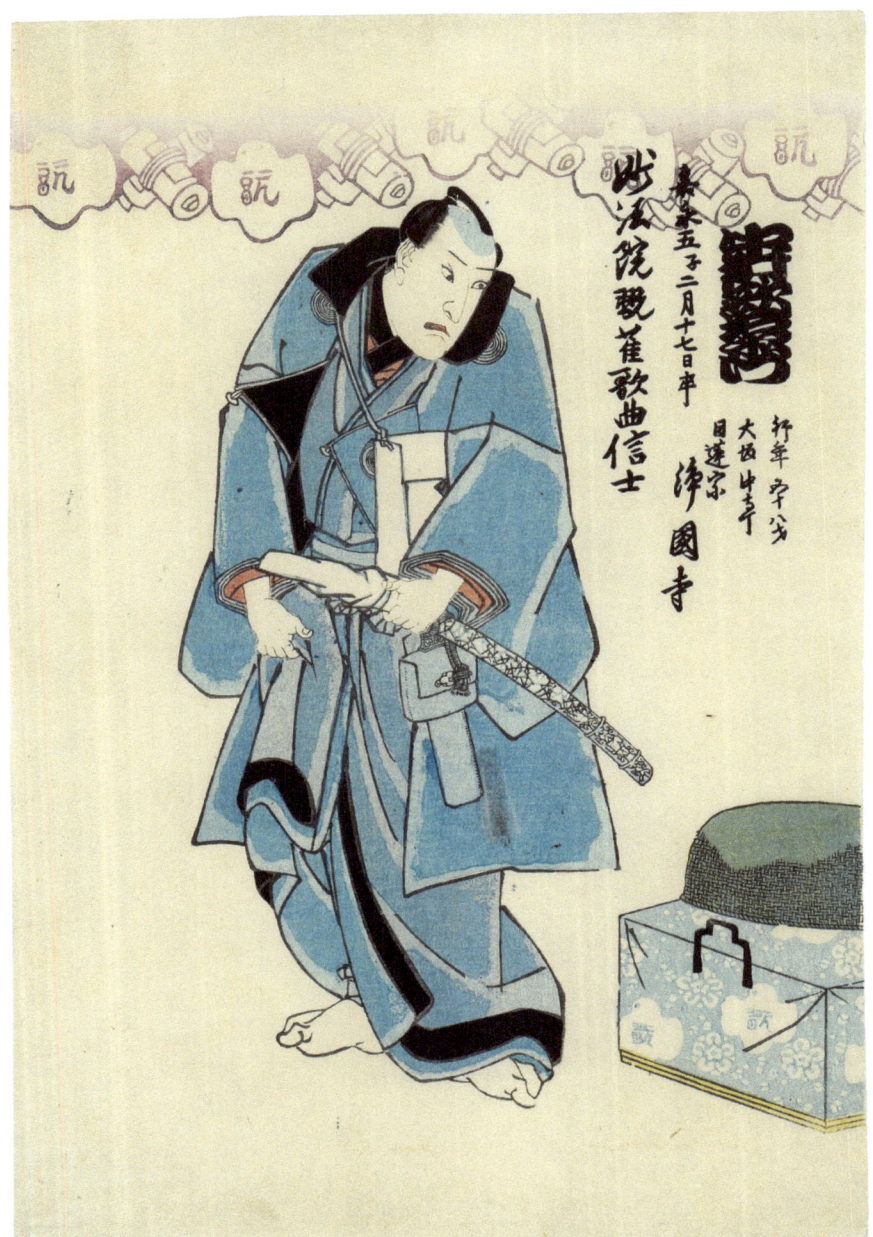

Yodaime Nakamura Utaemon

Nakamura Utaemon IV

Artist: Unknown
Publisher: Unknown
1852

94

This print was made as a memorial to Nakamura Utaemon IV. In the Edo period, especially in its latter part, such prints were made when popular kabuki actors died. They were made as a requiem for the dead or simply as a means to inform people of the actor's death.

In this print Utaemon IV is shown as being ready for a long journey to the nether land. The writing on the right tells the date of death, his posthumous Buddhist name, age at death, and the name of his family temple. He is holding a sword, and a tobacco pouch hangs from his sash. Perhaps the tobacco would comfort him during his last lonely trip. Above him are his kabuki clan symbols.

「四代目中村歌右衛門」
この絵は、四代目中村歌右衛門の追善のため出版された。江戸時代、特に後期には、人気の歌舞伎役者が没すると、追善として、あるいはニュースとして、このような絵が出版された。この絵で、四代目歌右衛門は、黄泉の国に向かう旅支度が出来ているように見える。この絵には、彼の命日、戒名、享年、菩提寺などが記されている。彼は、たばこ入れを提げているが、たばこは最後の長旅の友だったのだろう。

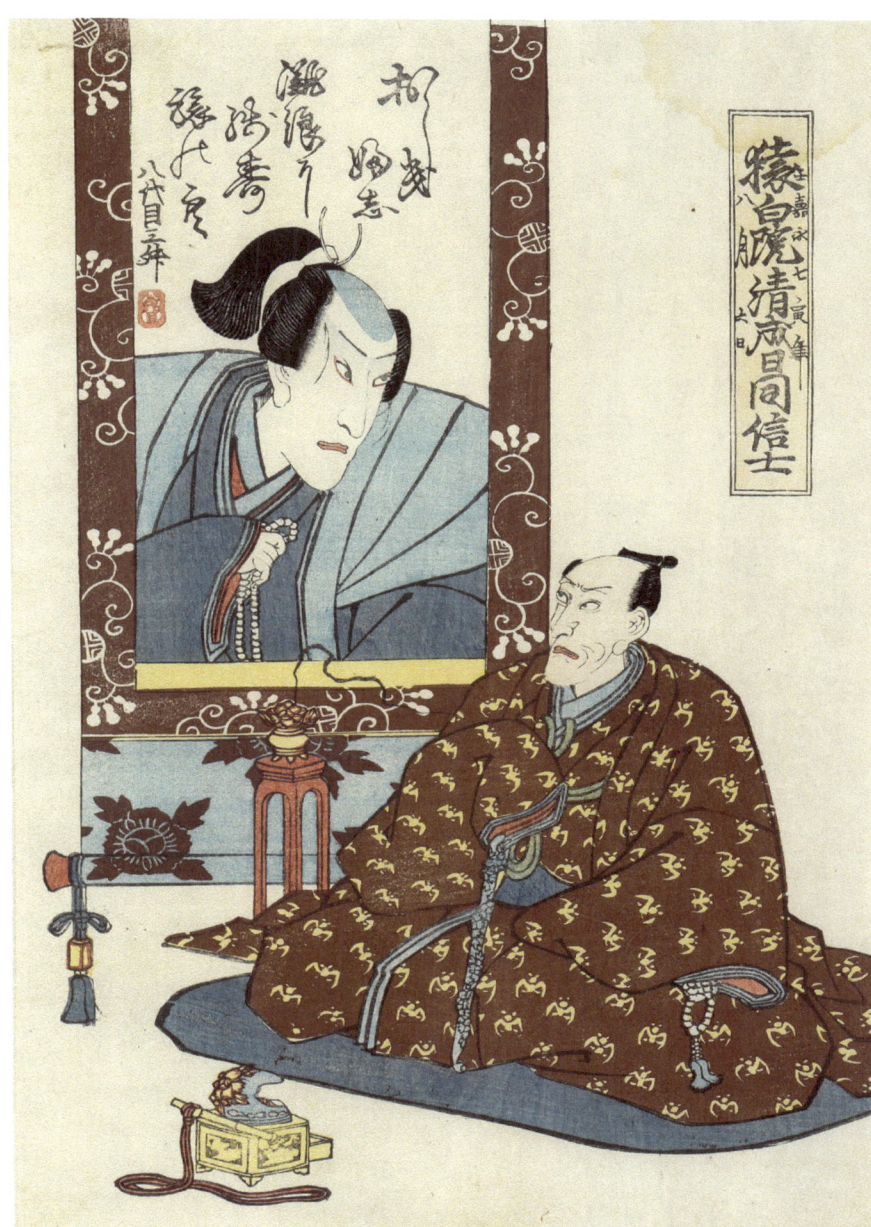

Hachidaime Ichikawa Danjūrō
to Godaime Ichikawa Ebizō

Ichikawa Danjūrō VIII and His
Father Ichikawa Ebizō V

Artist: Unknown
Publisher: Unknown
1854

95

Another print made in memory of a famous kabuki actor, Ichikawa Danjūrō VIII. He was very popular among women. This young man killed himself by slashing his neck in Osaka in 1854. The reason for his suicide was a complete mystery. It was a total surprise to the many in the Edo area, and they mourned his premature death.

About three hundred different prints were published at the time of his death. In this print his elderly father, Ichikawa Ebizō V, sits and stares at the portrait of Danjūrō VIII. Why did my son die? The Japanese writing above the portrait laments the untimely death of the popular actor. The writing on the right is his Buddhist name and the date of his death.

「八代目市川団十郎と五代目市川海老蔵」
この絵は八代目市川団十郎の死を悼み出版された。江戸時代、人気のある歌舞伎役者が亡くなると、このような絵が、追悼としてあるいはニュースとして出版された。

八代目の団十郎は、当時女性の間でたいへん人気があったが、嘉永7年（1854）に大坂で自殺してしまった。自殺の理由も見あたらず、江戸の人々は非常に驚き、その死を嘆き悲しんだ。彼の死を伝える絵は、300種ほど出版されたと言われている。

この絵では、八代目団十郎の肖像の前で、彼の父五代目市川海老蔵が、きせるを手に心を落ち着かせている。

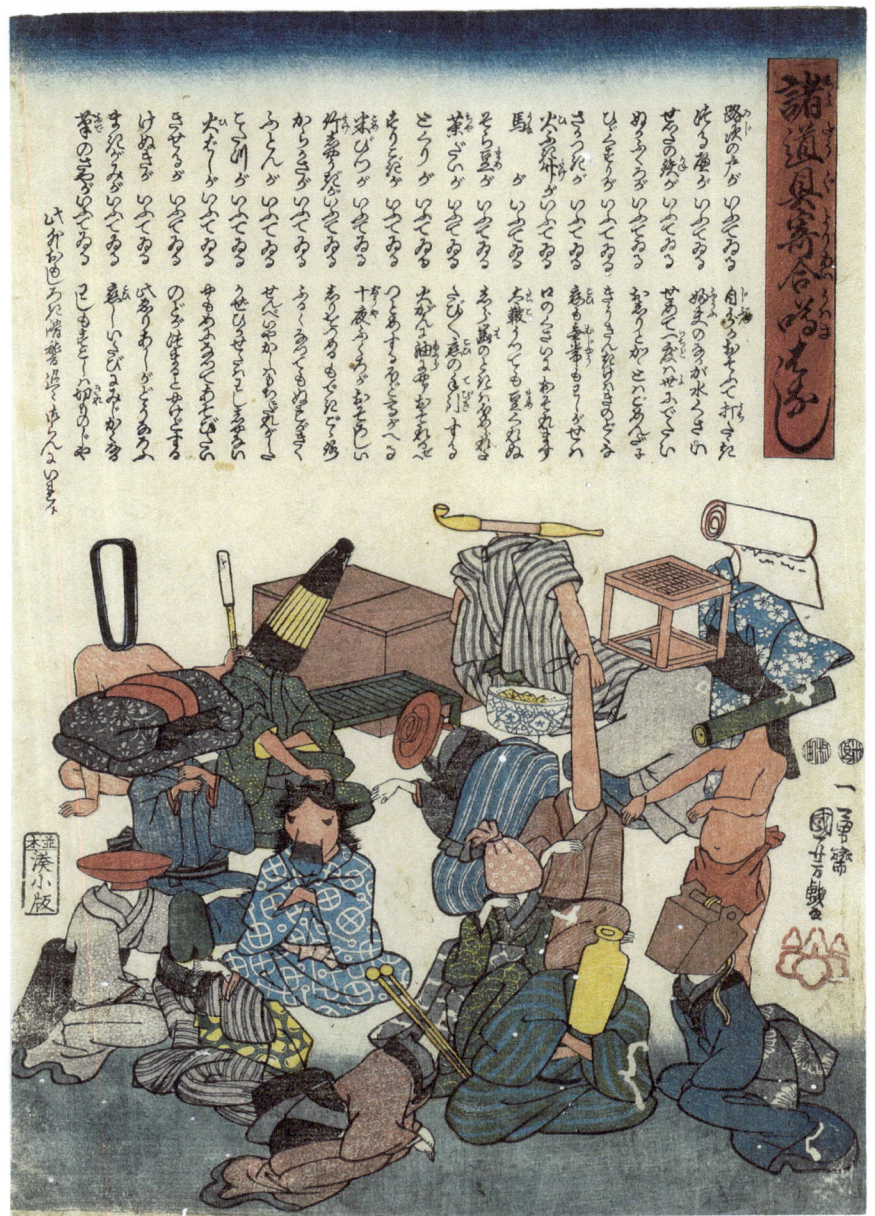

Shodōgu Yoriai Uwasa Banashi

A Meeting of Complaints by Humanized Household Goods

Artist: Utagawa Kuniyoshi
Publisher: Minato-ya Shōbē
ca.1848-1854

96

In this print, many household items are depicted as heads on human bodies. One can recognize a kiseru pipe, an oil-paper umbrella, a teacup saucer, a sake bottle, a sake cup, a pair of tweezers, a horse and so on. Most are typical household goods of the Edo period. They are holding a meeting. They all complain the way they are mistreated. For example, a pair of tweezers says that the neckline of my mistress will never be beautiful even if she uses me. A kiseru pipe grumbles that he is not cleaned often enough and warns the user that one can choke and burn.
The Japanese writing above them are their humorous complaints and soliloquies.

「諸道具寄合噂はなし」
世帯道具たちが、愚痴や独り言を言っている。例えば、毛抜きのセリフは「けぬきがいふてゐる　此ゑりあしがどうなろふ」となっており、きせるは「きせるがいふてゐる　のどがつまるとやけどする」となっている。持ち主の乱暴な扱いには、道具たちはいつでも不満だらけである。

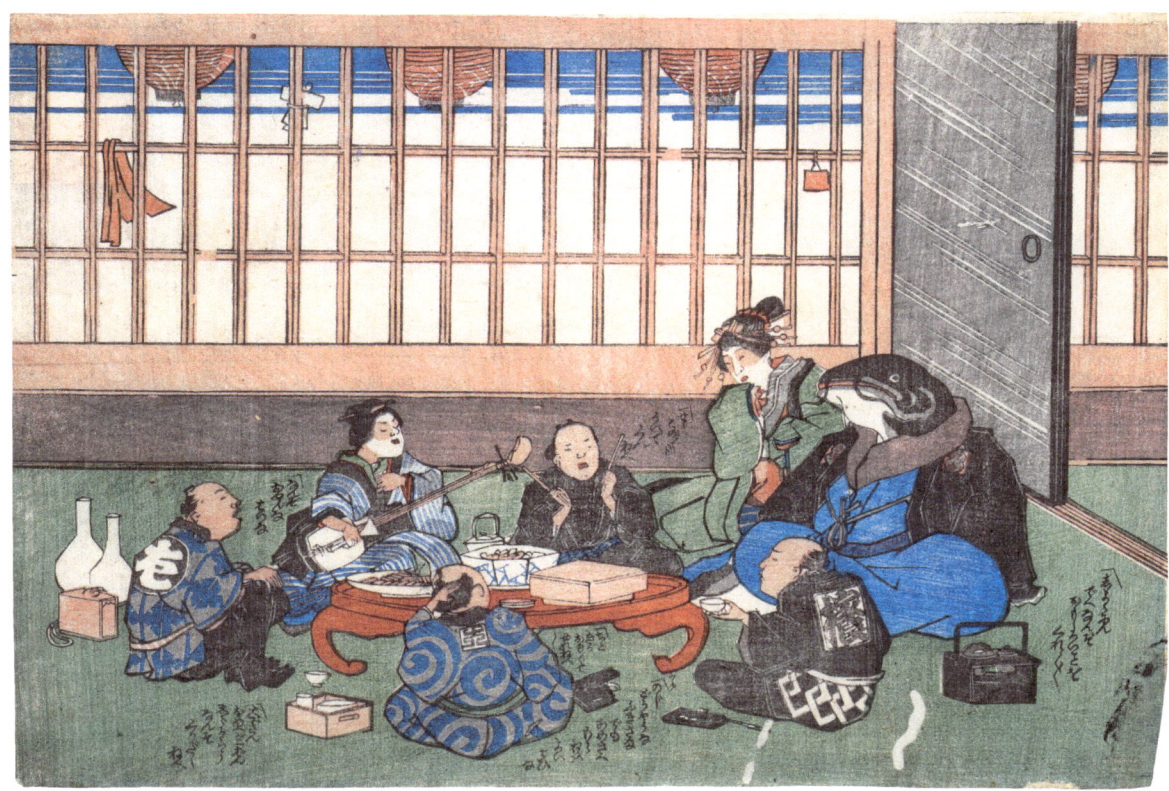

Namazu no Settai

Entertaining a Big Cat Fish

Artist: Unknown
Publisher: Unknown
1855

97

This is a satirical caricature. The huge catfish on the right is being entertained by some workers. They include a carpenter, a plasterer or a dauber, and a roofer.
On October 2, 1855, a strong earthquake demolished a large part of Edo. Many people died crushed or burned. After the earthquake the population began to recover. Carpenters, plasterers, roofers, and lumbermen were in great demand and became rich. One myth was that a huge catfish underground caused the earthquake. Hence the men who got rich by the earthquake are now entertaining the big catfish in appreciation. It is said that about four hundred prints of this kind were published after this earthquake.

「なまずの接待」
大工や左官、屋根屋が大鯰を接待している。
安政2年（1855）10月2日夜、江戸の町は大地震に襲われた。地震では、多くの人々が倒壊した家屋の下敷きとなり、また、火に巻かれ命を落としたが、地震後まもなく、人々は復興に向けて動き始めた。すると地震による特需で、特に建築関係の職人の手間賃が高騰し、材木などの価格も急騰した。当時は、地中の大鯰が暴れて地震を起こすと信じられていたため、この絵では、地震によってもうけた職人たちが鯰に感謝し、接待している。安政地震のあと、このような地震に関係する摺り物は400種以上も出されたといわれている。

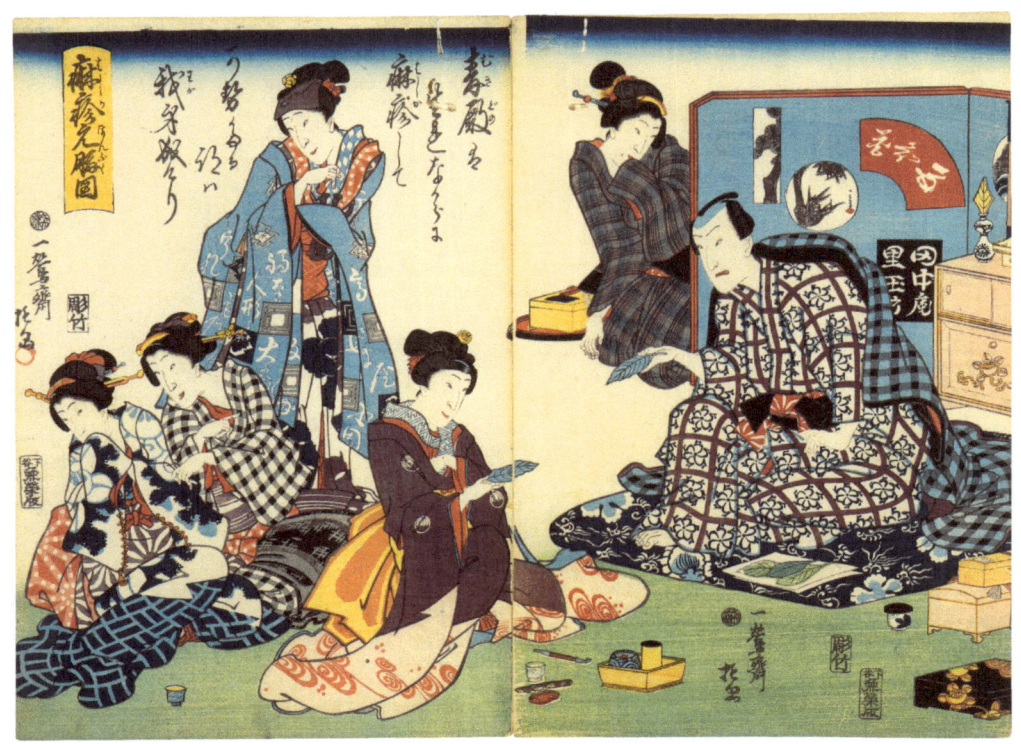

Hashika Genbuku no Zu

A Visit to Kabuki Actor Ichimura Uzaemon XIII Who Suffers Measles

Artist: Toyohara Kunichika
Publisher: Toto-ya Eikichi
1862

98

In 1862, there was in Edo a major epidemic of measles called hashika. Many people died. They didn't know of an effective cure nor its prevention. What they believed in was to cast a spell on the spirit of measles for a cure.

This print depicts some special tree leaves. The leaves were from the Tara tree. People wrote words of incantation and the patient's name and age on the back of the leaf, and threw it into a river. By so doing, they believed that the patient would recover soon.

In this print, three main figures are kabuki actors. The man sitting, Ichimura Uzaemon XIII, has measles. Sawamura Tanosuke III and Ichikawa Fukutarō I are in female attires. Sitting in front of Uzaemon is Tanosuke, standing behind Tanosuke is Fukutarō. Uzaemon is explaining to Tanosuke how he would use the Tara leaf. The other three women are also visiting Uzaemon.

A great number of prints relating to hashika were printed during the epidemic. These are now called hashika-e. The Japanese words on the left panel describe the special incantation against measles.

「痲疹元服図」

1862 年、江戸では痲疹が大流行した。この時多くの人々が亡くなったが、人々は、科学的な治療法や予防法を知らず、呪いで治そうとした。この絵には数枚の葉が描かれているが、この葉は多羅の樹の葉で、この葉の裏に呪いの文句と痲疹に罹った人の名と年齢を書いて川に流せば、痲疹が軽く済むと信じられていた。この絵には、十三代目市村羽左衛門、三代目沢村田之助、初代市川福太郎という三人の役者が描かれている。羽左衛門が痲疹で寝込み、田之助、福太郎、その他の女性たちが羽左衛門を見舞っているように見える。羽左衛門は、田之助に、葉を使った呪いを教えているのだろう。

この痲疹の流行時には、このような痲疹と関係のある絵が多数出版されており、はしか絵と呼ばれている。

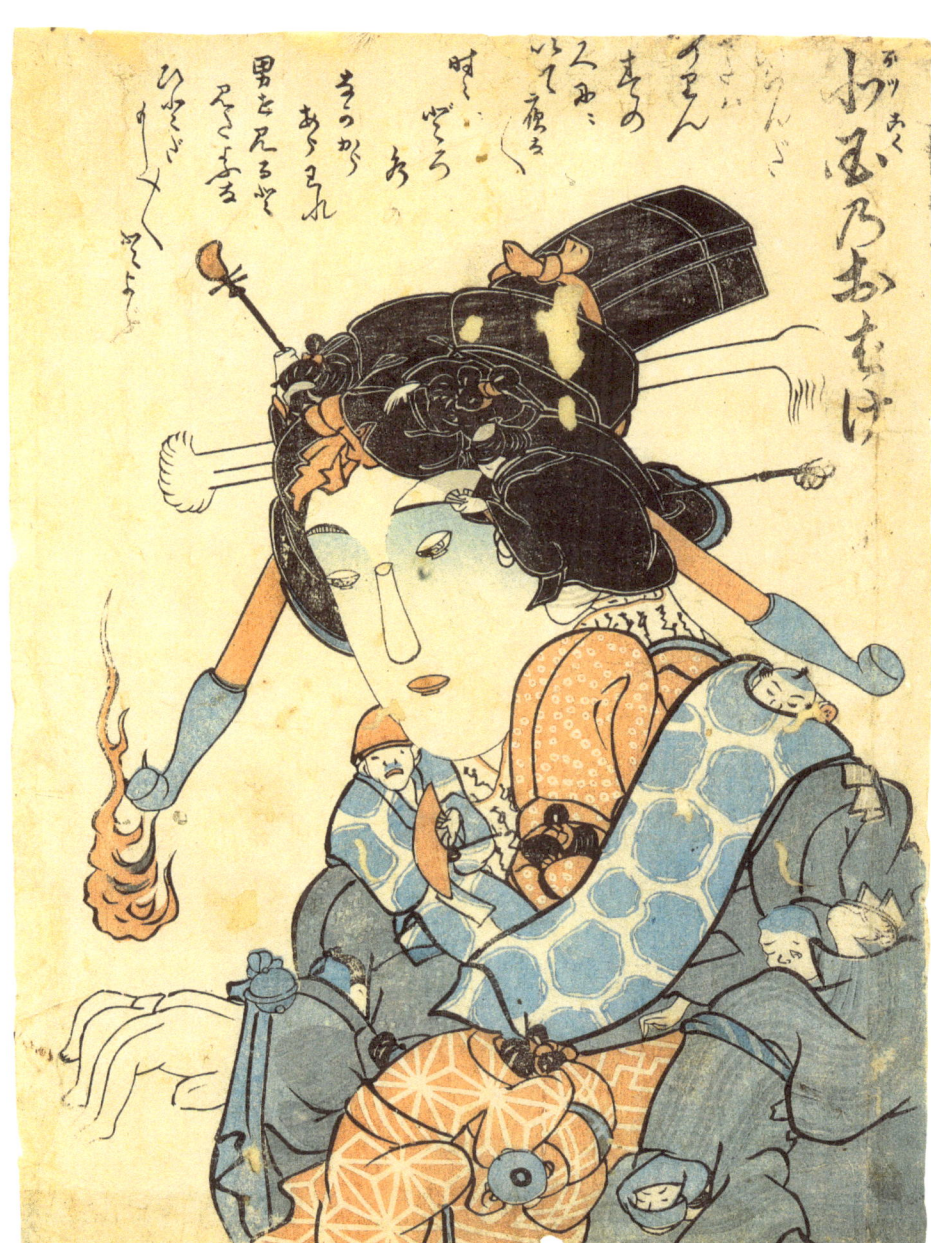

Hokkoku no Obake

The Monster from Yoshiwara

Artist: Unknown
Publisher: Unknown
ca.1865-1868

99

This is a satire of a Yoshiwara courtesan. She is made of little men, women and other miscellaneous items. Her mouth and both of her eyes are sake cups and her nose is a sake bottle. In her hair are professional jesters and geisha girls. Her ornamental hairpins are made of a shamisen, kiseru pipes, and a makeup brush. Around her neck, shoulders and chest are guests, a jester, a masseur and courtesans. The Japanese writing above says this monster appears every night in Yoshiwara and entices men.

In around 1850, artist Utagawa Kuniyoshi created such prints. It seems this particular print is not his, but an imitation of one of his prints. Some say Kuniyoshi got ideas like this from the Italian painter Giuseppe Arcimboldo (1527-1593).

「北国のおばけ」
遊女の上半身が男、女、吉原の諸道具類によって出来ている。目や口は盃、鼻は徳利、髪は幇間や芸者、簪は、三味線やきせる、化粧用の刷毛になっているのがわかる。1850年頃、浮世絵師の歌川国芳は、このような絵を描いており、この絵は国芳の絵の模倣であるように見える。なお国芳は、イタリアの画家、ジュゼッペ・アーチンボルドの絵から、このようなアイデアを得たと考える説もある。

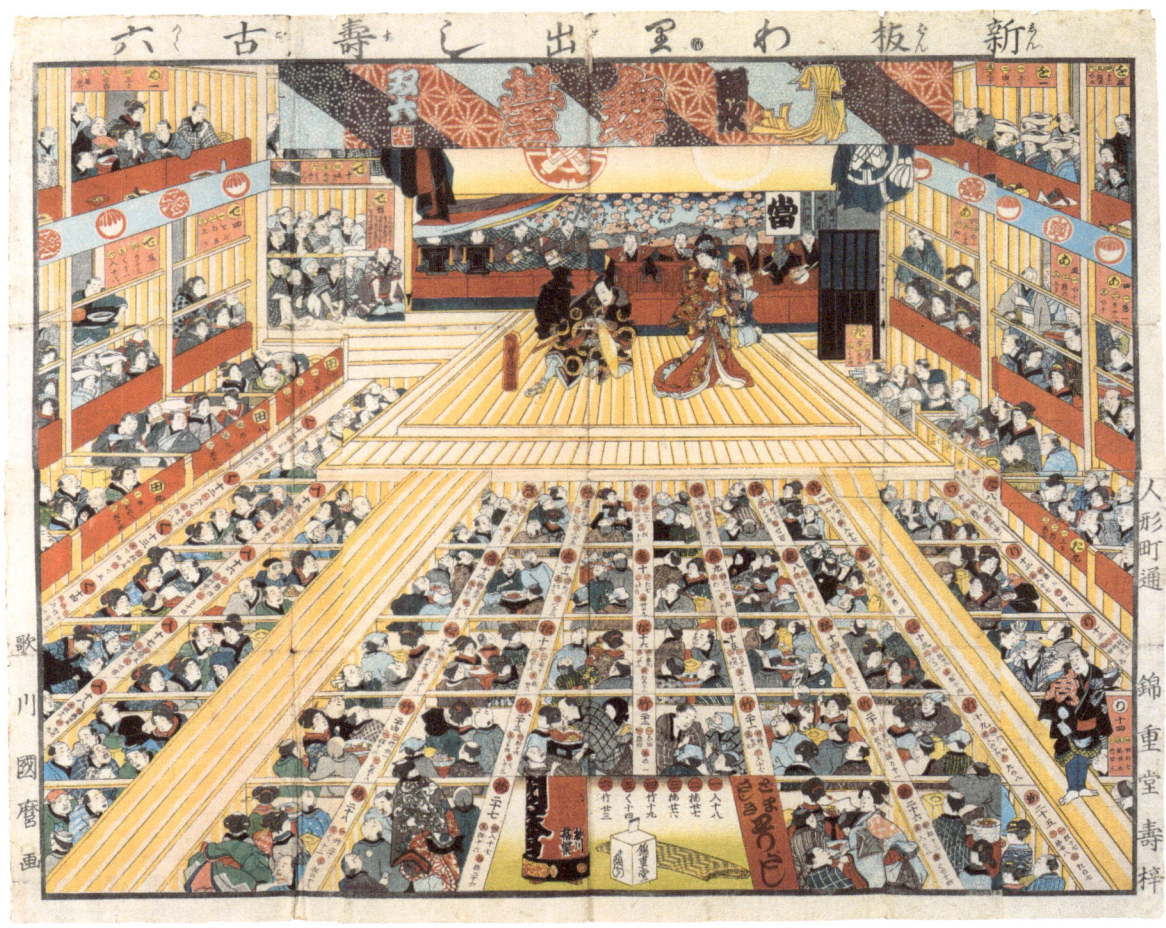

Shinpan Waridashi Sugoroku

A Sugoroku Game of Kabuki Theater Seats

Artist: Utagawa Kunimaro
Publisher: Jōshū-ya Jūzō
1860

100

The inside of a fully occupied kabuki theater is depicted. The square boxes in the foreground are for the normally priced seats. The elevated side box seats are the more expensive. Along the center square seats, one can see a wide passage on the left and a narrower one on the right. They are called hanamichi, a flower way, and kabuki actors walk over these passages to the stage. Therefore, the seats near the hanamichi are the preferred seats. To the upper left, a little space by the stage, some men are shown. This is the cheapest place to see a kabuki drama, but one can see only the back of the actors.

This print is also a sugoroku game. Players cast a die and move their pieces according to the number on the die to cheap, expensive, and normal seats. For each seat three numbers are given. They are allowed to move their pieces only when the number of the die matches one of the numbers given on the seat.

「新板わり出し寿古六」
満席の芝居小屋が描かれている。舞台から正面には数多くの枡席があり、左右には料金の高い桟敷席があったが、舞台の向かって左奥（下手）には羅漢台と呼ばれた安い席もあった。この羅漢台からは、役者の後姿を見ることになる。この絵は、飛び双六になっており、サイコロを振って出た目の指示に従いコマを進めて遊んだ。この双六の場合、コマは、高い席や安い席を行ったり来たりすることになる。

About the Tobacco & Salt Museum

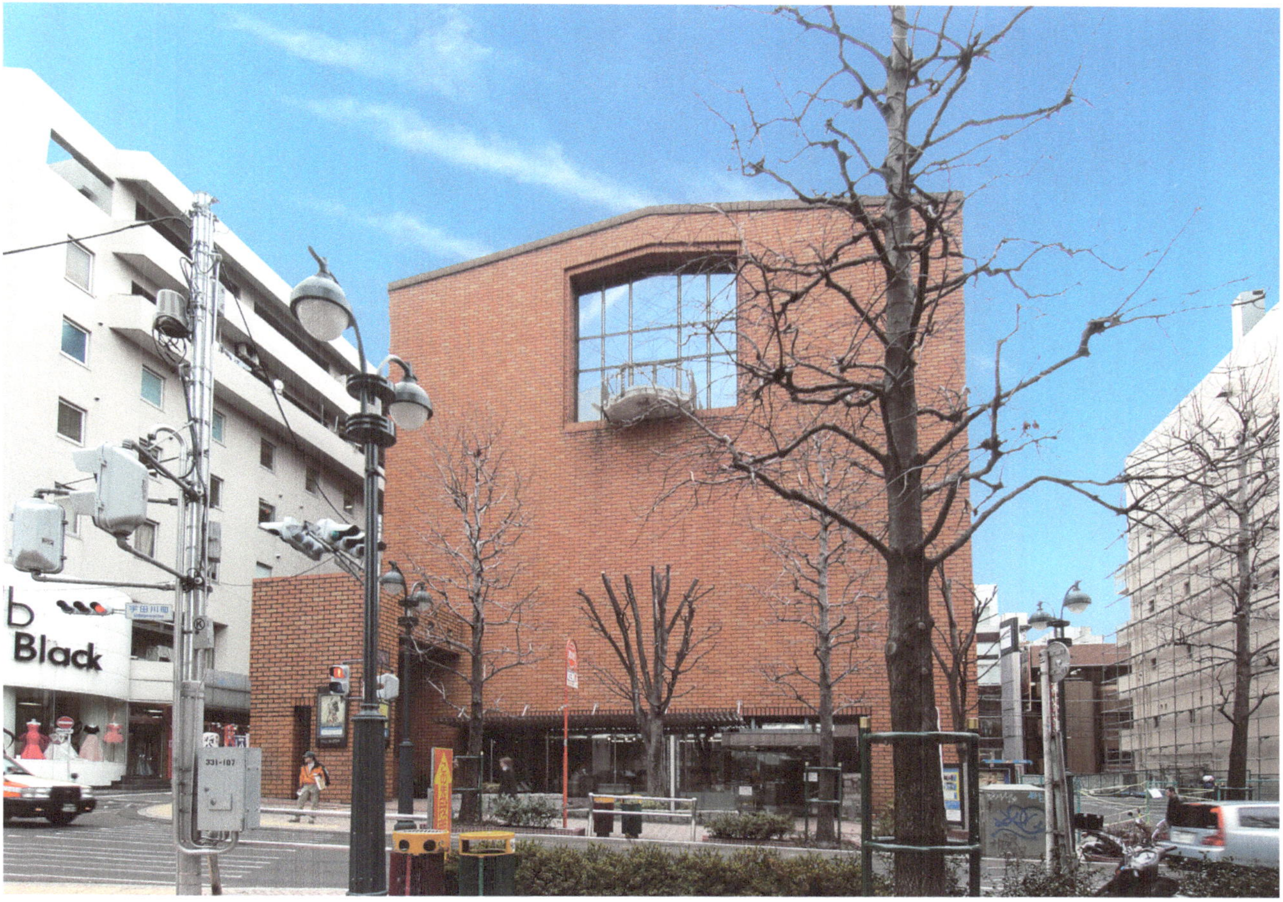

Address: Jinnan 1-16-8 Shibuya-ku, Tokyo Japan 150-0041
Telephone: ++3 3476 2041
Fax: ++3 3476 5692 (24hours)
URL   http://www.jti.co.jp/Culture/museum/WelcomeJ.html

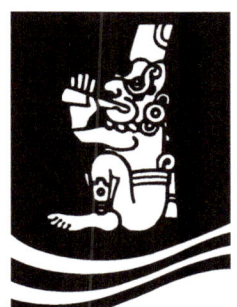

The Museum Logo

The logo is based upon a hieroglyph drawing from the early Mayan codex shown at right. The curving lines at the base of the logo represent the waves of the ocean, sole source of Japanese salt.

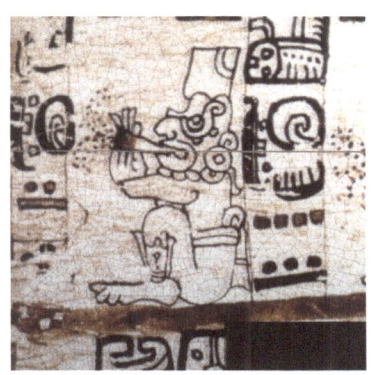

4F Special Exhibition Hall

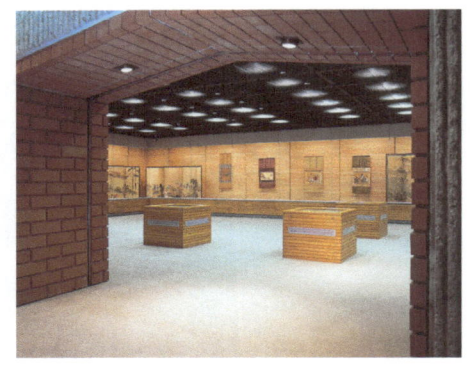

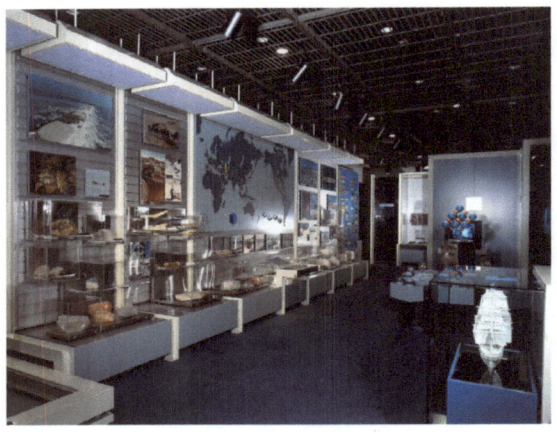

3F Japanese Salt and Foreign Salt
1 What is Salt?
2 World Salt Resources
3 Salt in Japan
4 Salt in Today's World

2F Japanese Tobacco
1 Tobacco in the Edo Period
2 Tobacco in Modern Times
3 Tobacco Manufacture
4 The Spread of Tobacco Culture
5 A Who's Who of Japanese Tobacco Devotees
6 Various Tobacco in the World

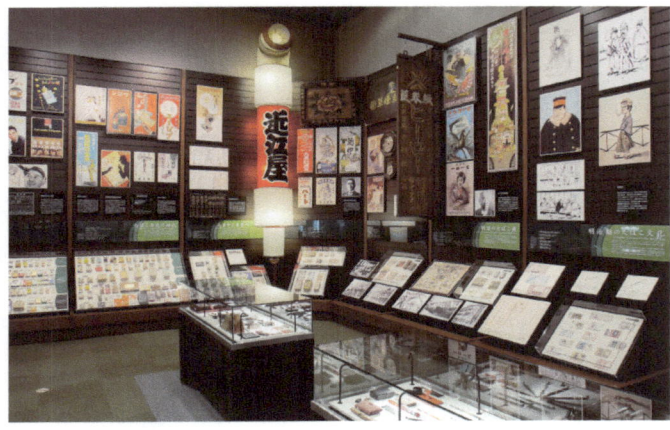

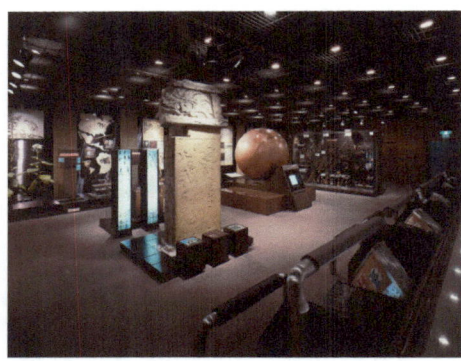

M2F The Route of Tobacco
1 The Origin of Smoking
2 The Spread of Tobacco
3 Tobacco's Arrival in Japan
4 Tobacco Implements Throughout the World
5 Yōzaburō Tsuchiya Collection
6 Cigarette Packets and Cartons from Many Lands

1F Entrance Hall

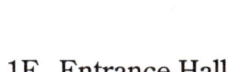

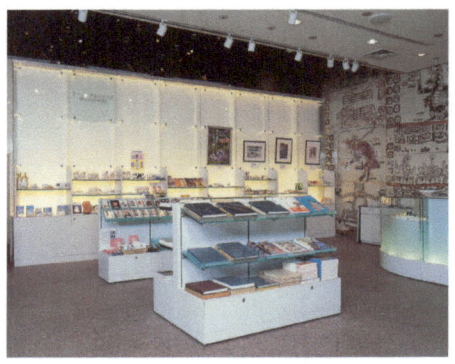

www.ingramcontent.com/pod-product-compliance
Lightning Source LLC
Chambersburg PA
CBHW050723180526
45159CB00003B/1118